*f*P

Also by Bob Drury and Tom Clavin

Halsey's Typhoon: The True Story of a Fighting Admiral,
an Epic Storm, and an Untold Rescue

The Last Stand of Fox Company: A True Story of U.S. Marines in Combat

Last Men Out

The True Story of America's Heroic
Final Hours in Vietnam

Bob Drury
and
Tom Clavin

Free Press
New York   London   Toronto   Sydney

Free Press
A Division of Simon & Schuster, Inc.
1230 Avenue of the Americas
New York, NY 10020

First Free Press hardcover edition May 2011

FREE PRESS and colophon are trademarks of Simon & Schuster, Inc.

For information about special discounts for bulk purchases,
please contact Simon & Schuster Special Sales at 1-866-506-1949
or business@simonandschuster.com.

The Simon & Schuster Speakers Bureau can bring authors to your live event.
For more information or to book an event contact the Simon & Schuster Speakers Bureau at
1-866-248-3049 or visit our website at www.simonspeakers.com.

Designed by Carla Jayne Jones

Manufactured in the United States of America

1   3   5   7   9   10   8   6   4   2

Library of Congress Cataloging-in-Publication Data
Drury, Bob.
Last men out: the true story of America's heroic final hours in Vietnam / Bob Drury
and Tom Clavin.
p. cm.
Includes bibliographical references and index.
1. Vietnam War, 1961–1975—Vietnam—Ho Chi Minh City.   2. Vietnam War, 1961–1975—
Evacuation of civilians—Vietnam—Ho Chi Minh City.   3. Vietnam War, 1961–1975—
Personal narratives, American.   4. United States. Marine Corps—History—Vietnam War,
1961–1975.   I. Clavin, Thomas.   II. Title.
DS559.9.H58D78 2011
959.704'3—dc22   2010029333

ISBN 978-1-4391-6101-2
ISBN 978-1-4516-1025-3 (ebook)

For dmcd
—rfxd

To my children, Kathryn Hamma Clavin and Brendan Hamma Clavin
—TC

U.S. Embassy Saigon 1975

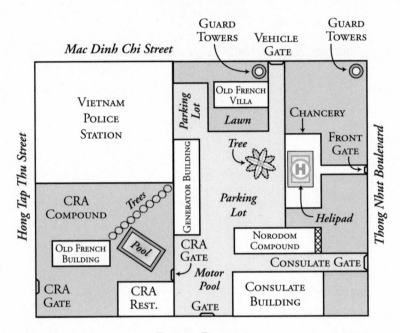

Courtesy of the Fall of Saigon Marine Association, Inc. A California Non-Profit Corp.

Contents

Contents

Prologue

Under the terms of the Paris Peace Accords signed on January 27, 1973, the United States and all foreign governments agreed to withdraw their combat troops from South Vietnam within sixty days; the South Vietnamese government agreed to negotiate with the National Front for the Liberation of Southern Vietnam—the Vietcong—toward a political settlement; and reunification of Vietnam was to be, in the words of the document, "carried out step by step through peaceful means." Exempt from the American military drawdown were the detachments of U.S. Marine Corps Security Guards (MSGs) posted at the U.S. Embassy in Saigon and at several U.S. consulates in various provincial capitals.

Less than two years later, the North Vietnamese broke the terms of the accords when, in late 1974, the North Vietnamese Army's chief of staff, General Van Tien Dung, began his push into South Vietnam with the intent of conquering it once and for all. To the surprise of most observers, General Dung marched his army though South Vietnam's fir-clad Central Highlands nearly without a fight. Dung had expected to triumph, but not against so little resistance. When U.S. forces pulled out of South Vietnam in 1973, they had left behind for their ally $5 billion worth of military equipment, including hundreds of tanks, 500 fighter bombers, 625 helicopters, and enough arms to equip a 700,000-man army. Thus, the initial ease with which his armies progressed south made Dung wary of a trap. Even when Dung's scout units returned to report that the South Vietnamese Army had, in fact, quit the fight for the Highlands, the general moved forward cautiously. It was only after his divisions captured Pleiku that he,

1

as one of his subordinates wrote, "decided to chase them as far as we could and as fast as we could."

Within days of Dung's first attacks, South Vietnam's president, Nguyen Van Thieu, recognized that he did not have the manpower to defend the Highlands. Instead, he ordered a defensive perimeter formed along the northern border of Da Nang in preparation for a counterattack, sacrificing the ancient city of Hue in the process. But Thieu had not counted on his army collapsing in on itself like a black hole. As Dung's divisions pressed onward, thousands of mauled Army of the Republic of Vietnam (ARVN) soldiers surrendered or deserted. For those remaining, the "orderly withdrawal" to Da Nang became a mass exodus, the poet's rueful "Convoy of Tears."

Ill-disciplined and starving South Vietnamese foot soldiers, many of them abandoned by their commanders, joined terrified throngs of civilians fleeing south. They plundered hamlet after hamlet, clogging roads, raping women, and stealing vehicles. Within days Da Nang was transformed from a once-thriving port city into an armed and desperate refugee camp seething with resentment—against the North Vietnamese, against Thieu and his cronies, against the U.S. allies who had abandoned them. In the minds of the 1 million Vietnamese overflowing Da Nang, hate and fear had replaced faith and hope.

On March 29, 1975, artillery shells began falling on Da Nang, in central Vietnam, as 35,000 North Vietnamese Army (NVA) troops prepared to attack. It was not necessary. Panic had done their job for them. Two days earlier, plane and helicopter airlifts had been cancelled when American pilots reported taking withering fire from rogue ARVN units; now these same South Vietnamese soldiers turned their guns on civilians as the latter clawed to reach rescue ships. Women, children, and the elderly were trampled in the rush to the sea. Fishing boats packed with civilians were confiscated by South Vietnamese soldiers, who tossed their countrymen overboard before shooting it out among themselves for the precious berths.

The six U.S. Marines detached to the Da Nang consulate, attempting to help people board at the docks, watched in horror as mothers who did manage to reach the water's edge set their babies adrift in small pails, hoping the tide would carry them out to boats, or toss them at already-moving barges. Most fell short and were drowned. One Marine witnessed a South Vietnamese Army officer shove women and children into the space between the dock and a boat, where they were crushed against the pilings as he scrambled aboard. Another Marine noticed several elderly Vietnamese disappear beneath a sea of bodies in an overflowing barge. By the time he dragged them out from the pile, they had been smothered to death.

That night, a deadly face-off between the Da Nang consulate's MSGs and an ARVN company was narrowly averted when the Marines, surrounded by their erstwhile "allies," joined the civilian consulate staff hiding in the back of a stolen garbage truck that made its way to the docks, from where they escaped on a leaky barge.

The final blow came when Thieu's top commander in Da Nang, Lieutenant General Ngo Quang Truong, abandoned his post to swim for the last U.S. naval vessel sailing from port. One hundred thousand of Truong's troops surrendered. With Da Nang gone, the southern coastal provinces soon followed. Within weeks, the North Vietnamese and their Vietcong comrades surrounded the capital city of Saigon and prepared to invade. For all intents and purposes, the long war in Vietnam was about to come to an end.

Except, that is, for a small number of Marines at the U.S. Embassy, who were not about to lay down their arms.

Part I
Dominos

We could be looking at an Alamo situation here.
—Major Jim Kean, addressing his fellow Marine Security Guards at the U.S. Embassy in Saigon

One

Saigon, 0300, 29 April 1975

The monsoon rains had arrived early.

They blew in from the southeast, and Marine Staff Sergeant Mike Sullivan stood on the roof of the U.S. Embassy watching the towering storm clouds scudding up from the South China Sea. He marked the difference between the distant bursts of heat lightning—sudden, silent detonations of white iridescence illuminating the jungle to the horizon—and the tiny pinpricks of orange artillery shells detonating near Bien Hoa, just twenty miles away. Tonight, however, the light show held little interest for Sullivan until he heard the North Vietnamese rockets whiffling overhead—heard them before he saw them, recognized their distinctive whine from long experience in the bush. One-Two-Two-millimeters, he knew. A 122's peculiar sound always reminded Sullivan of the muscular hiss of a narrow-gauge diesel locomotive. *Shhkerthunk-shhkethunk-shhkethunk.* The veteran staff sergeant knew his artillery, and he knew his railroads.

From instinct Sullivan pictured their makeshift launchers, ingenious ladder-shaped devices fashioned from thick bamboo stalks that could be toted up a steep mountain trail or across a muddy rice paddy. But, no, he realized suddenly. Not tonight. There were too many rockets. Which meant they had to be fired from the flatbed of a Russian-made six-by-six truck. Which meant a road. Which meant they were close. He craned his neck, scanned the sable sky, and pointed. *Got one.* He traced an index finger in a slow arc, southeast to northwest, following the red tail fire as it sailed in a graceful parabola toward Tan Son Nhut Airport.

"Hundred-pounder," he said to the scrum of young Marines knee deep

7

in shredded paper and barely visible through the smoke drifting out of the stifling rooftop blockhouse that housed the brace of cast-iron furnaces. "Smooth-bore launcher. Hard to control where that lands. Like a shotgun blast."

Within moments more rockets were overhead, and the half-dozen Marines of Sullivan's "burn squad," who had been destroying embassy documents on the rooftop, dropped their shovels and gathered about him, looking to the sky and bathing themselves in the soft, warm rain. For weeks the heat and humidity had lain over Saigon like an illness, sapping the will of the few Westerners left to do anything but find a cool room and a cold beer. Yet for seven consecutive days and nights, Sullivan's rotating teams of sleep-deprived embassy Marine Security Guards had taken shifts feeding all manner of documents into the maws of the white-hot furnaces: coded carbons of ambassadorial cables and secret CIA memoranda, classified military teletypes, American and South Vietnamese personnel records, some dating to 1954, when the French left. They were even burning paper money; thick, bundled stacks of crisp, new $100 bills. Five million worth was the rumor, a fortune in cash turned to gray ash.

The crimson glow from the unlatched furnace doors cast a sheen across the Marines' soot-streaked faces as they followed Sullivan, who now edged toward a pile of sandbags stacked haphazardly across the northwest corner of the asphalt roof. The staff sergeant took a breath and held it. The Tan Son Nhut airfield was six miles away. He knew he would see it before he heard it. *Flash. Boom.* He thought of the 3,000 Vietnamese refugees still crowding the airport—and the handful of U.S. Marines defending it.

For the past eight days Tan Son Nhut had been the busiest airstrip in the world, host to an assembly line of big-bellied U.S. military cargo planes landing empty and taking off with a menagerie of passengers—fleeing South Vietnamese men, women, and children fortunate enough to have landed a slot on the evacuation's "endangered" list. Some were worthy, and some had begged or bribed American sponsors, but 40,000 had exited the city over the past month. These refugees had mixed with American civilian contractors getting out: machinists, aircraft mechanics, weapons maintenance men, most of them retired military personnel, dragging clans in their wakes to form a sweaty, reeking ball of humanity. The smell was fear—and avarice. There was good money to be made ferrying newlywed "brides" and their families out of the disintegrating country. The last gold rush of Vietnam. As with all other gold rushes, this one, Sullivan sensed, was a tragedy waiting to happen.

Unlike his young MSGs, Sullivan had seen up close what a 100-pound rocket could do to a human being. *Tear a person apart like a meat grinder, is what it could do.* He remembered the jungle bases where he'd fought years earlier, directing artillery fire called in by the LURPs, the long-range Marine reconnaissance patrols. One night in particular stuck in his mind—the river camp at Hoi An, the North Vietnamese Army and Vietcong swarming over the wire from every direction. That attack had also begun with the whine of incoming 122s fired from bamboo launchers. The next morning he'd waded through mounds of American body parts scattered about the elephant grass.

The burn squad formed a semicircle around the veteran staff sergeant as the detonations from Tan Son Nhut came in rapid succession. The gunners were good. Sullivan had no doubt these were trained and experienced NVA regulars, and not VC farm boys. They "walked" their artillery from the U.S. Defense Attaché's Office (DAO) adjacent to the airport in a direct path toward the dual flight lines and then out to the helicopter landing zones beyond.

The Paris Peace Accords of 1973 had led to the withdrawal of all but a handful of U.S. troops from Vietnam as well as a general cease-fire between the United States and the NVA and VC. In the two years since that treaty, the DAO—an assemblage of huge gray buildings behind a high wire fence from which the generals William Westmoreland and Creighton Abrams had once commanded 1 million fighting men—had become home to hundreds of American civilian contractors and scores of U.S. Army, Navy, Air Force, and Marine personnel managing technical programs in support of South Vietnam's armed forces. They also worked on the agreed-on release of prisoners of war and, when and if possible, acted as official observers to adherence to the terms of the cease-fire. This included the withdrawal of U.S. and other non-Vietnamese troops from the country.

By 1975, as more POWs, or their remains, were accounted for, the U.S. military presence had drawn down at the DAO. According to the Paris Accords, officially titled "An Agreement on Ending the War and Restoring the Peace in Vietnam," there were now fifty military officers living at the vast, multibuilding facility, sometimes known as the "Pentagon East." The MSGs preferred another nickname that someone long ago had dubbed the DAO compound: Dodge City. Tonight it was living up to that provenance. The muffled *crump-crump-crump* of the explosions resounded like the echoes of a cowboy movie gunfight.

The Marines on the embassy roof stared dull-eyed as rows of South Vietnamese aircraft erupted in churning gouts of dirt, concrete, and steel. Suddenly Sullivan detected the hum of the heavier 130-millimeter shells accompanying the rocket fire. A moment later he saw an American C-130 cargo plane burst into flames midway between the munitions storage area north of the runways and the airport's main terminal. He instinctively flinched and took a step backward.

"How many of us out there?"

Sullivan did not even turn. He recognized the sharp Boston accent of Corporal John Ghilain, his voice thick as chowder—Big Blond John, perhaps the strongest man in the outfit. Four days earlier a platoon of Marine infantrymen from the Seventh Fleet had choppered into the DAO compound to provide extra security for an evacuation everyone knew was coming. But Sullivan knew that by "us," Ghilain meant MSGs.

"Seventeen," he said. "Including the two newbies."

Ghilain wiped his dripping forehead with his sleeve. "Jesus Lord," he said.

The "newbies" or "snuffys"—young Marines of low rank—were Lance Corporal Darwin Judge and Corporal Charles McMahon, who had only recently been deployed to Saigon straight from the MSG School in Quantico, Virginia. The twenty-one-year-old McMahon, eleven days in-country, was particularly raw, and Ghilain had taken a special interest in him when he discovered that they were practically neighbors back home in Massachusetts. McMahon had grown up in Woburn, a blue-collar mill town north of Boston that had already lost twelve of its sons to Vietnam. Although Ghilain was only a few months older than McMahon, his plan was to mentor the new Marine on the ins and outs of Saigon to ensure that number never reached thirteen. But his pet project was scotched a mere twenty-four hours after McMahon's arrival, when he and sixteen other MSGs, including the other new man, Judge, were transferred to the DAO to buttress the Fleet Marine presence.

Although loathe to let the others see it, the twenty-nine-year-old Sullivan was also worrying over the safety of the newbies. As the second-ranking noncommissioned officer in the detachment, it was his job to gauge each Marine's strengths and weaknesses. Yet he had never gotten a feel for McMahon. He just hadn't been around long enough. The eighteen-year-old Judge was a different story. The son of an Iowa mailman and looking every bit the part, Judge had been in Saigon seven weeks. On his second night in-country, he'd been posted to stand sentry as an adjunct to U.S. Ambassador Graham Martin's six-man personal security unit, or PSU, at Martin's residence on Dien Bien Phu Street, four blocks from the embassy. The next morning at chow, Sullivan had been corralled by Marine Staff Sergeant Dwight McDonald, a former MSG who had joined the ambassador's PSU. McDonald said that Judge had asked him if he ever gets scared.

"Told him, damn right I do. Then gave him a pat on the back and told him to keep his head down."

Sullivan had nodded and said nothing. The PSUs were a cocky bunch who looked down their noses at the embassy security guards. They dressed in civilian clothing, were allowed to let their hair grow over their collars, and were issued exotic automatic weapons such as Israeli Uzis. In addition, their multiple identification cards gave them nearly diplomatic privileges to roam freely all over the city and the surrounding countryside. To the MSGs, they projected an air of entitlement. Much of this, Sullivan suspected, had to do with the ambassador himself. The MSGs did not care for Martin. When he deigned to speak to them, or even acknowledge their existence for that matter, they found him off-putting and arrogant. But the Marines in his PSU were, by necessity, practically attached to the diplomat's hip. They adored him.

Yet to Sullivan, what McDonald had told him made sense. The same question Judge had asked crept often enough through Sullivan's mind, as well as: Why were we still here? In Sullivan's case, the answer was difficult to articulate. The winding trail the wiry, red-headed bantam rooster had taken from the rail yards and logging camps of Washington State to a foreign city under siege had been an adventuresome journey. It had not been so long ago, after all, that he had been a kid himself trying to avoid any military service that involved combat in Vietnam. Yet now here he was, a gung-ho Marine, willing to lay down his life for a disintegrating regime he neither liked nor respected.

It would have been one thing, Sullivan reasoned, if America's evacuation plan was all a ruse—if somewhere deep in the bowels of the Pentagon, the generals and admirals were planning a surprise invasion, an Inchon redux that would drive the North Vietnamese back across the Demilitarized Zone. But Sullivan was not a stupid man, and he knew this was not in the cards. Now, tonight, watching the NVA rockets sail over his head, thinking again about Judge and McMahon and the other MSGs out at the airport absorbing the bombardment, he simmered with anger. *If we're getting out, why wait until now? Why had we allowed our advantage, and our capability to do the job right, slip away?* To Sullivan this entire evacuation was simply a train wreck waiting to happen. And American Marines were standing on the tracks.

In his mind's eye, he pictured the tow-headed Judge with his piercing smile, and the long, gangly McMahon, the corners of his mouth still scarred from teenage acne. He tried to convince himself that they could fend for themselves. After all, they would not have been selected for the MSG battalion had they not had their wits about them. Marines had been protecting U.S. embassies and consulates since 1949, and the embassy guards were the elite of the Corps. Plucked from the top of their units and taught to handle situations as diverse as table etiquette and hand-to-hand combat, they were all smart men who knew how to think on their feet. Nonetheless, Sullivan had called in enough artillery strikes, much like the one now lighting up Tan Son Nhut Airport, to realize that incoming rockets played no favorites.

He wondered, not for the first time, if it had been a mistake to keep his conversation with the PSU McDonald to himself. He had never mentioned Judge's apprehensions to his immediate superior, Master Sergeant Juan Valdez. He and Valdez were the only two noncoms among the detachment who had served and fought during the war—the only two who had personally seen how a single strand of fear could steal a man's life.

"Like a light show out there, eh?"

Sullivan started at the voice. Valdez was standing beside him at the edge of the roof, the barrel of his M-16 rifle, its safety on, flush with the seam of his right pants leg. The gun looked like a child's toy in his huge hands. Sullivan had never heard him coming.

"Like old times," Sullivan said.

Two

Juan J. Valdez, the thirty-seven-year-old noncommissioned officer in charge, or NCOIC, of the Saigon MSGs, had been furious when Judge and McMahon were shipped into Saigon so late in the game. A notoriously understated Marine, Valdez had nonetheless griped loud and long to the MSG company commander, Major Jim Kean, about having to baby-sit a couple of newbies in the midst of . . . well, Valdez was also a religious man and did not like to curse, no matter how often the word *clusterfuck* crossed his mind.

"We have all we can do getting ready for the evac, and they're still sending kids over who don't have a clue about the operation," he told Kean when the major had flown in from the MSG company's Hong Kong headquarters a few days earlier. "I asked Battalion back in March not to ship anyone else over. Said they'd just get in the way, and I couldn't spare extra men to show them the ropes. They ignored me."

Kean understood and was more than a little sympathetic. He too saw no reason to be adding a trickle of inexperienced men to an already lost cause. If they were going to continue sending Marines to Vietnam, in Kean's opinion, they should have made it a couple of fighting divisions. The major also had a great deal of respect for his "Top," Master Sergeant Valdez, and the quiet authority he brought to his job. If Valdez said something was a mistake, then it was a mistake. But in his fourteen years in uniform, Kean had witnessed plenty of mistakes, some of which had cost men their lives. As much as he loved the Corps, he understood that it was not perfect. So as Valdez paced smartly before him—low-centered, irrefutable—he'd allowed the NCOIC to vent, all the while, and once again, taking the measure of the man.

Valdez, a twenty-year veteran, stood a trim six feet tall, his 190 pounds as hard as a sandbag.' Despite his bulk, he moved with a pantherish grace, and though innately gentle and retiring—an odd combination to find in a Marine master sergeant, now that Kean thought about it—when angered he could be menacing and gruff, his deep baritone voice hardening into a snarl and his cleft chin, large enough to grind stumps, jutting into the next county. He wore a jet-black mustache, as thick as a fruit bat and the envy of every young Marine in the outfit who had yet to start shaving. In his teens, Valdez had boxed as an amateur in his home town of San Antonio, Texas, and his time in the ring had left him with a cantilevered brow and flattened nose that Kean felt lent him the air of a man who had been run over by a tank and not fully reassembled.

Which was nearly true. Ten years earlier, Valdez had landed on a Vietnamese beachhead as the sergeant in command of a Marine amphibious transport craft, or AMTRAC, platoon. He'd served eighteen months in the bush at the height of the war, leading his forty-ton vehicles through hot spots from Da Nang to Chu Lai and points in between. Like Kean, who had seen his share of jungle fighting, Valdez knew well that men without proper training too often risked becoming dead men walking.

He remembered one inexperienced boy in particular, an AMTRAC driver just transferred into his platoon. One night, after they'd "swam" their vehicles ashore following a report of VC activity, the kid's tractor ran over a mine, rolled over, and sank into an NVA tunnel. It turned out to be a huge, underground field hospital, and the AMTRAC just disappeared from sight. Before anyone in the outfit could reach him, the young Marine had panicked and crawled out through the hatch—exactly what Valdez would have taught him not to do if only he had the time to train him. Wounded enemy soldiers sat up in their cots and riddled him with bullets.

Valdez put the thought out of his mind. Like Sullivan, he told himself that Judge and McMahon were trained MSGs, schooled too well to do anything so foolish.

Valdez had transferred into Saigon from the Budapest Embassy the previous September and did not talk much about past combat. But he never demanded that a Marine perform any task that he wouldn't do himself, and word spread among the detachment that he had seen hard action. The nickname that the men gave him was the Quiet Man. Kean had done his homework on his top sergeant; he had learned that Valdez's battle résumé and ramrod physical presence belied a tender heart. Valdez was an animal lover who could not pass a stray dog without wanting to adopt it, and as a Seventh Day Adventist, he did not countenance rodeos or horse racing or even the circus because of what he felt was their exploitation of God's lesser creatures. Once, as they'd watched Olympic highlights together over the Armed Forces Television Network, Kean did a double-take when Valdez confessed that his two favorite sports were gymnastics and ice skating. And the big NCOIC also had a weakness for syrupy Sinatra ballads and the schmaltzy black-and-white television fare of his youth such as *Father Knows Best* and *The Andy Griffith Show.* Knowing all this, it was not hard for Kean to appreciate Valdez's mother hen tendencies, particularly toward the youngsters Judge and McMahon. Hell, Judge even looked a little like the television character Opie.

"Do the best you can with them, Top," Kean said when Valdez had finished his rant. "Just try to keep them out of the shit."

To that end, Valdez had already opted to assign the new men to the small squad of MSGs headed to Dodge City to assist with the refugee stack-up. It was not an easy decision, but someone had to go. The terms of the year-old Paris Accords had by the middle of 1974 limited the number of armed U.S. military personnel in South Vietnam to fifty, exempting the embassy MSGs. In a Rube Goldberg–esque adherence to this decree, the platoon of Fleet Marines recently flown into the airport had left the helicopters dressed as civilians, in leisure suits no less, concealing their uniforms and weapons in bulky green duffel bags. Valdez had rolled his eyes. Forty young, military-aged men in buzz cuts wearing mufti. *As if that was going to fool Charlie.*

Yet despite this influx of firepower, the U.S. State Department still deemed security at Tan Son Nhut lacking, and ten days earlier, Ambassador Martin had specifically requested that Valdez supplement it with a squad of MSGs. The MSGs often worked posts at the DAO, and Martin reasoned that they were more familiar with the lay of the land. But Valdez sensed immediately that obeying Martin's request and splitting his command so near to the end was lunacy.

"They'll never make it back through the chaos come time to bug out," he told Kean. "And what if we have to fight? When it hits the fan, they'll be stranded out there T.U." *Tits Up.* "Doesn't anybody around here remember Da Nang?"

Kean knew the "Top" was right. But he also recognized that what was occurring in South Vietnam, in Saigon, was no longer America's war. It was a civil war the South was destined to lose. Kean walked a tightrope: his job was to protect American interests while keeping his young Marines as far away from the cross fire as duty allowed. Making his position more difficult was the fact that unlike any other unit in the United States Marine Corps chain of command, MSG detachments around the world reported exclusively to, and took their orders from, the U.S. State Department.

This meant that Valdez, and now Kean, were technically under the supervision of a civilian named Marvin Garrett, whom State had appointed as the embassy's regional security officer. From the moment he'd been interviewed by the RSO on his arrival seven months earlier, Valdez had considered the pink-faced Garrett a blister of a man, his personality unencumbered with charisma. He had also come to suspect, not without reason, that Garrett was incompetent. He'd kept that opinion to himself when Kean arrived and asked about Garrett. Valdez had merely warned the major, "Smiles like he just closed an orphanage. Just reason with him, drives him crazy." He'd read that line somewhere, and always liked it.

Kean understood. He nonetheless had to deal with the fiction of Garrett's authority as best he could. Which is why, after conferring with Valdez, he'd asked Garrett to accompany him to the office of Wolfgang Lehmann to plead his case against dividing his MSG detachment.

Lehmann, whose family had fled Germany and the Nazis when he was thirteen years old, was the embassy's deputy chief of mission, Ambassador Martin's number two, and a skilled bureaucratic infighter with a reputation for carrying out Martin's more furtive orders with a stiletto as opposed to a hatchet. When Kean entered his third-floor office, a blue fug of cigarette smoke hung over the room, and despite the whirring air-conditioner, it smelled like the inside of a powder magazine. The Marine major made his case. Lehman acted commiserative but could not help.

"If State wants MSGs at the airport, they get MSGs at the airport," he said with a shrug. Like nearly every other diplomat Kean had ever met, Lehmann seemed to speak in italics. As Kean turned to leave, Lehmann added, "Don't worry, Major; they're Marines. They'll be okay."

Kean frowned at the civilian's insouciance. His men were Marines, all right, but as tight as new boots. Hours later, when Valdez handed him a list of the sixteen MSGs peeled off for the DAO posting, he pulled out his duty roster and compared the names on the transfer orders to their length of service in Saigon. Valdez had done as he had asked: they were predominantly the men with the least experience in-country. He wanted his most savvy Marines here at the embassy. The major found a telephone and called the DAO. He was looking for an old colleague, a colonel he knew from Marine Corps headquarters in Quantico who was now billeted at Dodge City as a military liaison to the South Vietnamese Marine Corps.

"I need a favor," Kean said when he got him on the line. "Keep an eye on my kids for me. Make sure they don't slip through the cracks come time to evac. I know for a fact there is no way they're going to be able to get across town when this thing blows. Hell, we're just trying to best-guess everything here as it is."

The colonel promised to look after Kean's "kids," and in the meanwhile Valdez tapped a tough and cocky gunnery sergeant named Vasco Martin to command the DAO-bound squad. Martin himself had arrived in-country only two weeks previous, en route to become NCOIC of the Da Nang MSG deployment that no longer existed. Valdez tried mightily to rationalize his decision. After all, he told himself, Major Kean had directed him to keep the new troops out of harm's way, and the DAO might be the safest place in Saigon at the moment. If the North Vietnamese truly wanted every last American out of the city—"the enemy's last den," Ho Chi Minh had famously called it—there was no way in hell they'd be stupid enough to bomb the airport.

Three

The thirty-three-year-old Jim Kean was what the Marines called a "Mustang," an enlisted man who had been promoted through the ranks to officer and thus carried a worldview from the mud as well as the saddle. Two weeks earlier, as the situation in South Vietnam deteriorated faster than anyone in Washington had expected, he'd arrived in Saigon from Hong Kong to oversee America's withdrawal from the embassy, the last sliver of U.S. territory in Vietnam.

It was Kean's third trip to Saigon as commanding officer of Company C, a post that also included oversight of the MSG detachments across a broad swath of Asia. But the Saigon MSG detachment was the largest and most important in the world, and Kean was cognizant of the legacy he had been sent to sever—a legacy that stretched to the Corps' first amphibious landing near Da Nang a decade earlier.

At that time, when Marines came ashore on Da Nang's Red Beach in March 1965, Kean had been a $200-a-month "punk corporal" planning to elope to Reno, Nevada, with the former Rosanne Sorci, the daughter of an Italian-American fisherman from Monterey, California, he had met two months earlier. Eighteen months later, after successfully completing Officer Candidate School, he became one of them: a green second lieutenant—a "Butterbar" in Marine slang—trekking through the bush as an artillery forward observer for Delta Company of the 1st Battalion of the 7th Regiment of the renowned "Old Breed," the 1st Marine Division. The experience was simultaneously the greatest, the saddest, and the most terrifying adventure of his life. It was also nothing like what his dad had ever described.

The Keans were the progeny of a clan of hard-drinking and hard-fighting Scots-Irish who had emigrated to western Pennsylvania's steel country a century earlier and found jobs in the Carnegie mills. World War II broke the generational chain, and Kean's father, Donald, landed on Guadalcanal as a Navy Seabee in 1942, and two years later fought in southern France. Donald Kean went on to become one of the Navy's first frogmen, and his war stories held his oldest son, Jim, in thrall. Kean once wrote to his bride, "The drama of war was emblazoned in my mind forever through my focus on my father."

When Donald Kean chose to make the Navy a career, he moved his wife, Elizabeth, and five-year-old Jim to San Diego. Although Jim Kean was to return to visit his Pennsylvania relatives often throughout his lifetime, the winter bone-chill and smoky haze that overlay the rugged Allegheny hill country was forever supplanted in his mind by the smells of southern California's orange blossoms, honeysuckle, eucalyptus, and portulaca—as well as the constant sight of squared-away Marines in their sharp dress-blue uniforms entering and exiting nearby Camp Pendleton.

Though in time the Kean family was again on the road—Donald Kean's Navy deployments took him from New Orleans to Alaska and points in between—the electric memory of those Camp Pendleton Marines never left young Jim. After graduating from high school in Alameda, California, and attempting a brief, if futile, one-semester foray through college, he walked into the Marine recruiting office in Santa Barbara in 1961 and enlisted. Throughout his childhood, perhaps because of the family's frequent moves, he had always been a loner and rarely a joiner. But he considered this the best decision of his life.

Never much for book work, he had sailed through Encinal High as a star baseball athlete on a team that fielded three future major leaguers, including Hall of Famer Willie Stargell. But once in the Corps, Kean discovered in himself an aptitude for languages and, of all things, mathematics. He combined these skills to carve out a military niche in both Russian language studies and artillery training. He re-upped for a second four-year hitch and was sent to Vietnam in summer 1966. On one of his first reconnaissance patrols, he was cutting through a hedgerow with a dog trainer by his side when the dog triggered a booby trap. The explosion killed the dog and blew the trainer's severed hand into Kean's chest. "It happened so fast I didn't even puke," he wrote afterward.

As a young Marine back in the States, Kean had listened to the war stories told by the crusty veterans of World War II with an envy bordering on relish. He envisioned his Vietnam deployment in the same heroic terms, much like the violent old Irish sagas his grandfather and older uncles told—where good men always prevailed and the enemy was nameless, faceless, and dead. The booby trap incident was his initiation into the realities of war.

A month after the severed-hand incident, he contracted a severe case of dysentery and lost twenty pounds. After his recovery, Kean returned to his field artillery unit near Chu Lai and, feeling homesick, received permission to borrow a Jeep and visit his best friend from Basic School back in Quantico, another young Marine lieutenant named Sandy Kempner. Kempner was stationed only ten miles away, but the muddy slog across the only dirt road connecting the two outposts took Kean most of the morning. When he arrived, he was informed that Kempner had been critically wounded hours earlier when his convoy rolled over a minefield, and he had died of shock before he could be medevaced out. Kean was devastated. By this time in his deployment tour, he had seen men die before, but not someone so close to him.

On November 24, 1966, it was nearly Kean's turn. His unit had just off-loaded onto a hot landing zone when the Marine next to him stepped on a mine. The Marine lost his leg, and Kean was knocked unconscious by flying shrapnel. Flown to a field hospital in Chu Lai, he awoke with a severe case of amnesia. For five days he could not remember who he was, where he was, and why he was there. On the sixth day he awoke to a vision of his wife, Rosanne, and thereafter his memory gradually returned. He was back with Delta Company in time for Christmas.

Two months later, in February 1967, he added a Bronze Star to his Purple Heart when he returned to the scene of an ambush to rescue a wounded Marine inadvertently left behind after the firefight. But any such heroics—and he didn't think he had done anything any other Marine wouldn't do—were not what lingered in the recess of his mind about the incident. Instead, the exchange he had with his radio operator during the heat of the firefight was the story he came away with and loved to repeat over cocktails.

His platoon was pinned down atop an elevated causeway, several of his men were wounded, and Kean ordered everyone hunkered down to await the artillery fire he'd called in on the enemy positions. He then turned to his radio operator and jokingly hollered to the man to extend the device's long FM whip antenna in order to draw fire toward the radio and away from Kean. Whether the radio operator knew Kean was employing his morbid sense of humor or not, Kean found his response priceless: "Sir, fuck you, sir."

When he made it back to his base, he was informed that he was the father of a baby girl. He and Rosanne named their daughter Paige.

It was with mixed feelings that Kean departed Vietnam in fall 1967. He was anxious to see his new daughter, but he was also leaving good men and good friends behind. He recognized that America's war aims were far from being fulfilled, and he felt that if anyone could help secure victory, it was experienced soldiers such as himself. But the Marines had other plans for him.

Promoted to captain and serving as a Special Courts Martial Officer in San Diego, he fought through his restlessness by supplementing his Russian language expertise with courses in Mandarin Chinese. Much to his wife's dismay—the Keans were by now also the proud parents of Paige's younger brother, Edward Michael—Kean finagled a deployment back to Da Nang in 1970, first as a translator and POW interrogator and, later, as an artillery officer attached to a flattened hilltop shorn of vegetation, named Fire Support Base Ryder, southwest of the city. It was there, while riding shotgun in a reconnaissance helicopter, that he was hit in the butt by a sniper and earned his second Purple Heart. He was embarrassed by the location of his wound—"more holes in his ass than originally issued"—and at a small party after the award ceremony, his friends surreptitiously situated the commendation so that the medal was under the ribbon of the Purple Heart and thus the "cheeks" were down.

With the Marine drawdown from South Vietnam in full swing by 1971—the war was the Army's to win or lose now—Kean began a kinetic journey through the Corps that included Asian Studies courses and

Amphibious Warfare School. He wasn't sure where his future lay when, two years later, he was offered a job as the executive officer, the second-in-command, of Company C in Hong Kong. He jumped at it so quickly he volunteered to swim over. He moved his family to Hong Kong, where a second Kean daughter, Pamela Anne, was born, and settled into a routine of military diplomacy and travel on embassy and consulate inspection tours.

At the time, Company C oversaw MSG detachments at twenty-three embassies and various consulates, ranging from the Indian subcontinent to Beijing to Tokyo. The travel informed Kean as both a man and a Marine officer. Because of his security clearance, he sailed through a cryptic, alien world. Conversations with local political officials, CIA operatives, and U.S. State Department employees allowed him to gain a much broader perspective about what was the truth behind the headlines coming out of Asia. The prognosis for South Vietnam was grim.

From his new posting, he also followed the progress of the Paris Peace Talks with a chary eye. He felt Henry Kissinger had been fleeced by North Vietnamese Foreign Minister Le Duc Tho, and it hadn't surprised him when South Vietnam President Nguyen Van Thieu had to be pressured to sign off on the document. Thieu might have been corrupt to the marrow, but he wasn't stupid. He knew that the United States was now free to abandon his country. Kean also recognized that the psychological effect on the South Vietnamese was almost as devastating as the physical reality.

When a solemn President Nixon promised to prosecute any cease-fire violations by Hanoi, Kean had almost believed him. Perhaps, he thought, Nixon even believed it himself—until he was forced to resign in August 1974 over the Watergate scandal. When Congress cut the new President Ford's legs out from under him by slashing the Pentagon's Vietnam budget by two-thirds, Kean considered it the final stab. The enactment of a subsequent bill that prohibited the use of U.S. military force "in or over Indochina" was, in the major's view, Washington's way of twisting the knife. It was the word *over* that caught his eye.

The Americans had reconfigured South Vietnam's armed forces in their mirror image in terms of organization, logistics, and even maintenance. The one thing they could not provide for them was an effective air force.

Unlike in 1972, when Hanoi's full-bore spring offensive had been beaten back by Operation Linebacker, the first sustained B-52 bombing of North Vietnam by the United States in four years, this new congressional bill meant the end of U.S. air support.

In the summer of 1974, Kean took over Company C—at about the same time Hanoi began rearming and refurbishing the more than 130,000 soldiers, Russian-made tanks, and untold pieces of heavy artillery a controversial clause in the Paris Accords had allowed the North to keep in South Vietnam. Simultaneously, North Vietnamese work crews began construction on a network of roads to enable those troops to shift rapidly from sector to sector. When these acts of belligerence drew no U.S. reprisals, despite Secretary of Defense James Schlesinger's congressional testimony that Hanoi was breaking the Paris Peace Accords, North Vietnam's Defense Minister General Vo Nguyen Giap and his chief military commander, General Van Tien Dung, realized that America's response was all motion without action.

In December 1974, Kean made his second trip to Saigon to introduce himself to Sergeant Valdez and inspect the troops. "Adult supervision," the MSGs called it. They saw an officer only twice a year.

Kean took to Valdez from the moment they met and shook hands; he noted that Valdez's grip was like a hickory stick covered with sandpaper. The feeling was mutual. Valdez and a few of the MSGs had arranged a small welcoming party in one of the topless bars on Tu Do Street, but the major had shown no inclination to partake of the women. Instead, he drank each one of his Marines under the table. The next morning, looking no worse for wear, Kean warned his NCOIC that Dung's armies would not wait long before making an all-out sprint to Saigon: "With Nixon gone, all bets are off. I'm guessing a spring offensive. Almost worked for them last time."

To Valdez's questioning looks, Kean could offer nothing beyond the suggestion that the top sergeant ramp up weapons training as well as trips to the target range. He sensed that Valdez was underwhelmed by the directive. Three months later, not long after Kean's promotion to major, the dominos began to topple.

Reading the classified reports of the Communist surge south through

Da Nang and the coastal provinces, Kean felt a particular throb in his gut when he saw the ease with which the North Vietnamese had driven ARVN units from his old hilltop artillery camp, Fire Support Base Ryder. Not a single shot had been fired. He recalled, with a little bitterness, his carefree days as a Marine grunt yearning to be deployed to that hilltop artillery redoubt. Now the major was a man whose fire had been banked to an ember, but an ember carefully tended as he watched the destruction of a country he had seen so many young men die for. He couldn't quite articulate what bothered him more: the nearly 58,000 wasted American lives or the fact that here, today, his beloved Marine Corps was in retreat. He wondered, *How could this be?*

Four

One of Jim Kean's first orders on landing in Saigon was to abandon the Marine House on Hong Thap Tu Street, a converted hotel less than a mile from the embassy where the MSGs were billeted. The Marine House had been officially designated Marshall Hall in honor of an embassy guard, Corporal James Marshall, who had been killed during the 1968 Tet Offensive, and the Saigon MSGs had lived on Hong Thap Tu Street since 1969. Leaving it was a clear signal to all that the "bug out" was close.

It was not without sadness that Master Sergeant Valdez and Staff Sergeant Sullivan ordered the detachment to inventory and pack up all of its weapons and military-issue gear in large wooden crates and truck them to the embassy compound. The men were also allowed to take whatever personal belongings they could stuff into a single duffel bag, and as they filled their rucksacks, they moved at a desultory pace, stopping often to swap stories: about the time one MSG had scaled the outside of the locked building to sneak in an unconscious French hooker draped over his shoulders; about the marathon poker games; about the rowdy barbecues and fish fries they'd hosted on the roof. On their way out, the MSGs plied their longtime Vietnamese cooks, housekeepers, and drivers with gifts and thick wads of piasters. Sullivan made sure they also received whatever was left of the liquor from the fourth-floor bar after his Marines had combed through it.

"Don't want it going to some ComSymp," he told Valdez.

The NCOIC laughed. Half the Marine House staff probably fell into the category of Communist sympathizers.

Late in the afternoon, Valdez paced the sidewalk outside Marine House as the last of the boxes and bags were loaded onto trucks. Above him, the last flecks of the fading day mottled the twin spires of the Notre Dame Basilica, the great red-brick cathedral erected by the French. Streams of traffic merged and hooted and swirled along Hong Thap Tu Street as a few of the MSGs jotted stateside addresses for the local help should they manage to make it out. That no one truly believed this possible only added to their general gloom.

And then they were gone. Valdez stood alone before the empty building. He felt that he should make a gesture, perhaps salute, like they would in the Hollywood movies. Instead he turned, jumped into his Jeep, and drove away.

The Marines stowed their personal gear in a corner of the now abandoned canteen in the embassy's combined recreation area, or CRA, separated from the Chancery, the compound's main building, by a low wall, and spread their sleeping bags in the swimming pool dressing room on cots hauled up from a basement storeroom. On nights when it didn't rain, they carried the cots to the building's roof and slept under the stars. Kean, Valdez, and Sullivan found space in the Chancery itself, along the narrow hallways, in near-empty storerooms—wherever they could find an empty piece of floor. Valdez commandeered a small guard's office near the lobby elevators to use as an office.

Kean realized that the move was as symbolic to his Marines as it was to the Vietnamese, North and South, who surveilled them constantly. In the confusion and anarchy of these final days, the city had become a swamp of rumors and half-truths, and his men were not immune to them. There was already talk among the MSGs that the Communists had slaughtered every male over the age of twelve when they'd captured Da Nang. Kean knew this was not true, and he was determined to confront the hearsay head-on when he summoned Valdez the morning after they'd abandoned Marshall Hall. The straight dope wasn't much more comforting, but at least it was the straight dope.

"Men secure, Top?"

Valdez nodded.

"You, too?"

"I'm out."

Although Valdez kept a room at the Marine House, as the NCOIC he was also allowed to maintain separate quarters in a rented home closer to the embassy on Gia Long Street. He had lived there with his Vietnamese girlfriend, and after helping to secure her an exit visa, he had crammed all his personal belongings into a battered old steamer trunk and arranged for it to be shipped to the city's Newport Pier, on the Saigon River. There, barges leased to American contractors were supposed to be ferrying material out to the Seventh Fleet. The trunk contained all his memories from Budapest: personal photographs, a beautiful traditional Hungarian porcelain sword, a hand-embroidered arras depicting the sixteenth-century Ottoman siege. When he had locked up his home on Gia Long Street, the trunk was still sitting in the foyer. He knew he would never see it again.

"What have you told the men?" Kean said.

Valdez's shoulders shrugged ever so slightly. "Since the Highlands fell, Sullivan and me been pulling them together in small groups, reminding them to keep everything buttoned up. Since Da Nang and Phnom Penh, well, not much to say." The Cambodian capital had been captured by the Khmer Rouge on April 12.

"They know the shit's coming. Can't hide it. Refugee lines out the door and 'round the block every morning, longer each day. All the papa-sans trying to get in here to exchange piasters for dollars. Hell, the hookers downtown know more than we do. Still, we're taking the squad leaders aside all the time just to drill it in. You hear about Lehmann?"

Valdez nodded. The deputy chief of mission had been quoted the day before on Armed Forces Radio declaring, "Militarily, the North Vietnamese do not have the capability of launching an offensive against Saigon."

"That's bullshit, of course," Kean said. "General assembly tomorrow morning. Third-floor conference room."

Valdez shot him a questioning look. Who would man the posts? "All of them?" he said.

Kean smiled at his mistake. "Two assemblies, then," he said. "First one, an hour before shift break. Get half in. Then after shift break, the other half."

Kean added one more thing. "All liberty cancelled, Top. From now on, nobody leaves the compound except on official business."

At 8 A.M. the next morning, thirty-odd drowsy MSGs straggled into the large conference room adjacent to Ambassador Martin's office. The air-conditioning, powered by generators, was on full blast. It lent the atmosphere the clammy feel of a morgue. A moment later, Kean entered with an unfamiliar man wearing a tropical bush jacket, khakis, and desert boots. The major introduced the civilian as Frank Snepp, a long-time Saigon-based CIA operative.

"We could be looking at an Alamo situation here," Kean told the Marines. They all laughed. It died down quickly when the major did not smile. "I've asked Frank to give you the SitRep."

Snepp, worldly and confident, ambled to the front of the conference room, ran a hand through his thick, wavy brown hair, and opened a small notebook. He wasted no time getting to the heart of his situation report.

"Saigon is now encircled by at least ten, and probably fifteen, NVA divisions," he said. "Between 100,000 and 150,000 professional, battle-hardened soldiers. They outnumber the ARVNs three to one. They will not wait much longer for us to leave voluntarily."

Snepp paused to let the image sink in. He was describing ants picking a carcass clean, and the MSGs knew it. Then: "Another thing: a significant number of VC cadres and NVA forward artillery observers have already infiltrated the city."

This was no secret. The Marines knew that small, mobile flying squads of Vietcong had been roaming Saigon for months, if not years, to say nothing of the Communist sympathizers. A few weeks earlier, three MSGs—Corporal Ghilain, Corporal Steve Schuller, and Corporal Stephen Bauer—were returning to the Marine House from a night on the town when they'd paid off three cyclo-rickshaw drivers to let them stage a race. Ghilain ran his rickshaw into a wall, and when it tipped over, a cache of rifles and revolvers spilled out from under the seat. *Fucking Cong.* The rickshaw drivers all took off—the Marines were in no condition to chase after them—as the MSGs cursed and laughed.

Moreover, each night Valdez posted MSGs to the ambassador's residence to reinforce Martin's PSU, and each morning these men would return and detail for him the firefights they'd overheard, and sometimes witnessed, from the guard tower. Skirmishes between the VC and ARVN units had become commonplace in the huge cemetery across from the ambassador's front gates, and Valdez could only marvel over the fact that there remained any South Vietnamese soldiers still willing to engage the enemy. He had issued an across-the-board order that no MSG was to fire his weapon unless fired on, but he also knew that his frustrated young Marines, juiced on adrenaline and squatting helplessly behind sandbags, were itching to join the fight.

Now the CIA man, Snepp, brought the MSGs up short with the latest bit of intelligence: "Some of these NVA infiltrators have been apprehended wearing South Vietnamese army and police uniforms."

The MSGs exchanged glances. They worked side by side every day with the Vietnam National Police, the Canh Sat who had been nicknamed the "White Mice" by the Americans for their white gloves and the white stripes and large white precinct numerals on their helmets. The White Mice even patrolled the outside perimeter of the embassy.

As Snepp broke down the NVA divisions by the latest estimates of their strength and locations, Kean studied the faces of his men. In the days since his arrival, he had traversed Saigon often enough to sense the physical and emotional fatigue permeating the besieged city. Gone were the legions of strollers out for their evening *faire le promenade* through the town's grand boulevards; in their places trudged a small army of invalid war veterans— legless, armless, scarred by napalm, begging alms with tin cups. On his previous visits, he had been seduced and charmed by the fragile beauty of the Vietnamese people—particularly the women, whom he found brisk rather than chic in their flowery, form-fitting *ao dais* beneath bright parasols— and the sensuousness of their culture. But now a pall lay over the cafés and bars, the backstreet shrines and temples—what the local French had taken to calling *le petit mort*. The little death.

It was not, however, figurative deaths that made him anxious. It was the very possibility of the real thing. For despite the diplomatic dance about negotiations and last-minute cease-fires, he had studied the North Vietnamese well enough to understand them. He felt that once they had advanced this far, they had no intention of stopping. Frank Snepp said they had ten to fifteen divisions. Jim Kean had sixty-two Marines.

When Snepp finished speaking, he called for questions. The young Marines squirmed in their chairs, and then Kean saw a hand shoot up in the back. It belonged to Corporal Stephen Bauer, a handsome, dark-haired twenty year old who had transferred in six months earlier from his posting in Vienna. Bauer had been brought up short on his first day in-country when Valdez issued him a loaded M-16 rifle with an extra magazine and casually told him not to lose it. In Austria, the embassy security guards were unarmed most of the time. But here, Bauer soon learned, "regs" were a bit looser.

Bauer had grown up just outside New York City, on Long Island, the son of an aerospace engineer, and he was comfortable engaging his more experienced elders. Now he stood to address the civilian intelligence office. *Figures it would be a New York kid to call out the spook*, Kean thought.

"What about this hammer-and-anvil thing we've been hearing?" Bauer said. A few Marines murmured in anticipation. One rumor making the rounds had it that the ARVN generals—and by implication, U.S. military strategists—had purposely allowed the North Vietnamese to ring Saigon in order to bunch together, and target, the Communists in one place. When the time was right, the South would call up reinforcements from the Mekong Delta, drop them behind the NVA by parachute and helicopter, and hammer them on the anvil of the 60,000 ARVN troops stationed in the city.

Kean was grateful that Snepp did not laugh aloud at this fantasy.

"Good question," the spy said. "Short answer: ain't happening. The South hasn't enough men, and the North has reserve divisions up and down the country. If it were possible, Thieu would have tried it in Da Nang. Saigon will fall. And soon. Anyone else?"

There were no more questions. Kean sensed what each of his men was thinking. After Snepp loped out of the room, the Major added his own addendum.

"Every Marine a rifleman," he said, repeating the essential philosophy of the Corps, drilled into a grunt from the first day of boot camp. He jerked his chin in the direction of the embassy's front gate. "I don't know what's coming over those walls. Or how it's coming. Or when it's coming. But I can promise you one thing. When it does come, we will fight like Marines."

He paused to study the stony faces staring back at him. "And if it comes to it, we will not only fight like Marines; if we have to, we will die like Marines."

An ear-splitting roar filled the room.

Five

A s ranking officer of Company C, Jim Kean had also been charged with the supervision of four smaller MSG units, consisting of six Marines each, assigned to U.S. consulates in the South Vietnamese provincial capitals of Da Nang, Nha Trang, Bien Hoa, and Can Tho. The first two cities fell before the major's arrival in Saigon, and Valdez had absorbed these Marines into his detachment. The Nha Trang MSGs had come by chopper the night that city was overrun, the Da Nang contingent by a four-day barge trip down the coast. The sea voyage had allowed time for the ugly events they had witnessed to fester and boil.

When Valdez debriefed these new Marines individually, to a man they swore that they were squared away, ready to continue on as MSGs in Saigon. But the NCOIC was wary of integrating them into his command. He was a believer in the old battlefield adage: rarely believe a casualty, and never believe a straggler. And these were the ultimate stragglers. Not knowing what else to do, he'd housed them in the Marine House, and reports were soon reaching him of the night-terror screams echoing through its hallways. When Kean flew in, the NCOIC quietly pulled him aside one day about the problem. These men, he said, were so traumatized by the chaotic evacuations they'd witnessed that it was affecting the morale of his own MSGs.

Kean was dubious: they were, after all, highly trained U.S. Marine Security Guards. Then Valdez told him a story he had tried to hide not only from the embassy civilians but also from his own Marines. Since he was trying to keep it a secret, naturally every one of his men knew about it.

Early one recent morning, he told Kean, a young corporal from Da Nang had completely slipped his brake and begun hallucinating.

"Runs bughouse into the lobby yelling that Charlie is coming to get us all. 'The fuckers are coming, the fuckers are coming,' he's hollering. Attacks the Sergeant of the Guard. Doug Potratz. Thank God, the guy wasn't armed. Took three of my men to get him into a straitjacket. Shot him up with thorazine."

Hours later, Valdez continued, a small delegation of Saigon MSGs led by the squad leader, Sergeant Potratz, a twenty-one-year-old Marine with, at sixteen months, the longest-serving Saigon experience and one of the "old men" of the outfit—came to see him.

"Doesn't want to press charges or anything like that. Just tells me, 'They've seen enough already, Top. No way they're able to integrate and perform with us. Fact is, they're gonna infect us. Give 'em a medal and get 'em out of here.'"

Valdez let it sink in. "Tell you what, Major. I agree."

So, now, did Kean. He had most of the new men isolated for the night and flown out to the fleet the next day. Valdez's recounting of the incident bothered him, though. He knew there were more MSGs coming. Bien Hoa, just eighteen miles east of Saigon, was directly in the path of the North Vietnamese advance. And Can Tho, straddling the Mekong Delta's Bassac River 100 miles to the southwest, was also teetering on the verge as a combination of NVA and VC moved up from the south.

And, in fact, several days later, on April 23, NVA sappers infiltrated Bien Hoa, a virtual suburb of the capital city, and the artillery battle for the town began. The North Vietnamese gunners were careful to avoid shelling close to American positions, on orders of General Dung. Faced with the inevitable, the American consul in Bien Hoa, Richard Peters, gathered his small staff and his MSG detachment and bolted the consulate doors, and they all fled overland in Jeeps to Saigon. Over the next several days, Saigon itself was shelled regularly with 122s.

"Political rockets," Kean explained once to Valdez. "Warning us to stop evacuating South Vietnamese and go home."

So far, Kean noted, the demand was being ignored. He had monitored the evacuation of Phnom Penh from Bangkok, when U.S. helicopters had lifted 82 Americans, 159 Cambodians, and 35 third-country nationals out of the Cambodian capital one step ahead of the triumphant Khmer Rouge. The entire operation—"Eagle Pull" was its code name—had been such a textbook operation an observer might have thought it was a stateside training drill. A battalion landing team of Marines had flown in from the Seventh Fleet, formed a hasty perimeter around the embassy compound, and the Americans and their Cambodian staff were extracted in exactly two hours and twenty-three minutes.

But the Phnom Penh operation had been blessed by many favorable factors, from location near the sea to perfect weather to, not least in Kean's mind, the fact that the U.S. ambassador to Cambodia, John Gunther Dean, was a seasoned diplomatic veteran who had spent his career handling difficult scrapes. More important, Kean knew, Cambodia was a sideshow compared to South Vietnam. Its evacuation did not sting like the abandonment of Saigon certainly would. Nonetheless, back in the States, there were already small rumblings in and out of the media over the Cambodian civilians America had left to Pol Pot's butchers.

Jim Kean had done the math. President Ford had declared that it was U.S. policy to evacuate "those Vietnamese to whom we have a special obligation and whose lives may be endangered." In Saigon alone, American planners pegged that number at 200,000. It would take every airplane and helicopter in America's arsenal, operating around the clock for weeks, to get out all of them. Weeks? Half of Ambassador Martin's own staff, if not the ambassador himself, recognized that it was merely a matter now of counting down the days, if not the hours. Kean wondered, again, if he and his men would be ordered to make a last stand for the ones who would never escape.

Now, in the early evening hours of April 28, with Frank Snepp's SitRep fresh in his mind, Jim Kean invited Juan Valdez and Mike Sullivan to join him and his translator in an empty embassy office he'd commandeered for the occasion.

The three Americans gathered around a tinny Japanese radio to listen to the new president of South Vietnam, General Duong Van Minh, address his people for the first time in his inauguration speech. A finger of light from the waxing moon lit the horizon, where jagged bolts of heat lightning sheared the sky. Sharp salvos of thunder followed, causing bursts of loud static to drown out portions of the speech. Kean thought this appropriate. With the North Vietnamese knocking on his door, Minh, on the advice of his astrologer, had postponed his swearing in by twenty-four hours, waiting for the right stars to align. Kean gazed through the windows shielded by concrete rocket screens. It did not matter, he decided. What was there possibly left to say?

Forty-eight hours earlier, Ambassador Martin had vaulted Minh into the presidency with the aid of the French, who stilled pulled invisible strings in their former colony. The fifty-nine-year-old Minh was Martin's last, best hope—however delusional—for a negotiated truce. There were some in the United States who believed that the impoverished North would sit down with Minh not only because of their desperate need for international aid, but because of the one card he had left to play: his most loyal and professional troops still controlled Saigon and the Mekong Delta, the nation's breadbasket.

It was far above Kean's pay grade to comprehend why it had taken the politicians back in the States so long to dump President Thieu. Often in politics, the major understood, corruption was merely a sign of good manners. But Thieu's kleptocracy had taken the concept to new heights. Now all the years of distrust, incompetence, and outright theft had finally caught up to him.

Before Minh took office, Graham Martin had personally delivered the news to Thieu at Saigon's Independence Palace a few blocks away from the embassy, and Thieu's first instincts had been to fight the political coup engineered by the foreigners. But Martin was able to convince the man who for nearly eight years had held the divine "Mandate of Heaven" in South Vietnam that he was fortunate not to be leaving office feet first. The former president and his family were last seen the following morning at Tan Son Nhut in the company of Frank Snepp, lugging suitcases of gold bars aboard Martin's personal four-engine C-118 Liftmaster bound for Taiwan.

The new president had acquired the nickname "Big" Minh because, at six feet and 198 pounds, he towered over most of his countrymen. Now as Kean's translator fiddled with the radio dials, Valdez made a rare joke:

"Old Big's gonna need some big *cojones* to pull this country's chestnuts out of the fire."

Kean was tuned to the embassy scuttlebutt, and he knew that Martin's hope for fresh peace talks may well have held true six months ago. Hanoi had even hinted then that Minh would be an acceptable negotiating partner. But now General Dung and his armies would not settle for anything less than unconditional surrender. Even Minh appeared to recognize this, as Kean knew that he had already evacuated his daughter and grandchildren.

Kean passed out cans of beer and sandwiches as Big Minh's singsong voice drifted in and out through the static. Valdez and Sullivan ran the cold aluminum cans over their foreheads and necks before pulling the tabs. The major was drawing up machine-gun emplacements on an embassy map when his translator repeated one of the new president's declarations: "Our soldiers are fighting hard."

The Americans looked up from the chart and exchanged glances. It was too much for Sullivan.

"Hell, everyone in the city has been watching those cargo planes lifting out of Tan Son Nhut," he said. "Most of them carrying the South Vietnam high command. The other day some big-shot general stops a C-141 on the tarmac, pretends like he wants in to search it for draft-age men. Gets inside, buckles himself in, and leaves with the plane."

"Fighting hard," Valdez said. "Fighting hard to get on a Bird."

Valdez was in a sour mood. This was not how he envisioned his deployment ending. From his first day as a fifteen-year-old ROTC student at San Antonio's Tech High School, he had yearned to be a Marine, to storm a Pacific beachhead or a Nazi pillbox like John Wayne and Audie Murphy in the movies he watched every Saturday afternoon at the local theater. He hadn't seen much future as a Hispanic kid looking for honest work in Texas; picking strawberries or pecans held no allure, nor did following in his father's footsteps working as a maintenance man at the local golf course. He was a decent amateur boxer and a much better baseball player, yet even as a teenager, he had the presence of mind to realize that sports would not take him far in life. No, the Marines would be his ticket out of town.

San Antonio had been a hotbed of Marine recruiting since before

World War II. The intrinsic values of the Corps—men were judged by their ability, not the color of their skin or ethnic background—allowed for integration more easily than the other services. Every year when his high school ROTC drill team took part in the city's annual March of Flowers parade, he watched with a gimlet eye as the multi-hued Marine Corps Band stepped smartly to the front. And though Valdez had found school something to endure rather than enjoy, by his senior year he'd joined the Marine Reserves and become seriously indoctrinated into the service's *esprit de corps.* He knew how to break down and clean an assault rifle blindfolded, how to give and take an order, and how to march in step as well as that Marine Corps Band. At seventeen, upon his graduation from Tech High, he had only one goal in life, and he just had to convince his parents to sign the enlistment papers.

His father was not resistant. Salome Valdez had tried to instill in his son a set of moral values and principles, a respect for hard work and responsibility that mirrored the basic Corps precepts. He was happy for his son. But his mother proved an obstacle. Though the Korean War had largely wound down, the idea of Antonia Valdez's first-born son shipping off to some godforsaken country halfway around the world to fight Communists frightened her. It took some mighty convincing by the local Marine recruiter, a man named Joe Casillas, who would arrive regularly in his World War II–vintage Jeep at the Valdezes' clapboard house and take mother and son on long rides through the flat, rolling South Texas countryside, all the while extolling the virtues of the service.

The charm offensive finally broke Antonia, and the next day Valdez was on an American Airlines flight to San Diego and Camp Pendleton. It was his first time in an airplane. Twelve weeks of boot camp and four weeks of infantry training—"Every Marine a rifleman"—convinced him he had made the right decision; he enjoyed the torments more than his drill instructors would have preferred. When it came time to select his Military Occupational Specialty, or MOS, he remembered that Joe Casillas had been an AMTRAC man who had landed on the beaches of Tarawa, Saipan, and Okinawa during World War II. Valdez spent the next four years learning everything there was to know about the amphibious tractors of the 1st Marine Division.

He bounced from Hawaii to North Carolina's Camp Lejeune, back to Hawaii, and finally full circle back to Camp Pendleton on that first tour. Along the way, he married a Portuguese-Hawaiian woman named Adeline Demello in Oahu. By the time he reenlisted for another six years, the 1st Marine Division was already in the early planning stages for operations in Vietnam, and in early 1965 his AMTRAC platoon underwent jungle warfare training in the Philippines in anticipation of its landing in Da Nang.

Valdez now looked back at his eighteen months of fighting in Vietnam as if it had been a dream. He couldn't recall ever hearing the word *stalemate* during his tours in-country; America at the time was convinced it was winning and saving the world from communism. Over the ensuing years, watching from afar as Vietnam devolved into a political football and protesters filled American streets and campuses, the country's changing mood depressed him. He did not plan or want to go back to Vietnam. But he did not want to leave the Corps. He had also never forgotten the posters he'd seen in the Marine recruiting offices in San Antonio of proud leathernecks in their dress blues with the red piping posing before the Eiffel Tower, the Kremlin, the Tower of London. So when his company commander offered to recommend him for Marine Security Guard School, he happily accepted.

As with boot camp and infantry training, he took to the strict discipline of the eight-week school with a passion and graduated near the top of his class. His biggest complaint was the cold. Virginia had experienced an uncommonly frigid winter in 1972 and 1973, and Valdez, a Texas boy, hated the snow and sleet. Each morning as he trudged through the slush on his mandatory physical training runs, he fantasized about deploying somewhere warm, and at night when he thumbed through his world atlas, his index finger never strayed far from the equator. Tel Aviv would be an adventure, he decided. And Africa had always appealed to his wanderlust. Dar es Salaam in particular carried an exotic ring.

He was divorced from Adeline by this point—she could not abide the constant traveling and had settled in San Antonio with their two sons, Anthony and Michael; Irish twins, born a year apart. He supported Adeline financially and visited as often as possible, even helping to coach the boys' Little League team during one extended leave. But his family seemed literally and figuratively a world away when, in the spring of 1973, he arrived at his first MSG deployment at the U.S. Embassy in Hungary. Because of its location behind the Iron Curtain, Budapest was technically considered a hardship posting.

In truth, Valdez did not find anything about Budapest a hardship. He loved the country, the people, and its ancient culture, and he took to the MSG routine as if he'd been born to it. He had lucked out. It was an unwritten rule within the MSG Battalion that hardship posts were to be followed by tours to more favorable locations, and he felt he was enjoying the best of both worlds. When his year-long tour of duty expired, however, his battalion commander informed him that he was temporarily short of NCOs and asked him to extend in Hungary for another six months. It was Valdez's understanding that he and the commander had a tacit agreement: if he extended in Budapest, he would be rewarded on his next posting with one of the plum Western European capitals usually reserved for the more decorated veterans of the MSG Battalion.

By September of 1974, he had already bought street maps of Paris, London, and Vienna when his new orders arrived: Saigon. Not even another hardship post. Saigon was officially considered a combat deployment. Other than the extra sixty dollars a month in combat pay, he saw no upside to the order. He'd had his fill of Vietnam. But he accepted the deployment without complaint.

Despite his previous service, he had never set foot in the capital city. Da Nang was the closest he'd come to experiencing South Vietnam's urban culture, and for all that seaport's natural beauty, it was, in truth, not much more than a glorified backwater. Nevertheless, Valdez fell in love with Saigon nearly from the moment his plane touched down at Tan Son Nhut. It was monsoon season, and the water poured from the brim of his cap as he stepped from the terminal to meet his Marine escort, who greeted him with a bottle of French champagne. It was the first champagne he'd ever tasted, and it set the tone.

On the drive to the embassy, he drank in the city: its magnificent parks and flower gardens brimming with orchids and tulips, the elegant French colonial architecture from another century, its broad, teak tree–lined boulevards thronged with scooters, rickshaws, and bicycles. Despite the constant cacophony of a thousand blaring truck klaxons mixing with the high-pitched staccato of an equal number of two-stroke cyclo engines, Saigon, Valdez sensed, was a bubbling treasure. Where else in the world but Tu Do Street, after all, could a man hear the recorded voices of Janis Joplin and Patsy Cline trying to drown each other out within a single city block?

The U.S. Embassy was set perfectly in the center of this charming jewel, and after a few days of familiarizing himself with the local geography, he set out to discover what kind of men he commanded. He organized an MSG softball team and made a point of getting to know each of his young Marines personally by encouraging them to speak their minds and ask questions at the regular informal meetings he instituted. He accompanied them on weekly trips to the shooting range at the Vietnamese Royal Marine facility at Boomtown Beach on the South China Sea, and exercised with them during their physical training tests at the DAO complex. He also joined them on runs to and from the Marine House in the walk-in delivery vans that carried MSGs to security posts. These vans were universally known as "bread trucks" because of their size and shape.

At first the men were skittish. There was, and still is, a strict line of authority adhered to in the Marine Corps, and it was rare to find a corporal or even a sergeant with the gall to directly address a master sergeant without being spoken to first. But as the war closed in, Valdez made it clear that in order to perform their duties, the MSGs would all have to know and trust one another. Valdez constantly reminded himself that this wasn't Budapest, where the KGB ruled with an iron fist and there was never a danger of being blown to hell while sipping a beer in a bar or café. His Marines were vulnerable in Saigon; the enemy's presence was rarely seen, but always felt.

Although Valdez did not patronize the B-girls, he had been a part of the Corps for too long to suffer any illusions. He knew his Marines played as hard as they worked, and he felt they deserved it. Nevertheless, with the help of the CIA he put together a no-go list of public places likely to attract overt or covert Vietcong attention—including the entire neighborhood of Cholon, Saigon's Chinatown and a known hotbed of enemy activity—and ordered all men to travel downtown in groups while off-duty. Always assume, he stressed, that someone is watching you.

One reality Juan Valdez never forgot was that Saigon was a war zone. He sensed there was trouble coming, and coming soon, down Route One, "the highway without joy" that stretched from the Mekong to the DMZ and beyond, to the Chinese border. This was brought home by the occasional blast of a grenade tossed into a café from a passing cyclo or the *pop-pop-pop* of gunfire echoing across the city each night. Sometimes these gunshots were merely the sounds of the local curfew militia shooting rats on the rain-slicked streets with their small-caliber rifles. Sometimes they were a not-too-distant firefight.

In a way, Valdez felt like the title character from his favorite movie, *Shane*. He was surrounded by bad men in a beautiful setting, and he was here to keep the peace. Often he studied his Marines and assigned to their character and type the names of the actors he liked best. A sleepy-eyed sergeant might be Robert Mitchum; a handsome corporal, William Holden. But Juan Valdez was always Alan Ladd. Shane. The man in charge.

And as he sat with Major Kean and Mike Sullivan listening to Big Minh drone on over the radio, his mind drifted to this land of Hollywood make-believe. Not long ago the embassy theater had shown the war film *The Longest Day* on the weekly movie night. The epic was filled with big stars—Valdez's kind of stars, action heroes. But even Hollywood realized that in order to tell a realistic tale, some of those stars had to die in the end.

He was daydreaming about this when Major Kean slid a map of the embassy grounds across the coffee table. "Top, Sully, I think this is where we should put the machine guns." He had etched small, red X's at key points about the compound.

Master Sergeant Valdez cleared his head and went back to work.

Six

Pale shards of moonlight backlit the waning storm clouds as Mike Sullivan stood transfixed behind the pile of sandbags on the embassy roof. It continued to rain iron on Tan Son Nhut Airport—first a light patter, now a heavy downfall. Most of his burn squad had returned to shoveling, but as another barrage of explosions rocked the flight lines, Steve Schuller walked over from the incinerator room and joined Sullivan. Schuller was shirtless and dripping with sweat, and his bronzed chest and shoulders glowed as if they had been polished for the occasion. A frosting of black ash streaked his face and matted his short brown hair, thick as otter fur, and one moist clump had collected on his upper lip to form a tiny Charlie Chaplin mustache.

The detonations brought Schuller back to a time and place from over a year ago: sitting in the bleachers on a parade ground on Manila in the Philippines, the day he'd been selected for Saigon MSG duty. There had been explosions that day also—an artillery unit training on the next field. Then, as now, it reminded him of Fourth of July celebrations back home in Connecticut.

"Like fireworks," he said.

Sullivan just shook his head. *They all say the same thing*, he thought. *Even Top. "Like fireworks." "Like a light show." As if it's for our personal entertainment. No, not like fireworks. Not like a light show. Like artillery. Like artillery that'll kill you.*

"Yeah," Sullivan said, "like fireworks."

Sullivan was fond of Schuller. Out of all the MSGs, the young New

Englander may have been his favorite. The other Marines had nicknamed Schuller the "PT Monster" for his prowess at the mandatory physical training tests they endured twice a month at the DAO—push-ups, pull-ups, sit-ups, Schuller always scored at or near the top of the fitness reports. He was also perhaps the outfit's best swimmer, and if not its fastest, then certainly the runner with the most endurance. Over his thirteen months in Saigon, he had also proven himself one of the unit's steadiest Marines. It was not by accident. The Marine Corps consisted of 196,000 men, and if the MSGs belonged to the top 1 percent, Schuller was determined to climb into the top 1 percent of that 1 percent.

He had grown up on a small farm in northwestern Connecticut built by his mother's parents, who raised cows and pigs and tilled the stony New England soil for corn, cucumbers, and tobacco. He liked to remind the southerners in the detachment that Yankees had been cultivating to-bacco—without the use of slaves—long before Tobacco Road was much more than an Indian trail. This country childhood had also fashioned him into a natural outdoorsman, his shooting eye honed by the hours spent in the forests adjacent to the family's twelve-acre spread hunting squirrel, rab-bit, chipmunk, and skunk with his father's old .22 rifle.

Sullivan liked to rib Schuller that while he was tracking vermin with his popgun on the East Coast, he had come of age hunting mule deer, elk, and bear with a real gun in the rugged Cascade Mountains. But the staff sergeant also had to admit that Schuller's years in the woods had turned him into the most crack shot in the detachment, which Schuller took no end of enjoyment proving during the outfit's regular trips to the range at Boomtown Beach.

The male members of the Schuller family had served in the U.S. Navy going back generations, and young Steve was expected to do the same. But as a boy, he'd been awed by the gritty war movie *Pork Chop Hill,* and its scenes of heroic American infantrymen fighting through Korea were never far from his mind. He also never missed an episode of *Combat* or *The Rat Patrol* on his mother's old black-and-white Philco, although they didn't help his grades. He was a desultory student, and in 1971 he quit high school midway through his senior year and tried to enlist in the Marines. By this time, his parents had divorced, and his mother, Jennie, had custody—and legal guardianship—of seventeen-year-old Steve and his older brother and two younger sisters. She refused to sign the enlistment papers, instead making her son a proposition: if he returned to high school and earned his diploma, she would acquiesce. They shook hands on it, and Schuller graduated that June. One week later, with his mother's tentative blessing, he was inducted. His father, John, the old Navy chief, was livid that his son had spurned the seagoing service.

Although the idea of wielding a flamethrower like his role models from *Pork Chop Hill* had initially appealed to him, by now his goal was to join one of the Corps' elite Force Reconnaissance Companies, known colloquially as Marine Recon. His older cousin Bobby, a former Marine, had regaled him with tales of the derring-do of these "Super Grunts" in Vietnam, and he pictured himself decked out in full camouflage, his face daubed with green and black paint, slithering deep through the bush on elbows and knees and picking off Charlie like so many rabbits in the woods behind his farm.

He graduated with the third-highest ranking in his boot camp platoon, which ironically proved a temporary setback. Because of his physical prowess, his graduation rank, and his high scores on various Marine Corps aptitude tests, instead of being assigned to Marine Recon, or even an infantry company, he was sent to the Marine Air Traffic Controller School in Georgia. He hated it from the moment he arrived and deliberately flunked out.

Back in the infantry, humping a pack and rifle through the forests near North Carolina's Camp Lejeune, Schuller excelled. He was promoted from private first class to corporal, and soon thereafter made sergeant, well ahead of the usual timetable. It was on a Marine sea-duty "float" off the coast of Lebanon in 1973 that his rapid promotional record caught the eye of his company commander, who had once served as an MSG. The United States had already pulled combat troops from Vietnam, and though disappointed that he would not have an opportunity to fulfill his jungle fantasies, Schuller reset his career sights. The way his company commander described it, seeing the world as an MSG beat humping a rucksack, dollars to doughnuts.

He was recommended for MSG School by the same company commander, and after breezing through successive personnel screenings conducted by his battalion commander and regimental commander, he assumed the rest would be a lark—a few weeks of etiquette training, learning to use the correct silverware at embassy dinners, and he'd be off on missions of drama and intrigue. The grunts didn't call it "Knife, Fork and Spoon School" for nothing. At Henderson Hall in Quantico, the site of the MSG schoolhouse, he learned abruptly that he had been mistaken.

He was indeed required to differentiate between a fish fork and a dinner fork, but that was the least of it. The tasks and tests he endured over the next six weeks, both physical and mental, made boot camp feel like high school recess. Moreover, to simulate actual duty in a foreign and possibly hostile country, each prospective MSG was trailed during liberty by a plebe from the nearby FBI Academy. Any off-duty Marine entering a tavern was handed demerits the next day, and Schuller once received a reprimand when his invisible tail reported to his superior that he had cooled his feet in a Washington, D.C., reflecting pool.

What shocked him most was the attrition rate. By the end of the course, only half of the eighty or so men who had begun classes with him remained. He was puzzled when, before receiving his diploma, he was asked to sign a form stating that he was not married, that he would remain single, and that he would not become involved in a personal relationship with a female during his tenure as an MSG. The form was "officially unofficial," he was told. The Corps could not legally ban any Marine from getting married. But the rite was highly discouraged for MSGs. Schuller signed without a second thought. There were only two things that interested him—one was sex and the other adventure. He did not see how marriage factored into either.

He was even more surprised when he was deployed to Saigon for a twelve-month tour. The MSG Battalion offered every new graduate a "dream sheet" of posting preferences. There were three blank boxes on the form, and Schuller entered the same country in each: "Sweden," "Sweden," and "Sweden." He did not know much about Saigon other than it was a world away, but he was fairly certain that the city was not populated by beautiful blondes.

On the March morning in 1974 when he deplaned at Tan Son Nhut, the sky was so blue he felt as if he were walking into the interior of an overheated sapphire. Midway through the terminal, his khakis were drenched with sweat down to his boxers and undershirt, and outside on the sidewalk, the dragging weight of the muggy air dulled his wits. His head swam in the noxious fumes emitted from the hundreds of cyclos and scooters honking past the curb, their exhaust mixing with the sickly sweet smells wafting from the curbside food vendors hawking little coconut cakes cooked over smoky fires, oily fish in its ubiquitous nuoc mam sauce, and piss-colored rice beer. Dozens of stunted, cadaverous children, some missing limbs, clutched at his legs and shouted an indecipherable chorus of pidgin-English pleas for coins and candy. It was only the weight of war that brought him back to his senses.

The city virtually throbbed to a combat-zone beat. Groups of armed, pinch-faced Vietnamese soldiers congregated on every corner, and the airport was ringed with antiaircraft guns set in bunkers surrounded by sandbags. The roar of Phantom jets above was punctuated by the rotor whine of Cobra attack helicopters taxiing along the airport tarmac, and in the far distance somewhere beyond the hangars, he could pick out the distinct sound of machine-gun fire.

Schuller's initiation to the city coincided with the wilting dry season, and the dominant tactile sensation was of cheap building material deteriorating in the acidic atmosphere of Southeast Asia. Gritty, gray concrete dust spooled up by passing trucks mixed with the rust-colored native soil and black diesel exhaust to form an ever-present cloud layer that coated everything in sight. After a few deep breaths, he was certain he could already feel it eroding the enamel on his teeth. He had been under the impression that hostilities had ended in Vietnam with the signing of the Paris Peace Accords. He realized at this moment that, like Rick Blaine in *Casablanca*, one of his favorite movies, he had been sadly misinformed. He felt as if he had entered a prison during lockdown, and wondered if he would spend his next twelve months patrolling an enclosed embassy compound like a zoo animal pacing a cage. He thought of Sweden.

The tenseness in his jaw muscles relaxed when the tanned gunnery sergeant sent to meet him at the airport finally arrived. The "gunny" grabbed his duffel, clapped him on his soaking back, and led him to a convertible Jeep. He was a bit surprised that the sergeant had shown up wearing camouflage jungle utilities, but as they zoomed through the crowded streets, the air felt so good rushing against his face he pushed the obvious question from his mind. His transformation was complete when his escort took a roundabout route to the Marine House that detoured through Saigon's red light district. Schuller thought the man must have been reading his mind. To the new grunt, the flickering smiles of the B-girls loitering in bar fronts with new boob jobs bursting through Barbie doll dresses were a foreign, if not alien, wonder.

In short order, he came to love Saigon's lawless charm as much as he enjoyed its beautiful women—so much so that he happily signed extension papers when his first tour of duty expired. But it was more than that. Deep down he also harbored a secret ambition that someday he might be assigned to one of the consulates, on the outside chance the politicians back home came to their senses and decided to fight this war the correct way. Heroic fantasies out of *Pork Chop Hill* lay dormant in the recesses of his mind, and he was always the first to volunteer to make administrative runs to Bien Hoa, Can Tho, Da Nang. Driving to these cities, he scouted imaginary sniper positions. He was happy to re-up. There would be plenty of time left to meet a nice Scandinavian girl.

Mike Sullivan was aware of Schuller's reputation as a night crawler, bouncing along Tu Do Street from Club Tiger to Mimi's to the Moulin Rouge. It did not bother him. What red-blooded U.S. Marine would resist the temptations of a wide-open city like Saigon? Although the MSGs were expected to return to the Marine House each night by the city's 10 P.M. curfew, both Sullivan and Valdez thought it prudent to look the other way when their young Marines rode out the night in the back rooms of the downtown boom-boom houses where Filipino porn films broadcast continuously from screens above leather-padded bars. Schuller in particular possessed the kind of dark, handsome features that drew admiring glances from exotic women known to enjoy the companionship of a man in uniform. And he was far from alone among the Marines in returning those looks to the beautiful girls wobbling high on platform shoes who gave new meaning to the songs like "Cherry Pink and Apple Blossom White" that drifted from the ubiquitous café radios tuned to the Voice of America. After all, he had certainly been upfront about his nature; Sullivan had seen the "dream sheet" marked off, "Sweden," "Sweden," and "Sweden."

Moreover, since his arrival, Schuller had not let his personal proclivities interfere with his job. He was never late for an assignment and was always the first to volunteer for a new detail. His determination and devotion to duty were not only beyond question but also tremendous for morale. Schuller was a good man to have along in a pinch, Sullivan thought, and this was certainly a pinch they were in. Standing on the roof beside the staff sergeant, eyeing the fireballs mushrooming over the airport, the same thought struck Schuller. Things were different now. "No more fun and games," as his mother used to tell him when she meant business. He remembered the shooting range at Boomtown Beach, and considered that the next time he fired his M-16, it might not be at silhouette cutouts, but at men—men who would be firing back. When he finally turned to speak to Sullivan, his mouth was so dry his tongue stuck to the roof as if it had been soldered there.

"Guess it's starting. Like the major said."

Sullivan did not answer.

Sullivan detected a subtle tremor in the sergeant's voice, an anxiety he'd sensed building among all the MSGs. Not one of them would ever admit it. Hell, they'd been making Alamo jokes long before Major Kean mentioned it, going back to the fall of Da Nang. But Sullivan knew that it was one thing for a trooper to recognize that at any moment he could be called on to fight, and quite another to inhabit that gray netherworld where circumstances, not to mention orders, were nebulous. None of the MSGs had received a letter or telephone call from home, seen a newspaper, or heard a radio or television news report in days. Even the *Stars and Stripes* had ceased circulation in Saigon. Despite Frank Snepp's intelligence report—or maybe even because of it—a sense of groping blindly into combat against an unseen enemy pervaded their thoughts. And though Major Kean's gung-ho speech had buoyed them, it had not lifted the invisible weight each man felt.

"You know, like he said," Schuller said again. "if it comes to it, we fight and die like Marines."

"Yep," Sullivan said. "Like the major said."

He handed Schuller a handkerchief. "Here, wipe your face."

Before Schuller could grab the rag, both MSGs saw a series of large explosions rock the DAO.

Seven

The first rocket threw Sergeant Kevin Maloney out of his cot and deposited him on his butt on the warehouse floor. The entire building shook. The second jolted him back to his stocking feet. A nearby handheld radio squawked.

"Whiskey Joe! Whiskey Joe!" Code words for *incoming*. "Took a hit to the gym! We got casualties in the gym!"

Maloney, a member of the MSG detachment transferred to the DAO under the command of Gunnery Sergeant Vasco Martin, checked his watch: 03:58.

The gymnasium and bowling alley at the DAO compound had been converted into refugee processing centers. About one-third of the nearly 3,000 civilian "friendlies" still awaiting evacuation to Clark Air Base in the Philippines were formed up on the scuffed basketball courts and bowling alleys in compartmentalized blocks, or "sticks," of approximately 260 people apiece, enough to fill a stripped-down American cargo plane. From these sites they were to be escorted out to the flight lines and packed into the big C-130s and C-141s stacked up and arriving "hot" with the last of the American armaments allotted for the defense of South Vietnam—15,000-pound bombs, "Daisy Cutters," destined for the Royal South Vietnamese Air Force's munitions storage area.

Maloney had arrived in Vietnam only three months earlier, but despite his inexperience, "Gunny" Martin had appointed him one of his two squad leaders, and six hours earlier he had been ordered to post guards to the two gates off the airport road leading into the DAO compound.

He'd assigned the new arrivals, Corporal Charles McMahon and Lance Corporal Darwin Judge, to Post Number Two, on the southeast corner of the perimeter. Now, as the NVA rockets fell, he gave little thought to any civilians, Vietnamese or otherwise. His mind was focused on the newbies out on the wire. Still in his skivvies, Maloney grabbed an M-16 rifle and rushed for the door.

Outside, through the smoky chop, he spotted dozens of Fleet Marines converging near the concrete bomb shelters in front of the DAO head-quarters building. They were now in uniform and carrying their weapons openly. He instinctively ducked at the sound of a huge detonation and turned to see an American C-130, its fuel tank ruptured, erupt in flames on the main runway. A half-dozen Americans in U.S. Air Force jumpsuits ran across the tarmac toward another C-130 preparing to run the gantlet. Maloney assumed they were the crew of the dead plane. *Got out before it blew.*

He turned back toward the gates, and by the light of the red blossoms of fire consuming the cargo plane, he recognized the prone figure of Cor-poral Lamar Holmes, another MSG, twenty yards down the dirt service road. Holmes had been stationed at the DAO's Post Number One. He was splayed across the ground, holding his knee and bleeding from his head.

Maloney ran to him and bent over. "Holmes, can you walk? Holmes!"

The corporal shook his head, but did not speak. *Shock*, Maloney thought. He yelled for a corpsman and spotted several of his own Marines, MSGs led by Martin, tearing up the road behind him. They were trailed by Americans in civilian clothes carrying a stretcher and what looked like an emergency medical kit. Maloney left Holmes and sprinted toward the gate at Post Number Two.

A kaleidoscope of impressions raced through his mind. The baby-faced McMahon, captain of his high school football team, voted Boy of the Year at his Boys' Club back in his Massachusetts home town. The shy, wide-eyed Judge, the Christian proselytizer and proud Eagle Scout from Marshall-town, Iowa's Troop 310. When he reached the gate at Post Number Two—or, more accurately, where the gate should have been—there was nothing but a smoking hole. He guessed that the rocket had landed somewhere between Judge and McMahon and was about to yell their names when the whipcrack of bullets caught him up short. *Machine gun.* He dived into a drainage ditch by the side of the road. The VC had been snapping off rounds from the territory they controlled on the north side of the airport for nearly a month, but these gunshots seemed much closer. It took him a moment to realize that what he'd mistaken for hostile fire was actually an ammunition clip being cooked off in a pile of burning Honda motorbikes to the side of the Post.

He moved toward the Hondas and stumbled over a shiny new, black Marine-issue boot with barely a scuff on it but a foot still in it. A few yards away he spotted a flak-jacketed torso without any arms. The silky olive cloth that encased the armor plating was burned off, and the plating itself was dented and creased. He was bent over the remains when another rocket landed not far from the gate, so loud it was like the ripping of branches from trees in a tornado. Again Maloney hit the drainage ditch. It was from there that he spotted Judge buried under the burning motorbikes. He leaped to his feet and raced over. The boy's face was drained of color, his wide-open eyes like tiny black marbles, but he was in one piece. Maloney dragged his body from the flames, singeing his hands as he yanked him across the dirt by the collar of his blouse. Judge was dead.

Maloney was still kneeling over the lance corporal's body when Sergeant Martin materialized through the dust and smoke, more Marines and American civilians in his trace. They gathered as if in a trance around the corpses. Sergeant Martin broke the silence.

"Let's get this post squared away. Form up a body bag detail."

They bagged Lance Corporal Darwin Judge first. When they'd finished collecting all they could find of Corporal Charles McMahon, Martin ordered Maloney to take over guard duty at the now-evaporated checkpoint. He directed the remains of the two dead men to be loaded into an ambulance that had appeared out of the night.

Finally, Martin signaled all the MSGs except Maloney to follow him back to the warehouse. "Need a head count in order to file officially to the embassy," he said.

Maloney put a hand on Martin's shoulder.

"You can count heads for the record," he said. "But it's Judge and McMahon."

Eight

M ajor Kean took the news over an unsecured telephone line in Valdez's makeshift office in the embassy. Two MSGs KIA. The new arrivals Judge and McMahon.

"Judge's body pretty charred, McMahon blown to hell," Martin said.

Kean heard an explosion over the line. It went dead for a moment, then crackled back to life. Martin was still there.

"Still got incoming," he said. "But we've picked up as many pieces as we can find. Mission warden ambulance ran them to the missionary morgue." The mission wardens were civilian American contractors, predominantly retired military men, who hired local Vietnamese to drive shuttle buses, man firetrucks, and stand security at various American-owned aid agencies around the city. And drive ambulances.

Kean rang off and cradled the phone.

He had been fortunate. He knew that. Only two. Indeed, considering the bombardment, luck of the first magnitude. Still. He spun in his chair and headed for the lobby. He needed to find Valdez. News like this would travel fast, and he wanted to be the first to deliver it to the NCOIC.

As Kean suspected, however, word of the deaths was no longer a secret. Simultaneous to his conversation with Martin, four floors above him in the windowless communications center known as the "Bubble Room" because of the seamless and impenetrable Plexiglas lining the floors, ceiling, and walls, Sergeant Doug Potratz had been monitoring the chatter on the detachment's in-house Dragon Network radio frequency. He had picked up the news about McMahon and Judge. The Dragon Net was manned twenty-four hours a day by an MSG, and Potratz was the squad leader who had led the delegation requesting the evacuation of the disturbed Nha Trang and Da Nang Marines. It now struck him that Judge and McMahon should have been shipped out with them. His mind reeled for a moment before he was brought back with a start by the sound of weeping, followed by a soft moan.

"Oh, man, Judge. Judge. They got Judge. I went to MSG School with the guy. Oh-man-oh-man-oh-man."

Lance Corporal Jerome Thomas's head was buried in his huge black hands. His body convulsed. Potratz had forgotten he was there, sitting in a dark corner of the Bubble Room. Thomas was Potratz's machine-gun partner. When Major Kean first arrived, he and Valdez had paired off each MSG into two-man gun teams with instructions that they stay as close to each other as possible. The older Marine was momentarily at a loss. Thomas looked as if he was having a nervous breakdown. The idea of becoming a sitting duck in the middle of a civil war had not truly sunk in for Doug Potratz until he saw Jerome Thomas shaking like a wet dog. Someone had left an old copy of *Stars and Stripes* in the room, and the headline caught Potratz's eye. VIET BRASS FLEES FROM CAM RANH; DA NANG FALLS—SAIGON NEXT?

Potratz wrapped a beefy arm around the lance corporal's shoulders. "Calm down, man, calm down. This might be the beginning. Not the end, okay. This might just be prep fire. They might hit the embassy next. I need you alert, Thomas. We gotta be ready. Ready, Thomas. Okay?"

Thomas's tears slowed to a trickle. The two Marines sat silent, staring at the Dragon Network radio receiver, now emitting only static. Potratz rubbed his hands together. His palms were sweaty.

Jim Kean found Juan Valdez in the embassy lobby, hunched over in conversation with Mike Sullivan. Kean could not make out what they were saying, but he could guess. Valdez wheeled at the sharp snap of his footfalls on the polished marble floor.

"We hear two," he said. "Who?"

"Judge and McMahon."

The names struck Valdez like the downbeat of an axe. Did it have to be the kids? Then he remembered. The letter.

He handed Kean the day's duty roster and without a word took off for the old guard room he had converted into an office. He tried to recall the mail packet schedule; he could not. He reached beneath a pile of duffel bags and pulled out a brown cardboard accordion envelope the size of a briefcase. Inside were several manila file folders marked "Personnel." He found the one he was looking for.

Buried amid pay stubs, service records, and transfer orders—the detritus of a hasty exit from the Marine House—was a wispy sheet of carbon paper. A typed note, written eight days earlier, to the parents of Corporal Charles McMahon:

FROM: Marine Security Guards American Embassy, Saigon RVN 21 April 1975

Mr. C. McMahon:

Your son, Corporal Charles McMahon, has just arrived in Saigon, Vietnam for duty as a Marine Security Guard with the American Embassy here. As Non-Commissioned Officer-In-Charge of the Marine Security Guard Detachment, let me assure you that although he is new here, he appears to be the type of Marine who will make an important contribution during his tour of duty, and his efforts in helping to create among the people of Saigon, RVN and all Vietnam a favorable impression of the Marine Corps and of the American people, will be a source of pride to you.

Juan J. Valdez
Master Sergeant, U.S. Marine Corps

Valdez calculated the twelve-hour time difference between Saigon and Woburn, Massachusetts. He knew a Marine casualty officer would arrive at the McMahon home in Massachusetts with the official death notification no later than tomorrow. When had he sent the letter? Too late. The family would be reading his words long after they'd been informed that their son was coming home in a box. He wondered how it would feel. His boys back in the States were not much younger than McMahon. Anthony was thirteen, Michael twelve. How would he take such news? He did not need to answer his own question.

His hands shook as he reread the words one more time. He slid the letter back into the manila file folder and stuffed the folder back into the accordion envelope, which he jammed into his duffel bag. He tasted something metallic in the back of his throat. He left the office and walked toward the stairs.

He climbed to the roof, picked up a shovel, and began feeding shredded paper into the glowing incinerators. The burn squad was surprised to see the silent, stoic Top working beside them. An hour into his manual labor he paused and scanned the city's rooftops, gilded by the morning sun streaming in from the east. His eyes welled up. If anyone noticed, he would blame it on the smoky grit from the furnaces blowing into his face.

It was a rainy dusk in Washington, D.C. President Gerald Ford was having trouble focusing on the discussion at hand. He sat at the head of a finely grained mahogany table in the Cabinet Room of the White House as fourteen of his economic advisers bickered over oil tariffs and import taxes.

Ford leaned back in his chair and noticed Lieutenant General Brent Scowcroft, his deputy national security advisor and a member of his National Security Council (NSC), enter quietly through a side door. Scowcroft handed him a note.

The note advised the president that Saigon was about to fall and that the bombing of Tan Son Nhut Airport was making evacuation more problematic by the moment. When Ford finished reading, Scowcroft bent over and whispered into his ear. He told the president that two U.S. Marines had been killed in action at the airport. Ford nodded, reached for his own note tray, removed a pen from his suit jacket, and jotted a message. He handed it to Scowcroft.

It read, "Tell HK that we'd better have an NSC meeting at seven."

Ford suspected Secretary of State Henry Kissinger would not like the interruption. He and his wife, Nancy, were scheduled to attend a Noel Coward play that evening.

Part II
Delusion

My ass isn't covered. I can assure you when this thing is finally over I will be hanging several yards higher than you.
—Back-channel, "eyes-only" cable from Secretary of State Henry Kissinger to U.S. Ambassador to Saigon Graham Martin, 19 April 1975

One

Saigon, 0600, 29 April 1975

Major Jim Kean gazed out the window of the abandoned secretary's office on the second floor of the embassy in Saigon. The sky was the color of brushed aluminum, and the first of the cloud fortresses marching in from the sea had settled overhead. By tonight the loud *tack-tack-tack* of hot rain pounding the roof would echo throughout the building, deepening the furrows already graven in the major's broad forehead. Kean thought of the Santa Anas back home in California and remembered a detective book—*Raymond Chandler? Yes*—that described the winds roaring down through the mountain passes and making your nerves jump and your skin itch. Kean felt the same about the monsoon rains. They drove him crazy.

Now he was hunched over a desk half a world away, scanning the Marine Security Guard duty roster. He leaned forward in his chair and placed the fingertips of both hands on the polished wood in front of him. He had forty-six MSGs here in the embassy compound, fifteen across town at the DAO, and the remains of two KIA on a slab at the Seventh Day Adventist Hospital somewhere in between. He wanted those corpses recovered.

"I really thought they'd hit the embassy first, Top," he said. "I'm sorry about your two boys."

Master Sergeant Juan Valdez, seated across the desk, nodded and unconsciously kneaded his hands. Black ash floated from his cracked fingers onto the beige carpet.

Kean stood and faced the window. "You have to figure we're next," he said. "Which means we've got a logistics problem."

Valdez noted a dullness to the major's voice. Kean was one of those men whose erect posture, barrel chest, and square jaw line lent the impression that he was physically more imposing than his actual size. Valdez towered over the five-foot-nine, stocky major, but the NCOIC had never thought of his commanding officer as small. Until, perhaps, that day.

Kean's eyes were sunk deep into his boyish face, and his dirty-blond hair was slicked back with sweat. He was still wearing the same civilian clothes that he had thrown on two weeks earlier in Hong Kong—blue slacks and a soft pink, short-sleeved Arnold Palmer golf shirt with blue pin stripes—as grimy now as Valdez's drab green utility fatigues. Valdez wondered how much Kean had slept since. Valdez hardly had. As the non-commissioned officer in charge, the logistics headache would have been his without Kean's arrival. He could have handled it, he knew. Still, there was a sense of relief at having the burden lifted. He brushed a streak of ash from his sleeve.

"Know what I saw the other day?" Kean said. Valdez did not answer.

"Two locals, girls, hired to help process evac papers. They give them a little class first—technical stuff, how to do it, be precise with the forms and all that. So they listen real intent, nodding, and when it's finished they fill out their own forms and leave for the airport. Unbelievable."

Valdez recognized that Kean was trying to lighten the mood. It hadn't worked. "So what's next, sir?" he said.

Kean made a motion with his hands as if tearing up a piece of paper. "Options Two and Three, gone. It's too late to get people to the sea or the river. Repeat of Da Nang. And the airport flight lines, gone, too. No fixed wing getting in or out of Tan Son Nhut."

Valdez let that sink in. Tan Son Nhut. The last friendly air strip in Vietnam, once the hub of America's two-decade investment of blood and treasure in Southeast Asia. He thought back to his own arrival in Saigon and breathed an audible sigh. Kean paused as if waiting for the master sergeant to speak. He said nothing.

"That means it has to be choppers." Kean said. Option IV. Piling people into the fleet helicopters as fast as possible. There was no Option V.

Two years earlier, the Defense Department, despite repeated public declarations of support for the South Vietnam government, had put into place secret plans for the emergency evacuation of Saigon. The operation contained four options in all, with the fourth one given the unlikely code name "Frequent Wind." The first option assumed, perhaps naively, there would be time to fly out Americans, third-country nationals, and at-risk Vietnamese on commercial and military flights from Tan Son Nhut and other South Vietnamese–held air bases. When the provinces fell and foreign commercial air carriers ceased operations out of Saigon a week earlier, Option II, fixed-wing military airlift only, had kicked in. Given the state of Tan Son Nhut, that was now also by the boards.

Option III was a sealift from the ports of Saigon and designated landing areas along the South China Sea. But memories of the desperate, and fatal, Da Nang evacuation aside, the U.S. Navy had not counted on the swiftness with which the NVA advance had cut off access to the coast. Now, with enemy artillery batteries so near, the Joint Chiefs of Staff were loath to risk American landing craft—or to be blamed for starting a new war. The idea of a water evacuation was moot at any rate, as there was neither the means nor the manpower to move everyone to the piers along the Saigon River.

The final alternative, Option IV, was entirely a helicopter evacuation centered around, but not exclusive to, the DAO at the airport and U.S. Embassy. The small, twin-turbine, single-rotor Air America Hueys could land at various rooftop helipads and open spaces around the city, but only the landing zones in the DAO and embassy compounds could take the larger and heavier Marine CH-53 Sea Stallions and CH-46 Sea Knights. It would involve every chopper the Marines, Air Force, Navy, and Air America could muster. Kean recognized that a helicopter rescue of this magnitude had never before been attempted.

"That's what we have to start planning for," he said. "Despite what the ambassador says."

The major exhaled slowly. To Valdez it sounded more like a hiss. "I think he wants to burn with the city."

Kean was aware that just before sunrise, as the shelling at the airport tapered off, Ambassador Martin had hurriedly dressed at his residence, arrived at the embassy, and insisted on being driven out to the DAO in his armored Chevrolet Impala to personally assess the damage. Lambent light was leaking out of the sky to the east when, against the unanimous advice of his six Marine bodyguards, the Personal Service Unit, Martin ordered his car brought around.

The PSUs, dressed in chinos, bomber jackets, and a few even in safari suits, had crammed their Uzis into oversized leather briefcases and double-checked not only their handheld Motorola radios but the portable first aid kit before piling into Jeeps that buttressed the limousine front and back. Even as the small convoy reached the embassy's vehicle gate fronting Mac Dinh Chi Street on the north end of the compound, Martin's driver continued the protest. He pointed out that intermittent artillery was still falling on the airfield. The trip, he said, was too dangerous. Martin was adamant, and stony. At one point, he turned to the Marine seated next to him in the back seat of the car and asked what time it was. When the Marine answered that his watch had broken, the ambassador officiously informed him, "You will have one tomorrow."

In spite of his bodyguards' apprehension, Martin reached the DAO without incident. What he saw by the light of day at Tan Son Nhut was chaos. All semblance of military order had broken down. South Vietnam-ese officers had abandoned their posts, and panicked Royal Vietnam Air Force paratroopers and ARVN soldiers, many firing their weapons indis-criminately, roamed the flight lines, fighting among themselves to squeeze onto any remaining helicopters capable of lifting off. Thirty Royal Air Force pilots had descended on the DAO, pistols drawn, and demanded to be evacuated immediately. They were disarmed without incident when an American air attaché who had spent the previous few weeks helping their families to escape mollified them with promises to get them out as soon as possible.

Over a two-hour period that morning, General Dung's rockets and 130-millimeter shells had dropped at a rate of one per minute, and Martin, in a rare, and perhaps unhinged, understatement, regarded the bombard-ment as "an important signal." The ambassador was familiar with Dung's CIA file, which included a rare photograph of the strapping, clean-shaven general, his full white hair neatly combed back off his high forehead, the bright epaulettes on his broad shoulders seeming to gleam against his dark uniform.

Martin had known for some time that the fifty-seven-year-old NVA general had been handpicked by an ailing General Giap to lead the final assault on Saigon, despite a campaign of subterfuge that involved Dung's sneaking out of Hanoi in the middle of the night while lookalikes took his place at official public appearances and even at volleyball matches he hosted at his home, lest South Vietnamese or American spies notice his absence. The Hanoi Politburo had dubbed the southern expedition the "Spring Offensive," but two weeks earlier, following Dung's rapid roll-up of the Central Highlands, Le Duan, the First Secretary of the North Vietnamese Communist Party, had rechristened the military campaign in honor of the late Prime Minister Ho Chi Minh, whose name still reverberated like the clang of a sword.

Surveying the airport, Martin felt a grudging admiration for the accuracy with which Dung's artillerymen had begun the final stage of the Ho Chi Minh Campaign. The American ambassador may have despised all that Dung stood for, but as a former U.S. Air Force colonel and Army intelligence officer, he could not help but appreciate Hanoi's anaconda strategy from the moment Dung's divisions had poured across the border. They were slowly squeezing the life out of South Vietnam. What Martin did not know was that at this moment, as Dung reviewed the progress reports of the Tan Son Nhut bombardment in his underground bunker outside Bien Hoa, the NVA general had his own, ironic reasons to ponder its success.

To most of Hanoi's high command, the United States was merely the successor to a host of colonial oppressors the Vietnamese had battled for centuries. The Chinese had been followed by the French, the French by the Japanese, the Japanese by the French again, and now the Americans. Yet Dung had been present, and remembered vividly, those bleak days during World War II when the Office of Strategic Services, the CIA's forerunner, had parachuted operatives into his country to aid a then-obscure Ho Chi Minh in his guerrilla war against the Japanese. A U.S. Army doctor, Paul Hoagland, had even saved Ho's life in 1945 when he fell ill with malaria, and Dung had watched U.S. representatives accompany Ho's grand entrance into Hanoi as a liberator. Perhaps, Dung thought, some of those men were the very same he now trained his guns on.

A peasant by birth, Dung was not only the youngest member of North Vietnam's thirteen-member Central Political Bureau, the top decision-making body in Hanoi, but also the only one who could claim a farmer's "heritage of the earth." In 1939, at the age of twenty-two, he had been imprisoned by the French for his Communist resistance activities, but escaped jail to fight, first, the Japanese and, later, the postwar French puppet monarchy. Despite having little formal military training, his rise through the ranks was swift. He was soon appointed a permanent member of the Northern Revolutionary Army Committee and, after leading the successful siege of the French at Dien Bien Phu in 1954, was named Giap's chief of staff before his thirty-eighth birthday.

Later that same year, when the Geneva Conference conferred sovereignty on Vietnam with the stipulation that the South be ruled by a provisional government for two years, his opinion of the United States turned as President Dwight D. Eisenhower took advantage of the twenty-four-month window to install a pro-Western regime in Saigon. Dung would remember for the rest of his life the U.S. Air Force dropping leaflets intended to frighten North Vietnamese Catholics into defecting. "Beware!" the flyers read. "The Virgin Mary has fled South. Follow her or be slaughtered by the barbarian Communists."

Although not as educated as Giap and his cohorts, Dung did not consider himself a barbarian. Untold millions of his countrymen had been killed over the past thirty years, and he was not sure how many more wars of liberation he would have to fight. But he was certain of one thing: there would be no more against the Americans. They were leaving Vietnam, one way or the other. But not by plane. His artillery had seen to that.

Less than twenty miles from Dung's bunker, the U.S. defense attaché, Army Major General Homer Smith, was in total agreement.

"Unusable," Smith told Ambassador Martin as they peered through binoculars from the DAO headquarters building at Tan Son Nhut's cratered flight lines. Smith swept his hand from one end of the airfield to the other. Damaged hulks of planes and helicopters, some still burning, obstructed the runways. Unexploded bombs and spare fuel tanks, jettisoned by South Vietnamese pilots who had managed to flee during the shelling, also littered the tarmac.

As defense attaché, Smith had been appointed to monitor and maintain the flow of materiel and supplies to South Vietnam, including military support. Part of the Paris protocols called for the United States to continue to support the Thieu government in its fight against the Vietcong, who were considered rebels. But Smith, a former U.S. Army commander who had been stationed in Da Nang in 1969 and 1970, was technically forbidden to assume any military advisory role regarding operations, tactics, or techniques of employing the war materiel he funneled to the country. Given his experience in-country both during and after the war, when he watched the NVA conquer the Central Highlands a month earlier, he recognized that trying to revive the South's fortunes was as foolish as planting cut flowers. He was a military man through and through, and though it was far from his station to presume to advise a U.S. ambassador, this morning he could not help himself.

"Mr. Ambassador," Smith said, "it is time to call Option Four."

Martin's head snapped sideways. "That doesn't make any bloody sense." Option IV, Martin knew, meant leaving thousands behind. He pointed toward the runways. "You could take a Jeep and clear that debris in a half-hour."

"And who is going to provide security for that?" Smith hitched his thumb in the direction of a knot of South Vietnamese Air Force mechanics and maintenance men at the far end of the flight line. A pilot in an undamaged helicopter, one of the little Hueys, was attempting to lift off. The grounds crew, guns drawn, had it surrounded.

Martin barely glanced at the scene. As the ranking American official in Vietnam, he told General Smith, it was his duty to carry out the U.S. commitment to evacuate its former Vietnamese employees and any other locals threatened by the imminent Communist takeover. Helicopters would never get them all out. Fixed-wing arrivals, he said, would resume as soon as the flight lines were cleared.

The general listened with a mixture of patience and skepticism. Did the man not hear a word he'd just said? Smith felt as if Martin was reciting from a memorized, if dated, script. The ambassador's PSU team, standing off to the side and listening in silence, exchanged unhappy glances.

At the end of this terse back-and-forth, Martin demanded a secure telephone line to call Washington. He was put through to Brent Scowcroft, Kissinger's chief deputy. In front of Smith, he asked for, and received, a reconfirmation of his long-standing orders to continue with Option II, the fixed-wing evacuation.

"Resume processing passengers," Martin ordered General Smith after he'd hung up. He turned to leave, and hesitated. He had a final request. A squad of Marines, he told Smith, would be escorting his wife, Dorothy, and their cherished poodle, Nit Noy, from his residence to the DAO later this morning. Would it be possible to get Dorothy on the first plane out?

Smith was momentarily speechless. He recovered quickly enough to promise Martin that his wife would most certainly be on the earliest *aircraft* departing Saigon. The ambassador's limousine had barely cleared the DAO compound's gate before Smith was making his own telephone call, this one to Admiral Noel A. M. Gayler, the U.S. Navy's Commander in Chief, Pacific, or CINCPAC, in Honolulu. Smith relayed to Gayler the airport's condition, his disagreement with the ambassador, and the gist of Martin's phone call to Washington.

"What the ambassador is demanding cannot be done," he said finally. "The flight lines are untenable."

When Smith cradled the telephone, he was satisfied. Gayler had promised to persuade the Joint Chiefs to countermand any orders from the State Department that included a resumption of fixed-wing evacuation flights.

This much Jim Kean had picked up earlier this morning from his Marine sources at Tan Son Nhut, and this was where matters stood as he related the state of play to Master Sergeant Valdez over strong Vietnamese coffee back at the embassy. Kean told Valdez that the confusion, the pointless infighting, was a microcosm of what was happening throughout the city.

"And it doesn't matter what grand plans we have for an airport evac," he said. "When it comes to it, common sense says that people in a panic will run to the American flag. That means here."

Conversely, everything the major said struck Valdez as true to form. Despite his position as NCOIC, he had not had much personal interaction with the ambassador since a long, introductory interview when he had arrived a year ago. But the embassy was a small, gossipy community. He was not surprised by Martin's intransigence. He had heard enough about the man's stubborn streak, and had even witnessed his temper on more than one occasion.

"And this affects us how?" Valdez said.

Kean looked up from his roster. "Actually, there's more."

Valdez stroked the cleft in his massive chin. He had an inkling of what the major was about to tell him. The entire embassy was abuzz over the loud words Kean and Martin had exchanged upon the ambassador's return from the DAO.

When Martin's driver had dropped him at the embassy, he had marched through the lobby without a word to the security guards, gone directly to his vast third-floor office, and summoned Kean. There were no formalities. Martin was curt. He instructed the major that he was to delay informing Washington about the deaths of Corporals Judge and McMahon.

"They find out about those deaths, and they'll pull the plug here and now," he said.

Kean was irritated not only by Martin's instructions but by his haughty tone in delivering them. His disbelief was tempered by pity as he stared at the haggard diplomat standing before him. Pull the plug? Two of his men were dead, their plug already pulled. But he held his temper.

"With all due respect, sir, in this case, my chain of command clearly states I have to report these deaths. This is not a State Department concern." Kean's stomach knotted as he chose carefully his next words. "And the message is going to go out. If you don't allow me to do it here, I will go to the DAO myself and have them do it."

Martin glared at Kean, but said nothing. He waved his hand in dismissal.

Kean left the ambassador's office with his mind juggling scenarios, none of them good. Uppermost was the safety of his MSGs. His worst fears about Martin had just been confirmed: he was clinging like a badger to the embassy, to the American presence in South Vietnam. To Kean, Martin represented the old guard—the men who had taken the United States into this country in the first place but had refused to finish the job. Now their misbegotten adventure had reached its inevitable climax, and it was, as usual, left to the Marine Corps to clean up their mess. Kean was an experienced soldier. He already had two men dead. He wanted no more.

"He's delusional, Top," he said now to Valdez. "Thinks that he's the only man in the world who can negotiate some kind of peace treaty with the North."

Once, at a security conference shortly after his arrival, Kean had heard Martin make a promise that had become a sour running joke among the Marines. He'd sworn to his assembled staffers that he would abandon Saigon "only when the red flag is flying at the end of the block."

Well, Kean thought, *take a look out the window. There it is.*

Two

Jim Kean had no way of knowing that prior to his argument with the ambassador, prior to Martin's visit to Tan Son Nhut, prior even to the airport shelling, Martin had been buoyed by a cable from Henry Kissinger. Like Martin, Kissinger was a member of the Washington faction desperate for a face-saving denouement in Vietnam—if not for the sake of U.S. prestige, then certainly for his own. It was said that Kissinger would repeal the Enlightenment if it made him look good, and with Richard Nixon gone from office and President Ford's hands relatively clean of the failed war, it was Kissinger who stood to take the steepest political fall if South Vietnam was lost.

At 7 P.M. on April 28, twelve hours behind Saigon time, Kissinger attended a meeting of the National Security Council in which this dim conclusion was affirmed. The CIA director, William Colby, who had long contended that there was no chance of even stabilizing the South's position, much less turning the military tide, finally convinced President Ford that now, this moment, was the time to get out. The only question was, How? Secretary of Defense James Schlesinger and General George Brown, chairman of the Joint Chiefs, argued for the immediate implementation of Operation Frequent Wind. But Kissinger, sensing a public relations disaster should an American helicopter crash or, worse, be shot down, pressed for continued fixed-wing evacuations once the flight lines at Tan Son Nhut were cleared. The president, with the final word, sided with his secretary of state.

After the meeting Kissinger cabled Martin. He was careful to hedge his bets. Yes, he wrote to Martin, "If the airport is open for fixed-wing evacuation today, you are to continue the evacuation of high-risk Vietnamese by fixed-wing aircraft." But if the airport was unusable for planes, he added in a second paragraph, then Martin was to resort to an all-helicopter evacuation.

He also wrote, "While you should not say so, this will be the last, repeat last, day of fixed-wing evacuation from Tan Son Nhut."

In a subsequent private telephone call, Kissinger also reaffirmed to the ambassador that their last, best chance of avoiding catastrophe in Saigon was, ironically, the Soviet influence on Hanoi. Kissinger had spoken to the Soviet ambassador to Washington, Anatoly Dobrynin, who had promised to pass a message to the North requesting a peaceful settlement with the new South Vietnamese president, General Duong Van Minh. Dobrynin also intimated that if no settlement could be reached, the Soviet general secretary, Leonid Brezhnev, felt that the Americans had at least until May 3 to get out.

Martin shared this information with no one but his deputy, Wolfgang Lehmann. He sensed an opening. Word had also reached him via a CIA liaison to "Big" Minh that the Chinese were uncomfortable with the possibility of Hanoi's total control of Indochina and might try to pressure the North Vietnamese into forming some sort of coalition. If Martin could play the Russians off against the Chinese to save the South Vietnamese— deep down, this is how he had always hoped it would end, with himself pulling the strings behind a cease-fire. With a May 3 deadline, he had at least four days to make it work, although he begged Kissinger to somehow use his power to extend the deadline to two weeks.

Martin had returned to Saigon a month earlier from Washington— where he'd given congressional testimony arguing for more aid to Thieu— for precisely that purpose. His mission was one of the last legacies of Richard Nixon, who had appointed Graham Anderson Martin ambassador to South Vietnam in July 1973 with but one imperative: to keep the country alive. A "political solution," Nixon had called it. This meant keeping a vicious civil war in check until a deal could be struck. Since mid-March, when Dung's armies had joined the war, Martin had followed with sadness and alarm the piecemeal dismemberment of a country he had been charged with resuscitating.

Oddly, Martin was a political liberal by nature who had begun his diplomatic career during the FDR administration, and he had never lost his progressive streak. As ambassador to Thailand in the mid-1960s, he had been an early opponent of sending U.S. advisors into Vietnam, and he'd argued bitterly with then-Secretary of Defense Robert McNamara when the first Marine divisions had landed near Da Nang.

His sympathies had earned him derision in the American press. The influential conservative broadcaster Paul Harvey suggested Martin had "sense enough maybe to be Ambassador to Johnson Island, which is a thousand feet long and fifty feet wide, but not anything bigger." A more circumspect, if convoluted, description of the ambassador was offered by a Fleet Street foreign correspondent, who noted that "to describe Martin as a hawk would be to attribute to that bird qualities of ferocity it does not have."

Thus, Martin's fierce anticommunism struck colleagues and subordinates in the Saigon Embassy as an anachronism. Most were aware that Martin's nephew had been killed while serving as a Marine helicopter pilot in the early days of the war. This and his opposition to U.S. intervention, they reasoned, should have given him an even more realistic outlook on the futility of the South Vietnamese position. What they did not know was that when Kissinger and Martin had met at the State Department after his congressional testimony, the secretary of state had dispatched him back to Saigon with the words, "You have to get back there because the American people have to have somebody to blame."

Afterward, as Dung's NVA armies marched south, the embassy became more and more divided between two opposing camps. Martin and his young acolytes, who rarely left the city, believed unquestioningly in the wisdom of negotiations with an aid-starved North Vietnam, and the ambassador backed the efforts of a joint military team composed predominantly of current and former U.S. Army officers who had made repeated trips to Hanoi for just that purpose. On the other side stood experienced Vietnam hands who reflected Jim Kean's opinion that the ambassador was delusional. They viewed the joint military team's efforts as primarily a sordid trade-off of empty promises in exchange for the bones of dead American soldiers. They were convinced the North was merely stringing America along. One thing all agreed on, however, was that Martin had never fully recovered from a recent and severe bout of pneumonia, and it showed.

Once a smart, eloquent conversationalist—as long, it was said, as he was the center of the conversation—Martin had lately become a surly man. His courtly North Carolina accent was now often slurred by the medications he took for both his walking pneumonia as well as injuries he'd sustained in an old car accident, and he no longer spoke to people so much as spoke at them. As General Smith and Major Kean had seen this morning, his orders tended to escalate into harangues, and since his return to Vietnam, his health had seemed to deteriorate at a pace with the country.

Although still tall and spare, his posture was now stooped and his cheeks hollowed and skeined gray. The folds of his jowls had succumbed to gravity, and two dark smudges had settled permanently under his large pale blue eyes, so bloodshot now that they appeared to be permanently weeping. He was sixty-two years old and could have passed for seventy-five. Only his thick and perfectly coiffed white mane—and the constant cigarette dangling in a jaunty angle from his cracked lips—hinted at his former savoir faire. That, and his still-glowering stare, which, as one aide remarked, "could crack open an oyster."

President Thieu's decision to abandon the Central Highlands had come as a complete surprise to Martin, and since the fall of Da Nang he had implored Kissinger and Ford to ensure Saigon's survival by encircling the city with an "iron ring" of B-52 carpet bombing. This commitment to the survival of South Vietnam had nothing to do with his nephew's death, Martin wrote, "or an affection for the Vietnamese themselves. We [have] effectively given our word. And when you don't carry out your word you pay enormous consequences for it all over the bloody world."

To that end, he considered the use of any conceivable propaganda weapon fair game. He had even coached a Vietnamese dignitary scheduled to travel to Washington to testify in congressional budget allocation hearings to emphasize the recent crash of an Operation Babylift evacuation plane packed with South Vietnamese orphans. "If we can keep the [orphans] on the front pages," he'd advised the diplomat, "we'll swing the American public back to our side."

His intimations to Kissinger that bombs would already be dropping on

General Dung if Nixon had not been brought down by Watergate irked the secretary of state no end. He argued that all that was lacking to guarantee the complete obliteration of the approaching NVA and its VC proxies was more backbone from a craven U.S. Congress and a strong dose of vitamin B-52. Like most other newly turned converts, he could blind himself to facts through sheer force of will. The escalating cost of an unwinnable war, the economic burden on an America in recession, the demoralization of both American and South Vietnamese military draftees—a mere trifle.

Any evacuation, he maintained, would signal nothing more than a massive betrayal of a loyal ally, not to mention a betrayal of the thousands of brave young men, including his nephew, who had died for the cause. All for nothing.

On April 28, the day before the airport shelling began in earnest, Tan Son Nhut had been bombed and strafed by the NVA, which used A-37 gunships abandoned by the Royal South Vietnamese Air Force near Cam Ranh Bay. The physical damage had been minimal, the psychological great. Jim Kean, for one, considered the assault the exclamation point to the destruction of the facade of safety the city had largely enjoyed during the war.

A few hours after the incident, Kean and Valdez had been riding an elevator down from the embassy roof when Martin and the CIA's Saigon station chief, Thomas Polgar, entered in the middle of a bitter argument. At one point Martin slammed the elevator's Stop button with his fist, suspending it between floors. Kean suppressed a smile as he watched a red-faced Valdez try to make himself invisible in a corner of the small lift as Martin threatened to cut Polgar's balls off "and stick one in each ear."

Kean gathered that they were at odds over the CIA's supporting role in the recent defection of a large contingent of Royal South Vietnamese Air Force pilots who had flown a squadron of F-5 fighter jets to a U.S. base in Thailand. Moreover, for weeks the Agency's fleet of Air America helicopters had been making surreptitious flights to ferry its indigenous operatives out of the country, contravening Martin's specific orders. Despite the withdrawal of half a million American troops, the CIA's intelligence role in Vietnam had hardly changed, although Kean knew it was hard for the spies to accept their reduced importance. But at least they realized what was coming, he thought, and they were preparing for it. Martin, however, believed Hanoi would consider the Air Force defection a clear breach of the U.S.-backed promise to leave all of the South's military equipment in place in return for the North's future return to the negotiating table.

As the elevator shout-down intensified, Kean stared at the floor. Despite his embarrassment, Kean had no dog in this fight. Martin may have been tumbling off the deep end and endangering Kean's MSGs, but the Hungarian-born Polgar, a pug-faced, pear-shaped man with thin, lank hair and a perpetual air of smugness, was no favorite of the Marines. As far as Kean was concerned, the CIA had been on a first-name basis with the bottom of the deck in Southeast Asia for decades. It had run its own clandestine empire—fighting a war within the war, Kean called it—and its use of mercenaries, its own air force, and its murderous and probably illegal Phoenix Program (designed to identify and "neutralize" civilians sympathetic to the Vietcong) were anathema to everything he and the Corps stood for.

Closer to home—that is, closer to the safety of his MSGs—Kean knew that this was not the first time the ambassador and the CIA chief had butted heads. Polgar had been lobbying Martin for a long time to chop down the mighty tamarind tree overshadowing the compound's parking lot in order to make room for incoming rescue helicopters. The embassy's rooftop helipad was strong enough to support a small Huey and, at least according to the engineers, an even larger and heavier CH-46 Sea Knight, although such a Bird had never landed on it. More important, a CH-46, with its elongated fuselage, had never taken off from a roof packed with God knows how many people.

The Sea Knight, a twin-rotor assault helicopter also used by the Marine Corps for resupply and medevacs, was smaller and bore less load than the more ubiquitous CH-47 Chinook, flown throughout Vietnam by the U.S. Army. It was crewed by a pilot, copilot, crew chief, and one or two machine gunners and, depending on the altitude, temperature, and weather conditions—as well as on how many gunners were aboard—it could carry between a dozen and eighteen combat-ready Marines at a maximum speed of 160 miles per hour. Naturally, the more weight in the cabin, the greater the risk.

But the tamarind tree, planted a century earlier by French botanists, threw out huge, sweeping branches that blocked the only site on the grounds where an even larger CH-53 Sea Stallion, capable of carrying perhaps fifty people, could land. Parking spots for Martin and his top aides were reserved beneath the tree so their cars would stay cooler in its shade.

Once, Kean had learned that Polgar, in one of his more obsequious ploys, had approached the ambassador about the "tree problem" with honey instead of vinegar. "Listen to reason, Graham," he'd pleaded. "Those big choppers are going to have no place to land if that tree is still there. If we don't get rid of it, a lot of our people are going to be trapped; maybe some of them are going to get killed."

Martin responded with an imperial flick of his mane and a wag of his tobacco-stained finger. The tree, he said, was a powerful symbol of America's commitment to the South Vietnamese people. "Tom, there is no way I'm going to have that tree come down until it is apparent that we've lost every one of our options. If we've got to leave, we've got to do it with dignity. For God's sake, don't you see that once that tree falls, all America's prestige falls with it?"

The "tree problem" was no secret among the MSGs. The fiction that all evacuees—American civilians, refugees, Marines—would be bused to the DAO for evacuation was just that to everyone except, apparently, Graham Martin. Kean's men realized that the only way out was up. From the roof *and* the parking lot. Suspecting a conspiracy, or perhaps merely vandalism out of a sense of frustration, the ambassador had told Valdez that any Marine harming the tamarind tree would face a court-martial.

Despite this threat, a plot to take down the tree was nonetheless hatched. Its seeds had been planted two weeks earlier, on the Marines' last night of liberty, when MSG Lance Corporal Timothy Creighton was tasked by a State Department accountant with securing several cardboard boxes brimming with Vietnamese piasters. The money was bound for the rooftop incinerators, and Creighton locked the boxes away in a ground-floor storeroom. Later that day, as Steve Schuller and another MSG sergeant, Terry Bennington, organized a group bound for one final good time on Tu Do Street, Creighton remembered that he had "forgotten" to latch the storeroom window. He opened it from the outside, climbed in, and scuttled back out with bulging pockets.

The MSGs celebrated their ultimate night on the town by tipping rickshaw drivers the equivalent of fifty dollars in piasters for fifty-cent rides, ensuring that each bartender they encountered was equally and suitably reimbursed, and telling sweet lies to their favorite B-girls. Despite being conspicuously "overserved," the Marines made it back to the embassy before curfew. On their way across the compound, Bennington, a hardscrabble squad leader whose fists could hospitalize a brick, noticed that one of the Navy Seabees—attached to all American embassies as locksmiths and jacks-of-all-trades construction experts—had left an ax on the ground near the tamarind tree.

"Whack it," he dared Steve Schuller, who did not have to be asked twice. Wood chips flew.

Terry Bennington swung next, and a half-dozen MSGs in turn took their cuts at the tree's ten-foot base. Even the strongest of them was in no shape to do the tamarind any real harm; it would take more than a few drunken swings of an ax to wound the ancient growth. But it allowed the Marines to feel as if they were doing *something* in the face of impending catastrophe.

Subsequently, every evening when the ambassador left for his residence, MSGs lined up to gauge the tamarind. The tree became the place to gather on cigarette breaks, and even the Seabees joined in. They also left the ax tied to a low branch—on the opposite side of the trunk from the windows in Martin's office.

Jim Kean knew about these nightly forays, but after giving the matter some thought, he'd decided his most prudent course of action was to pretend that he didn't. To his way of thinking, the ambassador's "prestige" weighed against the obvious reality. The various consequences of this reality were running through the major's mind in the early morning hours of April 29 when Valdez departed his office with a list of orders.

Moments later Kean was interrupted by a State Department secretary, one of the few American women left in-country. She informed him there was a call for him on the secure diplomatic line. When he reached the young woman's work station, gales of rain were beating against the window. *Perfect.*

She handed him the telephone.

"Major?"

"Yes, Sergeant Nichols?" Kean recognized the voice of the Manila NCOIC whom he had charged with finding housing for the evacuating Saigon MSGs.

"Your wife's been trying to reach you, sir, but can't get through," Nichols said. "She got a hold of me, and asked if I could pass along a message."

Kean's heart skipped a beat. Rosanne was still in Hong Kong with their three young children. "What is it, Master Sergeant?"

"Well, she said to put it like this, Major. She's got news. She's pregnant."

For one tender moment, Jim Kean pushed thoughts of Vietnam from his mind.

Three

Mike Sullivan dropped to one knee on the corner of the embassy roof, the same vantage point from which he'd followed the airport shelling hours earlier. He watched the flag rise, again, atop a rough bamboo pole near the north end of the Newport Bridge. The cloth pennant hung limp in the rain, but its colors were clearly visible: red and blue, with a gold star. The National Liberation Front for South Vietnam. VC. The Newport Bridge, spanning the Saigon River, was a thirty-minute drive from Big Minh's Presidential Palace, where armored personnel carriers nestled among the flowering frangipani trees inside the spiked steel fence.

"Watch this," he said to Sergeant Duane Gevers. Gevers was standing in the doorway of the incinerator room, leaning on a shovel, letting the hot rain wash the grime and ash from his body. He dropped his tool, crossed the roof, squatted beside Sullivan, and wiped clean his prescription steel-framed aviator glasses.

Sullivan began a countdown. "Three . . . two . . . one." The pennant and the bamboo staff were decimated by South Vietnamese machine-gun fire.

"Third time this morning," said Sullivan. He pointed to an emplacement of concrete bunkers on the south bank of the river. "Some stubborn ARVN outfit still dug in down there. Don't know it's over." Sullivan was reminded of the days when South Vietnam boasted having "the world's fourth-greatest army."

"They know," Gevers said. "Just getting in their target practice before they turn the guns on us."

A rotund, jolly fellow with a quick smile and basso laugh, Gevers was the detachment's premier operator, a natural scrounger whom the others had nicknamed "Black Market King." One of his favorite ploys was to clean out the PX's liquor supply with ration cards won in poker games and turn around and, with the help of his girlfriend, sell the booze on Saigon's black market. And he could magically materialize a contraband AK-47 rifle, a beautiful French hooker, a rare Chinese silkscreen, or a tie rod for the motor pool at a moment's notice. No one ever knew where the contraband came from, and Gevers always demanded cash on the barrelhead—no trades or IOUs or "owe-sies." The anomaly of his personality lay in the fact that when someone was caught cash short in a pinch, Duane Gevers was the first to step up with a loan. He was, needless to say, hard for the other MSGs to figure out.

Now he walked away from Sullivan, back toward the incinerator room, and as he bent down to retrieve his shovel, he said over his shoulder, "Jesus, Mike, how'd a college man like you end up here, anyway?"

"Just like you," Sullivan said. "They lied to me."

"Nobody lied to me," Gevers said. "Unless it was when they told me I'd be shooting Charlie."

"Give 'er time."

Sullivan returned to studying the twisting contours of the Saigon River, now roiled muddy by the heavy downpour. Along its north bank, not far from where the VC had raised their flag, he could make out a brace of mortar tubes hidden from ground view by a spinney of cinnamon trees. He pushed a strand of lank red hair from his forehead and spotted a squad of black-pajama-clad figures scurrying behind the gun emplacement. They were wearing conical bamboo bush hats, with ammunition bandoliers criss-crossing their shoulders. It was the first good look at the VC he had had in years.

He strained to hear the tubing, the distinct, metallic *thrump* of the explosion in a mortar tube that propels the payload toward its target. It was a sound that struck fear into jungle grunts. But there was nothing, and he decided he was too far away. At any rate, no detonations ensued. *Just waiting,* he thought.

Almost a decade earlier, Sullivan had lost his college deferment and received his Army draft notice the same week. It was 1966, the war was nearing its height, and he had already attended the funerals of two high school buddies killed in Vietnam. He had spent two years at Bremerton Community College in Washington State, majoring in mathematics and talking politics with the war protesters deep into the night at the local burger joints. He was also an avid newspaper reader who hoped his good grades would earn him a scholarship to a four-year school. The United States Army was the last place he wanted to be.

Sullivan came from a line of railroad men and had virtually grown up in the rail yards near his hometown of Tacoma. While other kids were playing with building blocks or watching cartoons—there was no television in the Sullivan home—he was toting his father's lunch pail to the yards behind the Tacoma train station and hanging around to watch the big locomotives roll in. Everyone in the maintenance section knew Hank Sullivan's scrawny red-headed kid, and an electric current ran through him when he remembered his father's coworkers, big men covered in coal dust, carrying him on their shoulders out to the roundhouse to watch the giant turntables revolve the steam engines that struck him as machines from another planet. Sometimes they'd even hoist young Mike up into the cabs. "Pull the bell, Michael," they'd holler. "Pull the bell."

As a teenager he'd spent summers earning his college tuition in a Cascades logging camp until his father helped him secure his railroad union card, and while taking courses at Bremerton, he'd worked part time as a lineman. His dream was to earn a degree and find a job as a mechanical engineer, perhaps with the railroad.

His father had been a Merchant Mariner during World War II, a captain of a cargo ship in the Pacific, but he never pushed his son toward the military. When Sullivan received his draft notice, he tried to skirt the Army obligation by enlisting in, first, the Coast Guard and, later, the Air Force. It was too late. Neither service wanted anything to do with an Army draftee. On his father's advice, he tried the Navy. It was his last chance, he figured, to stay out of Vietnam. In the Tacoma Navy recruiting center, a grizzled Marine gunnery sergeant overheard him expressing his doubts about the Navy to another recruit.

"I can take you in the Marine Corps," the Gunny said.

Sullivan was wary, until the Navy also turned him down. He went back to see the Marine recruiting officer, who explained the benefits of joining the Corps—the same benefits Sullivan made clear to his incredulous parents later that night after he'd signed his enlistment papers.

"I'm going to Vietnam either way," he told them. "And at least the Marine Corps will train me better than the Army how not to get killed."

His mother cried, and his father, who had watched the slaughter of Marines on Okinawa from the top deck of his cargo ship, asked him if he had lost his mind.

Sullivan scored in the top ten percentile on his Marine Aptitude Test, and following boot camp and infantry training he chose artillery as his Military Occupational Specialty. Like Valdez with the AMTRACS, over the next year he learned the specifics of every possible piece of artillery, from the lightweight 60 mm mortars to the big 155 mm "Long Tom" howitzers, which could throw a shell out over fifteen miles. When he landed in Da Nang in 1967 with the 11th Regiment of the 1st Marine Division, his company commander made him a wire man.

"I've studied guns for 12 straight months and now they've got me laying telephone line, setting up switchboards, and operating radios," he wrote his father. "If that double-cross don't beat all. I thought I joined the Marines, not the Army!"

There was, however, a method to the Corps' madness. Sullivan was soon deep in the bush, communicating with Marine forward observers and reconnaissance outfits and directing shells at suspected enemy sites. Since he was proficient in both artillery and communications, he was the perfect man for the job. But he never lost his skepticism of U.S. aims in Southeast Asia. To the dismay of his superiors, he even asked his mother to mail him daily newspapers, including the *New York Times*. He did not like what he read, or saw, firsthand.

He sensed that the country was turning against the war—with good reason, in his opinion. On liberty in Da Nang, he recoiled at the excesses of the notorious R&R camp on the outskirts of the city abutting Freedom Hill, the 1st Marine Division headquarters. It was there where fat and happy military brass feasted on steak, beer, and ice cream while Marine grunts in the field suffered enormous casualties. It was a far cry from his father's descriptions of the World War II Pacific campaigns.

When his four-year hitch ended, he went back to the rail yards looking for his old job as a lineman. He'd made sergeant, but he was through with the Marines—or so he thought. The economy was in recession, and his job was gone. Confused and angry, he took the full ninety-day separation period before re-upping at his old rank.

After a tour at a U.S. military base in Spain, he was attending Marine Communications School in Japan when his company commander suggested Sullivan apply for Officer Candidate School. The memory of Freedom Hill and his distaste for officers still fresh, he tactfully declined. But MSG School was another matter. The more he learned about it, the more he thought that seeing the world might offer him a different side of military life. A year later—after requesting upon his graduation "dream sheet" deployments to Hong Kong, Buenos Aires, or Beirut—he found himself the NCOIC in Tehran, Iran, commanding a detachment of eighteen MSGs. His next assignment was South Vietnam.

Sullivan arrived in Saigon in March 1974, bound for Bien Hoa as the NCOIC of the consulate's six-man MSG detachment. He found the Marines at his new posting caustic and slack. For some reason—Sullivan could never determine why, even after combing through their service records—they considered the Bien Hoa deployment a form of punishment. He guessed that much of this had to do with the town's unofficial dusk-to-dawn curfew for Americans. It was no secret that while some twenty miles away MSGs were free to enjoy the pleasures of Saigon, gloomy Bien Hoa was rife with VC infiltrators and sullen ARVN draftees. Neither would hesitate to attack any Americans—contractors, State Department employees, aid agency workers, or U.S. Marines—who ventured into certain neighborhoods after dark.

On his second day on duty, he administered a Marine physical training test. Every Marine flunked it. They never failed another as Sullivan remade them into a crack unit. Not long into his deployment, Major Kean touched down in-country on his first inspection tour of the embassy and provincial consulates. The new commanding officer of Company C found the Bien Hoa detachment so "squared away" that he transferred Sullivan to the Saigon Embassy as temporary NCOIC while he looked for a more experienced man. When he found Juan Valdez in Budapest, he asked Sullivan to stay on as Valdez's assistant.

Sullivan agreed, with one request. His MSG deployment was scheduled to end in the spring—he'd been ordered back to California to resume his MOS duty in an artillery company—and he asked the major if he might fly his fiancé in from Tehran and marry her in Saigon. Kean gave him permission, and as an afterthought asked Sullivan what date he was shipping out.

"Thirty April, sir."

Now, standing on the roof of the U.S. Embassy, watching a Vietcong mortar team dig in across the Saigon River, Sullivan fingered the transfer orders in the cargo pocket of his utilities and pondered the irony. Tomorrow was 30 April. At least his wife was safe.

He'd flown his new bride, the former Camy Mohregi, out of Saigon a month earlier, before Da Nang fell and only days after they were married in Saigon's Queen of Peace Church. Twenty-four hours after their wedding, he'd been visited in the home he rented with Camy by an old friend from Bien Hoa, a former sergeant major in the Vietnamese Army who now worked as a CIA operative. The old soldier was one of the toughest men Sullivan had ever met—"the ultimate survivor" he called himself in his thick Vietnamese accent. Sullivan had never seen him so nervous and out of sorts. He warned his American friend that the NVA would be in Saigon sooner than anyone could imagine.

"They will come by the old route," the spook said—the Ho Chi Minh Trail, formerly a series of bicycle paths and now a one-way gravel highway with its own oil pipeline and pumping stations. The one way it headed was south. "Get your wife out now."

Sullivan was impressed and not certain how alarmed he should be. He had not seen the old soldier since Bien Hoa, and certainly never told him he'd gotten married. Yet like everyone in Saigon, he'd heard the rumors of North Vietnamese armies massing on the border. They were just that. Rumors. Moreover, he still harbored the fantasy that Washington would never let the South fall. America had made a promise, and the Seventh Fleet was sixty miles offshore. One sustained naval bombardment would have the Communists running like rabbits all the way back to Cambodia.

But he trusted his friend's judgment, and had never known his sources to fail him. The next morning he called his parents in Tacoma, told them to make up his old bedroom, and drove Camy out to Tan Son Nhut.

A Vietnamese customs officer had just processed her paperwork and was about to stamp her exit visa when two large explosions rocked the airport. Everyone dove for cover except Sullivan, who pushed Camy under the table, reached across, stamped the visa himself, and pocketed it. After Camy's commercial flight departed, he returned to the embassy and headed straight for the Bubble Room. Corporal Steve Bauer was manning the Dragon Network.

"What the hell was that?"

"Sitting here when a plane comes in so low it shakes the building. Thought the ceiling was coming down."

Sullivan looked up and saw a fine layer of plaster dust coating the Plexiglas.

Bauer continued. "Turns out some ARVN fighter pilot decides to defect and lets two bombs go on the Presidential Palace before flying north. Scared the shit out of all of us. Thought we were next."

Sullivan turned to leave; Bauer stopped him. "Hear something funny? After the explosions the ambassador runs in here wanting to know what happened. He's wearing a dress shirt, real pressed, and a tie."

"So what's so funny?"

"Only other thing he's got on are boxer shorts, black knee socks, and shoes. Think he forgot his pants?"

Sullivan walked out of the Bubble Room without responding. The incident settled things for good in his mind. That night he met with Valdez, and the two formed the first burn squad. It was time to begin destroying official embassy documents lest they fall into enemy hands.

He may not have realized it, but Staff Sergeant Mike Sullivan and Ambassador Graham Martin had reached the same conclusion, albeit via roundabout routes: the mess in South Vietnam was the fault of the spineless politicians back in Washington. Sullivan had witnessed firsthand what an American fighting unit could do to Charlie in a straight-up, mano a mano confrontation. He also knew his history. *We took out Dresden. We took out Hiroshima. What the hell made Hanoi so special? Why didn't we make the North fight or surrender?*

Somewhere deep in his gut, however, he knew it would never come to that. He laughed at his own naiveté and checked his watch. It was nearly 8 A.M. He decided to make his rounds, and headed for the stairwell.

Four

The United States Embassy, known officially as the Norodom Compound, encompassed over three acres of prime real estate at the intersection of Thong Nhut Boulevard and Mac Dinh Chi Street in downtown Saigon. Constructed in 1967 along the city's Embassy Row several blocks west of the Presidential Palace, it faced the British Embassy across Thong Nhut Boulevard, and its southern flank abutted the venerable gardens of the French Embassy.

This inviolable slice of U.S. territory was actually two separate compounds, a consulate and the embassy Chancery proper, which were divided by an eight-foot wall bisected by a steel gate. The three-story consulate was located in the southern third of the grounds and took up about an acre of land. It was here where mundane day-to-day commerce—processing visas, promoting and protecting American business interests, coordinating aid activities—was conducted. An MSG was stationed in the consulate lobby Monday through Friday during office hours, but local Vietnamese hired by the mission wardens patrolled the grounds and the front gate.

The larger area to the north housed the six-story Chancery building. Two MSGs manned Post Number One at a lobby desk twenty-four hours a day. From there they were able to see both the main entrance, the front pedestrian gate on Thong Nhut Boulevard, as well as the rear entrance coming off a courtyard adjacent to the large parking lot. The second floor was given over to State Department employees, the third to offices housing Ambassador Martin and Deputy Chief of Mission Lehmann. The fourth floor, an odd dovecote of Plexiglas and steel that included the Bubble

Room, was dedicated to communication specialists and equipment from both the State Department and the CIA. Various security agencies, including the CIA, dominated the top two floors, with Polgar's sixth-floor office sitting atop the edifice.

Northwest of the Chancery, past the parking lot and motor pool and beyond another small wall, was the combined recreation area. The CRA, with its trimmed lawns, swimming pool, canteen, bar, and small theater, was an attempt, as per the custom of American innocents abroad, to transport Main Street to Mac Dinh Chi Street. This smaller outer compound also contained an elegant two-story French villa that overlooked a small, squat Vietnamese Police blockhouse outside the wall. The villa had been nominally used as a residence by the U.S. mission coordinator to Saigon but had since been requisitioned as living quarters for Colonel George Jacobsen, a retired World War II veteran who was serving as Ambassador Martin's field operations overseer and evacuation coordinator. It was also in this building that Major Kean had installed the two-man machine-gun team of Doug Potratz and Jerome Thomas.

Both the consulate and embassy grounds were pocked with multiple warehouses and utility sheds built into a second eight-foot wall, embedded with glass shards and topped with concertina wire, which sealed the entire complex.

The main embassy building, the Chancery, was one of the tallest structures in Saigon, and as Mike Sullivan descended the stairs he noted, not for the first time, the irony to its construction. In contrast to the city's quaint, stucco French colonial ambience, the Chancery had been built of glistening white concrete, an architect's idea of a symbolic beacon of American strength and values. It truly was an imposing construct, yet its beauty was marred by an ugly gray concrete lattice facade, a rocket screen to deflect incoming projectiles that testified to the reality of America's role in Southeast Asia.

Before Major Kean's arrival, Sullivan and Valdez had decided that if and when it came time to defend the grounds, the consulate would be emptied, closed, and the gate separating it from the embassy locked and barred. When Kean studied the plan, he agreed, although the Marines kept these informal contingencies secret from the State Department.

There was no reason to go out of their way to bu
ambassador.

Since the bombing of the Presidential Palace a
Son Nhut by the captured South Vietnamese a
however, contingency had become reality, and t
stood. This still left three other gates to be forti
walkway in front of the embassy on Thong Nh
gate off Mac Dinh Chi Street, and a combined p
trance into the CRA area.

On his way to check on this back door, Sulli
ond floor of the Chancery and popped into an o
ner. Sergeant Phillip Babel, whom Valdez had in
was seated behind an M-60 in a room Major I
machine-gun post.

The M-60 was the standard-issue Marine ma
ing five hundred 7.62-millimeter rounds per mi
of over two miles, although—as every machine
knew—such sustained firing would soon burn
inside the embassy compound the maximum firi
nothing. Babel's gun emplacement covered the
as the vehicle gate, mere yards away.

Kean had issued handheld Motorola walkie-
and the four MSG squad leaders in order to ke
share updates twenty-four hours a day. One of
1968 Tet Offensive was the unreadiness of most
South Vietnam, including those guarding the
January 31, a nineteen-man VC sapper team ha
near the Chancery and charged through. For s
had held them off until Marine reinforcement
killed or captured them all. Ambassador Mart
Jacobsen, was present for the attack and was cre
Vietcong soldier in the compound. But the MS
killed in the six-hour firefight, and Kean had vow
were to happen on his watch, it would not be fo

This morning, Sullivan peered over Babel's sl

s one of his first acts in office, President Minh had declared martial
an extended curfew, but the city's civilians had not even treated
tions as a suggestion. In front of the main gate on the rain-slicked
Nhut Boulevard, a huge crowd, the largest yet, had already begun
e and flow, like water coming to a boil. Beyond the throng, an or-
e of mostly better-dressed and middle-aged Vietnamese still hop-
ply for exit visas stretched around the corner and out of sight. The
walls and gates were substantial, but there was no way they would
ill-blown siege, even by unarmed civilians.

van wondered if any of the NVA sappers Frank Snepp had warned
hiding among the masses converging outside. He was also troubled
nordinate number of ARVNs milling about in various vestiges of
l. He assumed they were deserters—the remnants of the defeated
n armies had been drifting into the city for weeks. More ominous,
heard rumors about the city's young Cowboys, boys really, members
e gangs and often VC sympathizers, hanging around the docks near
on River and just picking up the abandoned M-16 rifles of soldiers
o flee by boat. There were only three MSGs posted at the main
d he knew they would be quickly overrun if the disgruntled South
nese soldiers instigated a riot—or worse.

jor and Top know about all the Cowboys out there today?" he said.
el grunted. "Yup, guess so, since I told 'em." Coming from Babel,
considered this a soliloquy.

re was a saying in the Corps, "A Marine on duty has no friends."
e MSGs, Babel had most taken this to heart, seemingly on and off
abel, a former infantryman, thrived on the Corps' predilection for
ne and precision and took his position as one of the more senior
ts very seriously. He wasn't one to socialize with any Marines under
mand or beneath his rank, and Sullivan understood that many of
, most especially the lance corporals and corporals, but even some
ther sergeants, considered him a taciturn sort. He rarely attended
ftop barbeques and fish fries they used to hold at the Marine House,
ess joined in on the downtown sojourns. His visits to the roof were
limited to his tai kwon do lessons, which he took from a local mas-
eventually resulted in his earning his black belt in the martial art.

Most of the Marines chalked this up to Babel's barely concealed disappointment at watching his dream job, an MSG deployment to London, slowly slip away. His tour of duty as an MSG was nearly up, and the Marines Security Guard Command in Quantico had indicated to Babel the previous autumn that following his Saigon posting, before returning to his infantry MOS, the U.S. Embassy in London would be his next, and final, deployment. But as the situation in Saigon deteriorated, his superiors, citing his experience in the field as a grunt, found more and more excuses to extend his Saigon duty. When one of his oldest friends, Sergeant Tony Tucci, another MSG, had been transferred from Saigon to Rome several months earlier, Babel was too angry to even accompany him downtown to buy parting souvenirs. "You're going to leave and I'm going to be stuck here," he'd told Tucci.

Despite all this, there was something about Babel that had grown on Sullivan. He knew that the native of San Antonio, Texas, came from a military family; on the rare occasions when Babel spoke of his father, an Army veteran—usually to Doug Potratz, probably his best friend in the detachment now that Tucci was gone—he never used the familiar "Dad," or even the more formal "Father." It was always "The Major." And Sullivan suspected the young man was trying to model himself after Valdez, although he inherently lacked the softer, more flexible side of the veteran Top.

Valdez had apparently noticed this too, which is why he had made him a squad leader. Beneath Babel's blunt exterior Sullivan detected a caring Marine whose inexperience did not allow him to show it. The closest he came to being one of the guys was the pride he took in his wardrobe of tailored safari suits, articles of clothing that, for all of Babel's fondness for them, just did not seem to suit the man's personality—like putting a pirate in spats. The bottom line for Sullivan was that he knew he could rely on the Marine in a tough spot and had total confidence in him as a squad leader. Beyond that—well, at this point in the game, there was nothing much beyond that.

Still peering out the window, Sullivan put a hand on Babel's shoulder and pointed to two ARVNs slouched in front of the abandoned British Embassy with M-16s hefted over their shoulders.

"Look," he said. "I don't trust them. Some definitely carrying. The rest probably hiding their weapons. For now. Hot day out there already, and doesn't it look to you like there's too many of them wearing ponchos? What do you think?"

"Yessir," Babel said. Sullivan smiled as he walked out the door. That was more like the squad leader he knew.

He jogged down the stairs, exited the embassy's front door, and eyeballed the vehicle gate as he crossed the lawn. Last night's shelling of Tan Son Nhut had riled the city into a frenzy, and he was put in mind of a rogue grizzly that had once wandered into his logging camp in the North Cascades. The mass of people outside the vehicle gate was larger, and more vocal in their pleas, than the crowd in front of the main gate.

When he reached the CRA entrance, the situation was much the same. This "back door" was the gate through which all Vietnamese embassy workers came and went, and everyone in town knew it. He decided that when he spoke to Valdez and Kean, he would recommend that any Fleet Marine reinforcements choppered into the compound be deployed back here first.

Gunnery Sergeant Bobby Schlager was one of the MSGs manning the CRA post this morning, and when Sullivan spotted him cleaning his rifle, he was pierced with pangs of envy. In the midst of the mounting anxiety of the past few weeks, through all the hurry-up-and-wait endemic to any military operation, Schlager had at least taken one small piece of action into his own hands.

The blond, balding Schlager had succeeded Sullivan as the NCOIC at the Bien Hoa Consulate. When he'd arrived in Saigon by Jeep with the rest of the consulate's escaping contingent, Sullivan had asked Kean to keep him on. Schlager was a cool hand in a pinch, Sullivan told Kean, the sort the detachment would need. He also possessed a crazy streak, as evidenced by the plot he had fomented and carried out not long afterward.

When Schlager reached Saigon, he realized that in their haste to abandon Bien Hoa, the U.S. consul, Richard Peters, had forgotten to strike the colors. He asked Peters for permission to return and retrieve the flag, but Peters forbade any such "wild adventure" and told Schlager that by now, the NVA "owned" Bien Hoa. But the MSG was persistent. It didn't sit right in his stomach leaving an American flag behind. He took the matter to Major Kean, for whom the notion of retrieving a symbolic piece of the United States held a half-cocked attraction.

"If Marines could risk their lives standing it up on Mount Suribachi," Kean told Top Valdez as the two discussed the idea, "we can sure as hell risk taking it down in Bien Hoa."

The major ordered Schlager to come up with a mission plan. Schlager obliged. And Kean signed off on it.

Schlager knew a former Marine helicopter pilot now working for the CIA's Air America. He asked around after him, and found him driving a little UH-1 Huey "Slick" on delivery runs between the CIA apartment complex and the Seventh Fleet. The Bird had almost no armament or firepower, but the pilot was game for a detour. The two arranged to meet on the embassy roof's helipad near sunset. When the Huey landed, Schlager was waiting. So was a young civilian, a former deputy consul in Bien Hoa who had learned of the hare-brained mission and insisted on riding shotgun. The two boarded the Bird, and soon the view of the shanty rooftops of northern Saigon, visible through the Huey's Plexiglas floor, were replaced by the green canopy of jungle separating the two cities.

The sun had nearly set when the aircraft approached Bien Hoa from the southwest. It was immediately apparent there was no place to land. Schlager was seated in the rear of the chopper, his feet dangling from the sliding side door, when the pilot grunted over the intercom and pointed to the half-dozen Soviet-built T-55 tanks parked in the lee of the former U.S. Consulate. A squad of North Vietnamese infantrymen lolled about the treads, smoking cigarettes and laughing. Above them, the Stars and Stripes was still flying from its staff on the roof of the little building. The Communists had apparently never noticed.

Both Schlager and the pilot had anticipated this, but the young diplomat strapped into the copilot's seat had no idea what to expect. Before he could protest, the Huey had dipped over a stand of high trees and was hovering like a mosquito above the flagpole. Schlager cinched the gunner's safety belt tight to his waist and stepped out onto a skid. He leaned backward, braced himself against the tension of the safety strap, and let his hands fall free. His body was suspended at a forty-five-degree angle to the helicopter.

The flag was buffeting wildly in the Huey's prop wash when Schlager snatched it with both hands. Bunching it into his left, he used his right to unsnap his Marine-issue Ka-Bar knife from its sheath and slice the thick nylon rope holding it to the flag staff. By now the NVA soldiers were firing indiscriminately. Only God knew how they missed, and above the ear-splitting rotors, Schlager could hear the subsonic boomlets of AK-47 rounds whizzing past his ears. Once he signaled that he had the flag secured, the nose of the little Huey dropped as the pilot let the throttle out full.

Gunny Schlager was still standing on the Slick's skid, the flag clutched tight in his left hand and his Ka-Bar now between his teeth, as he raised his now-free right hand toward the angry and humiliated Communists. He made a fist and slowly extended his middle finger.

"Give 'em something to remember us by," he told Major Kean on his return. Kean allowed Schlager to keep the flag.

Five

A prearranged signal for the evacuation of Saigon—known to all Americans, civilian and military, and thus to just about everyone else in the city—had been worked out some weeks earlier and was to be set in motion whenever an announcer for Armed Forces Radio read the words, "The temperature in Saigon is 105 degrees and rising." This code phrase was to be followed by a Bing Crosby recording of "I'm Dreaming of a White Christmas" playing continuously on a loop. "White Christmas." In hot, humid April in South Vietnam, no one doubted that this was a military operation.

The two now-defunct fixed-wing evacuations from Tan Son Nhut Airport, Options I and III, were, like all other military ventures before a shot is fired, designed to be quick, easy, and safe. Kean had instructed Valdez and Sullivan to go over the plans with the detachment so many times that the MSGs had taken to greeting them with raised hands and pleas: "No more evac talk. I got it already."

It was not hard to get; the planners had tried to keep it as simple as possible. Refugees and evacuees, including the majority of the MSG detachment, would depart the embassy either on small Hueys shuttling to and from the DAO compound or in a convoy of olive-drab, Japanese-made Isuzu buses. At the same time, additional convoys of buses and minivans, led by automobiles painted to look like Vietnamese National Police cars, would fan out through the city to a dozen prestaged pickup points where American civilians and "endangered" Vietnamese had been told to gather. These routes had been designated "trails"—as in "Santa Fe" and "Oregon"—and dry runs had already been conducted.

Once inside the DAO compound, the embassy MSGs would fall in with a company of Marines scheduled to be flown in from the Seventh Fleet. Together they would form a security perimeter protecting military cargo planes arriving and departing Tan Son Nhut. When all American civilians, Vietnamese refugees, and third-country nationals had lifted off, MSGs and Fleet Marines would board the final two C-130s while a team of demolition experts blew the communications equipment and set fire to the DAO buildings.

Simultaneously, the ambassador's six-man PSU team and a truncated squad of MSGs, no more than a half-dozen led by Kean and Valdez, would remain at the embassy and accompany Martin when he lowered the colors and was choppered off the roof.

Kean had left the decision to select the MSGs for that squad up to Valdez, who had not yet decided who would remain. The major and his NCOIC were certain, however, that it would have to be a CH-46 that picked them up. The scores of Marine CH-53s awaiting "L Hour" on the flotilla of American ships floating offshore with the Seventh Fleet—three Marine helicopter squadrons and ten U.S. Air Force Jolly Green Giants on ready alert sixty nautical miles from Saigon—were too heavy to land on the small rooftop helipad.

Now, with the fixed-wing airlift plan abandoned, it was almost 9 A.M. when Valdez found Sullivan near the back gate and told him to pass the word among the MSGs that the entire embassy evacuation, civilians and military, was going to have to somehow be accomplished by choppers: Navy and Marine CH-46s, Marine CH-53s, the Air Force contingent, plus whatever Birds the spooks from Air America could scrape together. Although all Americans and designated refugees except the ambassador and his small party were still technically scheduled to fly out from the DAO, hardly anyone at the embassy believed that possible. Helicopters, and lots of them, would eventually have to land at the embassy. It was going to be sporty, even if they ever got that goddamned tamarind tree out of the way.

"Major says everyone stays professional this morning," Valdez told Sullivan. "Business as usual. Posts at all three gates open at nine. Repeat, business as usual."

Sullivan raised an eyebrow. Hadn't Kean or Valdez seen the size of these desperate crowds? What about the ARVN Cowboys? Snepp's infiltrators? Opening the gates, "business as usual," was insane. The Marines had received instructions from the embassy's regional security officer, Marvin Garrett, to admit only those carrying American passports, foreign allied passports, and Vietnamese with stamped evacuation authorization documents. Which of these documents were real and which had been forged, the Marines would never be able to tell.

People were already slipping through cracks all over the compound and losing themselves in the crowd of previously admitted "friendlies" camped out on the lawn by the embassy pool. With the burn squad pulling double shifts on the roof, there were not enough Marines to plug every hole. And then at some point, everyone was supposed to board buses to cross town to the DAO compound? A joke. Sullivan knew all this but said nothing to Valdez. He did not have to. The NCOIC knew it also. He shrugged.

"Gotta at least give the appearance," he said. "Martin's orders."

He was careful to emphasize the word *appearance*, just as Major Kean had instructed.

Six

The ambassador's intransigence was now becoming a tactical thorn beyond Saigon and Washington. Out on the South China Sea aboard the light cruiser USS *Oklahoma City,* Vice Admiral George Steele, commander of the Seventh Fleet, made a terse entry in his diary. "Ambassador Martin's unrealistic attitude towards the evacuation is exemplified in the delay in his personal authorization to cut down the tree in the Embassy compound," Steele wrote. "That prevents helicopter access. Having failed to initiate the evacuation in a timely way so that the majority of evacuees could be taken from Tan Son Nhut Airfield as the plan envisioned, the Ambassador is still not taking those actions large and small to facilitate matters."

But Steele was helpless to do anything about it. His fleet, dispatched from ports as far-ranging as Okinawa, Pearl Harbor, and San Diego, had only just coalesced off the coast to supplement the smaller Navy Task Force 76 which had sailed from Subic Bay following the fall of Da Nang. That task force, commanded by the man-mountain Rear Admiral David Whitmire, had been cruising the coastal waters for days picking up Vietnamese boat people. Now that the entire U.S. naval force was arrayed in a 100-mile arc in international waters—thirty-five ships of the line including five aircraft carriers surrounded by dozens of tenders, seagoing tugs, and reconnaissance craft—it was expected that Option II, the sealift, could be implemented. No one had counted on the situation ashore falling apart so rapidly.

In the communications room of Whitmire's command-and-control ship, the USS *Blue Ridge,* Marine Brigadier General Richard Carey felt the cold steel beneath his feet vibrate from the ship's engines as he also fretted over the narrowing of evacuation options. A compact man with a long, hangdog face, Carey had been chosen to command the helo lift. He also had at his service the 9th Amphibious Brigade of 6,000 armed and restless Fleet Marines billeted below decks. An affable, soft-spoken fifty-two-year-old who seemed the antithesis of the growling, cigar-chomping Hollywood Marine, Carey had been handed this assignment because of his experience as both a combat infantryman and a Marine aviator.

Known to his peers as a pleasant racquetball partner and a delightful raconteur at base happy hours, Carey also possessed a temperament of flint—hard but easily sparked. As a raw first lieutenant, he had been decorated numerous times for leading a platoon ashore at Inchon, South Korea, in 1950. Sixteen years later, having transferred to the Corps' aviation component, he'd led an F-4 fighter command based in Chu Lai. Carey was qualified to fly thirty-seven different types of aircraft, and his record as the only Marine to complete day and night carrier qualifications piloting a CH-53, a CH-46, a Huey, and a Cobra gunship—all in one day—still stood. He had seen enough war for one man's life and took to heart the old British Navy adage that battleships were cheaper than battles.

Since sunrise Carey had watched hundreds of desperate South Vietnamese in every type of helicopter—and even the occasional light plane—blotting the dove gray sky above Steele's ships. The small Cessnas and Piper Cubs would swoop close to an American craft, throttle down, and a door would fly open through which men, women, and children would jump into the sea before the pilot ditched the plane as close to a ship as possible. Scores died.

The military choppers, meanwhile, frantic to land somewhere, anywhere, would hopscotch among the fleet looking for open space on any deck. Many ran out of gas during the search and also crashed into the sea. When aircraft did manage to find safe haven, their passengers were rushed out of the helicopters to be processed on hangar decks as teams of U.S. sailors pushed the Birds overboard to make room for the next descent. Among the helicopters that set down on the *Blue Ridge*, it was reported to Carey, was one flown by the South Vietnam Air Marshal, Nguyen Cao Ky. Even in this time of crisis, the Americans could see the black humor in

Ky's escape. The flamboyant, mustachioed air marshal, once the country's prime minister and Thieu's former vice president and political rival, only days earlier had vowed to remain and fight the Communists "to the end."

"Anyone who flees our beloved country while the enemy advances upon us is a coward," Ky had announced to a crowd of some 6,000 followers at a political rally near the Presidential Palace the night before Thieu sneaked out of the country. Now here he was, strutting the deck of the *Blue Ridge* in his tailor-made flight suit and combat boots, a white silk scarf tied rakishly about his neck, as U.S. seamen hauled his personal Huey to the edge of the deck and tipped it over into the South China Sea.

Watching this flying circus unfold, Carey recognized that once his Marine pilots took to the air the sky-borne traffic jams were going to make the goal of an evacuation by sunset impossible. He would have forty to fifty choppers over the city at any given time, and there was no radar to guide them in and out. Navigation would be predicated on line of sight, and he knew the weather was turning. That meant flying at a low ceiling, making them fat targets for antiaircraft and missiles. Nonetheless he had eighty helicopters and the best-trained Marine pilots and crews in the world, and he champed to use them. Soon. This, he knew, would be no Phnom Penh.

A few miles away, pacing the deck of the converted aircraft carrier USS *Dubuque,* Marine Flight Leader Gerry Berry was chewing over much the same problem as the warp and weft of the South China Sea rose through the soles of his boots. Berry, another Phnom Penh veteran, had led a squadron of four CH-46 Sea Knight helicopters overflying the sea on emergency search-and-rescue, or SAR, missions during the evacuation of the Cambodian capital—the more powerful CH-53s, with their stronger "legs," had done all the long-distance ferrying. But that day there had not been a cloud in the sky and they'd flown under Visual Flight Rules, or VFR. Now he scanned the northern horizon, where the sheeting rain lent the late-morning sky the macabre formality of a steel engraving. Thick, viscous clouds formed a towering wall that seemed to reach to the troposphere. The storm was moving inland fast, and he was certain that the more dicey

Instrument Flight Rules, IFR, would be in effect even before dark. Unless the brass planned on pilots flat-hatting close to the ground under those clouds . . . and making themselves easy targets from ground fire and RPGs.

Moreover, for reasons Berry could not fathom, the *Dubuque* was steaming west, alone, toward the Gulf of Thailand. As the bulk of the American armada, silhouetted against the dark sky off the stern, receded further in the ship's wake, he remembered from one of his history classes that the weather had been much the same during Dunkirk.

For the last three days, the thirty-year-old Berry and his flight crews had sat idle, on alert, awaiting the commencement of Operation Frequent Wind. They had taken their meals, bitched, and even peed over the side of the ship under a bright yellow sun that pushed temperatures to 110 degrees and drove the humidity to near 90 percent. And now, this morning, the payoff they'd been waiting for was imminent. Yet here they were sailing away from the fleet.

Handsome and heartland raised, Berry was a virtual recruiting poster for Marine aviation. With his blond buzz cut, prominent cheekbones, and boyish face that tapered to a strong jaw line, he looked as if he had come out of the womb wearing a flight suit. Nothing could have been further from the truth, and he was aware of the disconnect.

A former high school and college quarterback from Des Moines, Iowa, Berry had flown in a plane precisely once before enlisting—when his Simpson College football team had visited Colorado College for a road game in his senior year. Upon his graduation in 1967, he received his draft letter from the Army. Like the MSG Staff Sergeant Mike Sullivan, Berry saw no future in humping an eighty-pound pack through the jungles of Southeast Asia as a pogue grunt, and on the advice of a fraternity brother, he dropped into the local Marine recruiting center. A poster hung on the wall depicting a god-like pilot in an orange flight suit standing beside a Phantom jet.

"Could I do that?"

The Marine recruiter handed him a pen and a sheaf of papers. "Take the test."

Berry passed the aviation aptitude exam easily, and after ten weeks of Officer Candidate School, he was surprised to be chosen as the first Marine ever to attend the U.S. Army flight school at Fort Wolters, Texas, while the rest of his classmates were shipped to basic training before heading for Navy Flight School in Pensacola, Florida. At first Berry had been flattered by the attention. However, it gradually dawned on him that when the military spends time and money on you, they weren't necessarily trying to save your life; rather, they were trying to find some way you could lose it while working for them. It was 1968, and not only was the Army desperate for helicopter pilots to send to Vietnam, the service was also angling to take a bite out of the Navy's domination of the war's air service.

The point was almost moot. During his first few weeks at Fort Wolters, Berry considered himself a "shitty pilot." He worried over being shipped back to basic school with his tail between his legs. Then, one day after class, an instructor pulled him aside and told him to relax.

"You think they're gonna flunk you out? Forget about it. You're the first Marine down here. Never gonna happen."

The advice eased the pressure he felt, and in January 1969, months ahead of his Marine and Navy classmates, he graduated with honors and was deployed to Vietnam. Now, standing on the flight deck of the USS *Dubuque,* he recalled with a wry smile the man's exact words. *Never gonna happen.* He couldn't count the amount of times that respected officers, smarter than him, had assured him of the same thing about the collapse of South Vietnam. *"Never gonna happen," my ass.* Berry had been visualizing this day for months, since the first rumblings of the NVA offensive. But it had dawned on him as long ago as flight school.

And though he had no idea why the *Dubuque* had separated from the fleet, he suddenly felt that it did not matter. What did were the orders he'd been given earlier in the pilots' Ready Room, when he and the others had been told that today was the day they were finally going in to sweep up the mess begun so long ago. For most of the young pilots, it would be their first sojourn over Vietnamese territory. For Berry, it was a sad return. Judging by the storm clouds, it would also be a dangerous one.

Berry had long been accustomed to flying according to the law of unintended consequences. It was one of the first things the old timers had taught him when he'd arrived in Vietnam: "You fly in and you think something's going to happen one way, and it invariably happens the other way."

He'd joked at the time that it sounded like quarterbacking a football team: what could go wrong, would go wrong. The veteran flyers had looked at the new kid like he was crazy. "This is a much more dangerous game, son," a tough old gunnery sergeant had told him. The gunny had been right about that.

Berry had been sent to war as a twenty-four-year-old second lieutenant, the youngest CH-46 pilot in his squadron. "Brown Bar," the other Marines nicknamed him, after his rare single insignia—heretofore all Marine combat pilots graduating from Pensacola had come over as first lieutenants. He'd been assigned to I Corps at Quang Tri, near the Demilitarized Zone, ten miles south of the border with North Vietnam. He hadn't waited long to see action. Nor did it take him long to sense that something about this war was, as he put it, *dicked up*.

On one of his first missions, he'd offloaded a Marine recon team on a mountaintop just west of his air base and blanched as the infantrymen took heavy fire from the moment their boots hit the ground. One of his squadron's helicopters was shot down during the insertion, and Berry's Bird made eight more runs into the area to try to rescue the crew. He had not trained on 50-caliber machine guns in flight school, and it was the first time he heard how loud they were. Finally, his helicopter too shot up to continue, his crew chief wounded, he returned to his base only to discover that both the recon team and the flight crew of the downed chopper had hiked out to safety.

Not long after, his squadron was ordered to reinsert another recon team near the same location. Again they were met by heavy fire—*the enemy isn't stupid*—and again the recon team leader radioed for an extraction almost immediately. Berry had been a wingman back then, and his squad commander had turned their Sea Knights around just as the top of the mountain appeared to explode with gunfire. Although they were flanked by two Cobra gunships, flying low and raking the hill with rockets and their own machine guns, even after three passes Berry's squad could not find a hole in the enemy defense. Enemy bullets had perforated the clear canopy surrounding him, his copilot was dead, and both his crew chief and his door gunner were wounded. The squad commander had finally radioed the recon team leader, "We can't get you off the top of the hill. You gotta get over to the other side."

The Marine grunts descended the slope to about midway down the mountain, but even there, the choppers continued to take incoming. Finally, as Berry hovered on the hillside, his right skid almost touching the ground and his helicopter tilted askew so his rotor blades would not clip the tree tops, the recon team was able to leap through his open side door. Two of them were thrown in. Limp. Dead.

At the time, he'd been a kid, and despite the killings, it was all one hell of an adventure. He'd flown over 900 missions in his thirteen months in-country, yet somewhere in the back of his mind, he always wondered if this was any way to run a war. He wasn't much for politics, but he couldn't help but notice that he was repeatedly dropping different troops onto the same mountain, as it were, and firing at the same enemy each time he did it.

Now, back in Southeast Asia for the first time in six years, floating off the Vietnamese coast, he remembered those first few forays in-country and realized that they were the reason he had seen "now" coming for some time. He had lived the ignoble history—in September 1969 when the United States closed the base at Quang Tri and I Corps fell back to south of Hue City, and then a year later when they had moved farther south, all the way to Da Nang.

In the years since he had set foot in that luscious, green country, Vietnam had provided him with a different sort of education, and his outlook on human nature, and how it applied to this war-torn country, had evolved from a Hobbesian "nature red in tooth and claw" to a more enlightened version of live and let live. Now here he was, standing on a flight deck, come full circle from the college jock who had joined the Corps to escape the Army draft, from the brash young pilot cleated up in both helicopters and jets, to the mature officer who now wondered what would have happened if the United States had just learned its lesson from the French at Dien Bien Phu in 1954 and left the damn country and its people to their own devices. And if he read the scuttlebutt correctly—and he was certain that he had—we couldn't even get our own people and our friends out by boat, ship, or cargo plane.

Still, if his life in the Corps had imparted to him one overriding philosophy, it was that once the Marines gave a war, it was your duty to attend—even if things, here, now, still seemed pretty dicked up.

"Got weather moving in," he said to his crew chief.

The crew chief popped his head out from the cabin of the CH-46. His hands and face were smeared with gun oil. He glanced toward the monsoon clouds scudding across the South China Sea.

"Well, at least we got something to hide inside when we get in the air," he said.

Seven

Could there be such a thing as too many riches? This was the question General Van Tien Dung contemplated in the roofless structure that his staff had now set up as headquarters in the jungle near Ben Cat, less than twenty miles outside Saigon. He began to compose a response to the mass communiqué dispatched from Hanoi earlier this morning over the names of General Giap and First Secretary Le Duan. The message read, in part, "We call on all cadres and fighters, party members, and all members of mass organizations to strike with the greatest determination straight into the enemy's final lair with the heroic spirit of an army with a hundred victories in a hundred battles, smash the enemy's power to resist, and completely liberate the city of Saigon-Gia Dinh."

No stranger to florid prose, Dung could also read between the lines. He knew that the transmission was directed to him. He also knew he had fulfilled his role. His army, at 800,000 strong the third largest in the world, occupied most of South Vietnam. Saigon was completely encircled, his divisions aligned in the shape of a five-point star around the city. All roads and most bridges leading into and out of the city were in his hands, and the few that were not, such as the Newport Bridge, still stubbornly defended by ARVN units, would soon be secured. Tan Son Nhut's flight lines were unserviceable, and his troops were advancing from the south on the provincial capital of Can Tho, in the heart of the Mekong Delta.

If it had not been completely obvious over the preceding months, Dung thought, it certainly was now: the South was losing the war faster than his troops could win it.

Events had unfolded differently than he had envisioned. At age fifty-seven, Dung was still a fit and athletic soldier, and the aggressive manner in which he played volleyball with his officers mirrored the way he ran his campaigns. But he was also a meticulous planner, and when he had first slipped into the Central Highlands from Hanoi, his stated intention had been to secure the countryside before the rainy season began, dig in for the summer, and resume military activities in the fall. Saigon would be taken, at the very latest, by early 1976.

But the enterprise had changed with each succeeding victory over Thieu's forces, and by early April, Dung had reported to his superiors that the opportunity to end the war before the monsoons had arrived had come. He was determined not to commit the same errors his predecessors had made during Tet in 1968, when what he considered their timidity had snatched defeat from the jaws of victory. He had been appointed to lead this campaign precisely because of his ferocity, and he was not about to lose the upper hand.

As little as three weeks earlier, the Politburo had refixed the date for the "liberation" of Saigon as May 19, Ho Chi Minh's birthday. But seven days ago, on April 22, that date too had been moved up at Dung's discretion when he'd received a private cable from Le Duan: "The military and political opportunity for launching the general offensive on Saigon is ripe. We must make sure the best use of each day and launch the attack against the enemy from every direction without delay. If we grasp this great opportunity firmly, our total victory is sure."

Dung was in complete agreement. The only impediment to this challenge would be another intervention by the United States: a fusillade from the Seventh Fleet or a return of the B-52s and their full-scale bombing runs. And what about the U.S. Marines guarding the U.S. Embassy? Would they put up a fight? He recognized that he walked a tightrope. The Politburo had been closely monitoring events in Washington, D.C., and some of its members had taken at face value Vice President Nelson Rockefeller's recent declaration that "it is far too late for us to do anything to reverse the [military] situation in South Vietnam."

Dung was not so certain. In his view, the United States was ruled by running dogs, albeit sly running dogs. And just as he had initially believed

President Ford's and Henry Kissinger's "pathetic and touching" promises to defend the South Vietnam regime, he remained wary, he wrote, of the "obstinacy and cunning [that] had always been the characteristics of the U.S. imperialists and their flunkies." In short, he worried that the "war-crazed" American government would hatch a final plot, perhaps involving those very same Marines guarding the embassy, to save face and "to prevent a second Waterloo which could bury the prestige of the ringleaders of U.S. imperialism."

To avoid just such an occurrence, he realized he needed a plan of his own not only to secure victory over the South but to allow the Americans a safe withdrawal from the capital. It went against all he had lived and fought for to allow the capitalist oppressors to escape without penalty. But it was the only way. He hoped that his shelling of Tan Son Nhut was a sharp enough poke with a stick to move them along faster. If not, they would pay.

But for now, Dung decided, he would wait, at least until the day was out. He was in the middle of dictating his thoughts to Hanoi when an aide interrupted with news that two American planes had entered Vietnamese airspace. The prominent laugh lines at the corners of Dung's mouth disappeared, his thick white eyebrows twitched in agitation, and his broad, squarish face clouded over.

Eight

The news spread rapidly through an embassy compound where secrets no longer existed. Two American C-130s from Clark Air Base in the Philippines were vectoring at 16,000 feet over the tiny airport on the Vung Tau peninsula. The small spit of land, extending into the South China Sea like a wart on a witch's nose, was forty-five miles southeast of Saigon. Through his Marine contacts at the DAO, Jim Kean learned that Ambassador Martin, fulfilling a long-standing promise, had unilaterally ordered the cargo planes to land and pick up the families of a unit of Vietnamese Royal Marines who had been bused to a former Australian military base on Vung Tau.

Kean knew that Martin felt he needed the support of the South Vietnamese Marines, the country's last, best fighters, to secure the American evacuation. If they were to turn on the Americans, no one would ever get out. The defense attaché, General Smith, had just received a report that two platoons of NVA infantry had been spotted setting up mortars in a cemetery a half-mile north of Tan Son Nhut Airport, and a unit of South Vietnamese Marines was the only force that stood between them and the DAO.

Kean also knew that the cratered runways at Tan Son Nhut not only remained a sporty proposition for landing big cargo planes, but that airport security had gone to hell. A South Vietnamese Air Force pilot who had managed to get his F-15 off the ground during the shelling had returned, landed on the main runway, and abandoned the jet with the engine still running. He'd then commandeered a Jeep and driven off to find

107

his family. Simultaneously, the parallel flight line was now clogged with a truckload of ARVN soldiers threatening to ram a South Vietnamese C-130 in an attempt to block its escape through the rubble.

So it had to be Vung Tau. It all made sense. The major had to admire the ambassador's moxie. He may have been sick, he may have been dead tired, and he may have an atomic ego, but that tough old sonofabitch sure was something else when he was angry. And he was still giving the orders. When Admiral Gayler in Honolulu heard about the planes, he tried to call them back. But Martin overrode the CINCPAC, and they were now preparing for a descent onto the peninsula.

Up on the embassy roof, MSG Sergeant Bobby Frain thought he heard the hum of the plane engines and looked up to try to spot them. The cloud cover was too thick. No matter, he thought. He was certain they would not be carrying any new girls for him to meet. The last three months had seen to that.

The twenty-year-old Frain had grown up in one of the smallest incorporated villages on record in Pennsylvania and had joined the Marines to see the world. A natural social animal, he'd arrived in Saigon the previous year, and though he was soon as open to the city's nightlife as any of the rowdiest MSGs, he had one quirk that set him apart: he preferred, as he put it, "round-eyed girls." Tall, dark, and handsome—the other MSGs made constant sport of his facial similarity to the actor Rock Hudson—he was also dubbed "The Body Beautiful," for his naturally sculpted torso. He would eschew the local B-girls in favor of the more Western-appearing half-French women left over from the colonial days, and he also had an internal radar, the envy of the detachment, that alerted him whenever the sisters or daughters of embassy workers or the myriad American civilians working for private companies in Saigon flew in for visits.

No matter who they were or where they worked, sooner or later every visiting American woman ended up at the embassy to dine at the CRA canteen, swim in the pool, or just withdraw cash from the bank. And no matter how soon any Marine thought he'd received word of "fresh blood in the compound," by the time he arrived to make his play, Frain would already be out by the pool, showing off his washboard stomach and posing in his tight bathing trunks.

One of the senior political officers whom the MSGs suspected of being a CIA spy was the father of two gorgeous twin daughters in their late teens. Before the city became too dangerous, the man's wife and the twins would visit him at Christmas, during spring break from college, and over long periods in the summer. Frain applied his good looks and his roguish, appealing personality to the mathematical problem and wound up dating them both at the same time.

The only taboo, well known to every MSG, was the ambassador's comely daughter, a stewardess for TWA. During the peaceful years, she had been a regular around the embassy, and during one of her visits late in 1974, Martin had caught an MSG and his daughter flirting. The offending Marine was shipped out the next morning—Martin had gone over Kean's head to make it happen so quickly—and rumor had it that he was now posted to the consulate in Nuuk, Greenland. Even Frain wasn't that adventurous.

Frain was recalling that poor MSG's fate as the C-130s landed successfully at Vung Tau. They were on the ground no more than fifteen minutes before lifting off with the Vietnamese Marine families aboard. Upon their departure General Smith again telephoned Admiral Gayler. "The helicopter evacuation should begin now," he said. "Or I don't know what."

Whether coincidence or not, a few moments later, a squad of Air America Hueys was circling the DAO, preparing for descent. Six miles away, Jim Kean had joined Bobby Frain on the roof. The two watched as the little helicopters buzzed the DAO compound like a swarm of angry bees. The major knew one thing was for certain: the loyalty of the South Vietnamese Marines now belonged to the ambassador.

Kean also sensed it was time to take matters into his own hands. On his way back downstairs, he had spotted the CIA spooks running around as if they had all seen ghosts, and there was a rumor spreading that the NVA had issued an ultimatum demanding the departure of all Americans from the city by sunset or else they would turn their artillery on the Presidential Palace, the DAO, and the U.S. Embassy.

Over the past week, before the crowds had truly begun to surge, he had scouted several possible locations for helicopter landing zones outside the embassy walls, and written them all off as too inefficient or too dangerous.

Now he asked Valdez to round up a couple of Seabees and ordered the Navy construction men to find cans of luminous paint and mark both the rooftop helipad and the parking lot with a giant "H." For night landings. He thought of the shelling rumor. *Maybe add a bull's-eye too.*

Next Kean directed the mission warden fire chief to soak the ground around the parking lot to keep any debris from being lifted into the prop wash of arriving helicopters and to keep the hoses running. Finally he told Valdez to collect the MSG machine gunners and have them take up their prearranged positions.

The little Air America Hueys had already started to land on the embassy roof to begin ferrying out secretaries and lower-level diplomats when the RSO, Marvin Garrett, summoned the major to his office. Kean wore a lion tamer's look as Garrett dressed him down for "panicking" and ordered him to have his MSGs resume "normal operations."

Kean listened, nodded, left Garrett's office, and decided to ignore him. He thought the man had been drinking. And in any event what Garrett had referred to as a "controlled facade" was now closer to uncontrolled pandemonium. There were already between 1,500 and 2,000 jumpy refugees within the embassy walls and another 5,000, by Kean's rough estimate, pressing against the gates. More were arriving every moment.

Kean was not sure who exactly was directing the Air America choppers to the rooftop helipad, but he did not like it. It only attracted the civilian crowds. Bypassing Garrett, he loped to Ambassador Martin's office and requested that he call them off. There would be time, he explained, to get everyone out when the CH-46s and CH-53s began arriving. Martin called Garrett's office and ordered him to discontinue all landings on the roof. Kean was not certain if Martin actually agreed with his reasoning, or was merely spiting the CIA's Polgar.

Nine

At 10:30 A.M., Ambassador Martin was informed that General Smith and Admiral Gayler were on his secure telephone line. He summoned Wolfgang Lehmann and Colonel George Jacobsen to his office and took the call. Martin was exhausted. He seemed to physically shrink even further as Smith and Gayler, in turn, told him it was time to make a decision: NVA troops were less than a mile from Tan Son Nhut. The two American military men could barely conceal their anger at Martin's disconnect from reality.

"We still have time," Martin told them.

This was too much for Gayler: "Ambassador, in the bluntest terms, no, we do not."

Martin hung up and, for the first time, admitted the obvious to Lehmann and Jacobsen: "Hanoi has no interest in negotiations."

The two aides knew that Martin took this as a personal betrayal. They were still in his office ten minutes later when, at 10:45, Martin took a call from Kissinger. The aides suspected the secretary had telephoned at the prompting of Admiral Gayler. Kissinger's tone was more circumspect—he was, after all, just as reluctant as Martin to cede State Department authority over Saigon to the military—but his message was much the same. He'd spoken to the president, he said, who had ordered Option IV.

Martin held the telephone receiver to his ear and reread the hand-delivered letter he had only just received from President Minh:

Dear Ambassador Martin:
I respectfully request that you give an order for the personnel of the

111

Defense Attache's Office to leave Vietnam within 24 hours beginning April, 29, 1975 in order that the question of peace for Vietnam can be settled early.

"Yes, it is time," Martin told Kissinger, and rang off to compose his reply.

Dear Mr. President:
I have just received your note. This is to inform Your Excellency that I have issued orders as you have requested.

At 10:51 A.M.—thirteen years, four months, and one week since the death of U.S. Army Specialist Fourth Class James Thomas Davis, the first American killed in open combat with the enemy in Vietnam—Ambassador Graham Martin officially relinquished civilian control of South Vietnam and formally executed Operation Frequent Wind's Option IV. It was now a military operation.

Frank Snepp, panting from his dash down three flights of stairs from CIA headquarters, found Ambassador Martin slumped against his secretary's desk in the reception area outside his third-floor office. He handed Martin a smudged teletype, the transcript of an intelligence report filed moments earlier by one of his local station officers with sources in the NVA. In the garbled syntax of translated Vietnamese, it announced that NVA gunners were preparing to lob 200 rounds of 130-millimeter shells into the heart of downtown Saigon at precisely 6 P.M. today.

Snepp told the ambassador that General Dung was not only enraged by the two cargo planes landing at Vung Tau, but also over the fact that Americans still occupied the DAO. Dung had received messages from Hanoi informing him that there had been a pullout of American "military advisors" from the airport compound, yet his own forward observers near Tan Son Nhut were reporting what looked to be business as usual at the DAO. Dung suspected the Americans of some type of duplicity.

Martin remained expressionless as he read the missive. He shrugged, handed the paper back to Snepp without a word, turned, and walked into his office.

In his office in the White House, Henry Kissinger was handed a sheaf of cables sent to him by General Smith. The general described the growing panic among the Vietnamese refugees at the DAO compound and his fear that for each hour the evacuation took, the odds of getting out all American civilians as well as the Vietnamese on the endangered list would decrease.

At this point, Kissinger was not worried about Vietnamese, endangered or otherwise. The longer it took every American to leave Saigon, the greater the chances of hostages. Even if their lives were spared, the public relations nightmare would be horrifying. He wondered, again, how much faith he could place in the Soviet promise to pressure Hanoi into delaying the capture of Saigon for four more days. And even if the North agreed to Brezhnev's request, could the NVA keep a leash on the Vietcong?

He also questioned Martin's stability. That the ambassador had finally agreed to the initiation of Frequent Wind was a major step but not completely reassuring. Martin was under enormous mental and physical strain, yet had requested to stay behind, at the French Embassy, with two volunteers in order to supervise an orderly transfer of power from President Minh to General Dung. That was all America needed: a U.S. ambassador held hostage.

As the secretary of state pondered these depressing thoughts, he turned to Vice President Rockefeller, who was also studying the cables.

"We'll be lucky to get all the Americans out now," he said.

Rockefeller looked aghast. The thought had never occurred to him. "Really?"

"Well, you know," Kissinger said, "it depends how quickly the mob can get out of control."

"You hear?" Mike Sullivan wore a sour grin.

Juan Valdez looked up from the cot in his office, disoriented. He hadn't slept in sixteen hours and was trying to catch a short catnap. He was in that liminal state—the free-fall zone between wake and sleep. He checked his watch. He'd been down for three minutes. To Valdez the filthy Staff Sergeant Sullivan looked like one of those Mexican movie banditos just about to spit on the cantina floor.

"What?"

"Tree's coming down. Lehmann gave the order."

"Overrode the ambassador?" Valdez doubted that. Lehmann had brass, but not that much.

Sullivan shrugged. "Beats me. But it happened. Major's out there now with a bunch of our guys and a couple Seabees."

Option IV, Valdez thought. *Finally. Official.* He jumped from his cot. "Let's go," he said.

The rain clouds had dissipated, and a cloak of gray, wet humidity had settled over the city when the burn unit on the roof heard the news. A half-dozen MSGs coated in grime exited the incinerator room and trudged past a growing pile of circuit boards, radio transmitters and receivers, crypto gear, and thousands of laminated name cards the CIA had planned to use as seat tickets for high-risk Vietnamese. It was all classified garbage now, destined for the burn barrels—large drums of sodium nitrate used to destroy material that would not burn fast enough in the furnaces.

The Marines lined up along the western rampart and peered down at the tamarind tree. They resembled a row of black turkey vultures waiting for a wounded animal to die.

Someone broke out the last of the heat tabs, the one-inch chemical wafers used to warm up the C-rations, and passed them around. Despite the noxious fumes from the trioxin, a picnic-like atmosphere ensued as the Marines ripped open the thin cardboard C-rat containers and dug into their first hot meal in days. Schuller had drawn a B2, which included a large can of spicy meatballs, a smaller can of pound cake, and pimento cheese spread and crackers. He tried to trade the cheese and crackers for a can of fruit cocktail or peaches. There were no takers.

They ate and watched as, below, Bobby Schlager and a big Seabee wielding gasoline-powered chainsaws dug into the tree trunk from either end. A few feet away, a squad of MSGs stood beside a two-ton mission warden fire truck. Within ten minutes, the ancient tamarind toppled across the parking lot with a great crash. The MSGs scattered as one of its larger branches barely missed crushing the truck.

The Seabee continued to saw the old tree's trunk into four-foot sections while Schlager and another Bien Hoa MSG, Sergeant Ronald Duffy, connected grappling hooks to the ends of two thick chains attached to the truck. They dragged the larger pieces toward the vehicle gate while more Marines hacked away at the branches with handsaws and axes. Steve Schuller imagined that the towering pile of cordwood would heat his mom's Connecticut farmhouse for an entire winter.

Schuller tossed his empty C-ration tin toward the furnace room and lit a Lucky Strike.

"Hated that fuckin' tree," he said to no one in particular.

Graham Martin sat in his office, his back to the closed window. Despite the loud whirring of the air-conditioner he could not help but hear an exaggerated, gleeful scream carrying the trace of a Hungarian accent.

"Timberrrr!"

The CIA's Tom Polgar could not let it rest.

Ten

One hundred miles to the southwest of the besieged capital, Marine Staff Sergeant Boyette "Steve" Hasty scanned the gunmetal gray sky from the end of a planked river pier and watched the spooks break the deal. The CIA's silver-and-blue Air America helicopters, shimmering in the noonday heat of the Mekong Delta, were not heading to Saigon as the American consul had ordered. They were fleeing for the sea, for the fleet. *Typical,* Hasty thought. First, the Agency had stolen the small speedboats the Marines had planned on using for their escape. Now this.

Hasty, the twenty-four-year-old NCOIC of the six-man MSG detachment guarding the U.S. Consulate in the small regional capital of Can Tho, followed the choppers with his eyes until they were specks on the southern horizon. He then returned to loading an assortment of weapons onto the crowded and rickety boats. What, after all, was a pirate fleet without plenty of guns? Hasty had been in periodic telephone contact with Jim Kean, back in Saigon, for the past twelve hours. Simultaneous to the NVA shelling of Tan Son Nhut, the city of Can Tho had also been bombarded. And though no Americans had been killed or wounded, a good portion of the town, including the central market, had burned. When the winds picked up, Hasty had crawled out onto the consulate's pitched, tarred roof with a garden hose to try to keep the flames from jumping the wall separating the American compound from the marketplace. The task looked hopeless until a providential morning rainstorm swirled up and doused the fires.

A few hours after the shelling, at just past 10 A.M., Can Tho's American consul, Francis Terry McNamara, had received a call from Saigon. After he'd cradled the telephone receiver, he summoned Hasty into his office. It was time, he told the Marine, to get out. Down the river. An evacuation, as McNamara had predicted, predetermined by the CIA's cowardly bug-out. Hasty had been prepared for any contingency. In his seven years in the Marine Corps, he had learned to live by one overriding adage: "You can never have too many weapons or too much ammunition." The philosophy had served him well since he had volunteered nine months earlier to leave Thailand and "stand up" from scratch the security for the new consulate in Can Tho. Now the Americans were running, and he felt that he and his detachment were as prepared as possible for what Kean had warned him was the looming "shit storm."

Hasty had known he was in for a different kind of Marine security job even before his arrival in the Delta. Can Tho was literally a backwater—a rowdy river town on a tributary of the Mekong that served as a commercial gateway to the northern interior for ships and barges hauling, and smuggling, everything from rice to tractors to guns. Kean had offered him the NCOIC position with a caveat: he'd be getting the most inexperienced MSGs to man the new detachment. "You got to staff this new consulate out of hide," the major told him. "Carve off a hunk of yourself and there you go."

But Kean had never warned him about the hastily frocked U.S. consul general designate. Terry McNamara was cut from a breed Hasty had never before encountered. Arriving in Can Tho, the MSG had not so much met McNamara as hunted him down—their first introduction took place in the back room of a local geisha house, where he found the forty-seven-year-old career Foreign Service officer enjoying a young lady's company as well as a magnum of French champagne chilling in an ice bucket. Surrounding them was a carpet of empty bottles of Ba Muoi Ba, the notorious hangover-making Bierre 33 whose secret ingredient was said to be embalming formaldehyde.

Hasty had since been inundated with rumors about the charming, handsome, and thoroughly divorced McNamara—specifically that he was, in the words of a diplomatic colleague, "the world's biggest liberty risk." Yet since his deployment, the MSG had performed due diligence on the man and discovered that there was more to McNamara than met the eye.

Vietnam, for instance, was far from McNamara's first brush with the exigencies of civil war.

McNamara was one of the State Department's most experienced Africanists, having served in seven countries across that tumultuous continent beginning with his 1957 appointment to the U.S. Embassy in Salisbury, Rhodesia, at the age of thirty. Four years later, while posted to the breakaway province of Katanga in the southeastern portion of newly independent Republic of Congo, he had engineered the evacuation of American missionaries and Foreign Service workers in the midst of one of Africa's frequent bloodbaths—in this case, an exceedingly brutal assault by Congolese government troops on the rebel stronghold. Studying the episode, Hasty was impressed not only by McNamara's tactical know-how but also by his personal bravery. As firefights between the government troops and Katanga's mercenary-backed militia erupted around the consulate, he had managed to gather all American nationals in one place, commandeer an armored personnel carrier from a nearby U.N. Swedish peacekeeping unit, and drive everyone to safety through a roaring gunfight.

Afterward he remained behind, alone, until the Congolese assault was beaten back. Since then he had attained a reputation as something of a fixer, albeit a wild-card fixer, in State Department circles.

Since Africa, McNamara had served three postings to Vietnam, the first in the late 1960s in the Mekong Delta for the U.S.-run pacification program Civil Operations and Rural Support (known as CORDS), a hybrid military and civilian operation reporting to the State Department and larded with rear-echelon paper pushers. McNamara was anything but, getting into the field and often exposing himself to danger, and he had been rewarded with an appointment to a senior Foreign Service officer post in Da Nang from 1969 through 1971. And unlike Graham Martin, McNamara harbored a deep affection for the country and its people. Africa had fascinated him, but Vietnam, for reasons he could not quite articulate, had exerted on him an even stronger emotional pull. He traveled often through the delta by helicopter, by sampan, by Jeep, and sometimes even in an unmarked Peugeot, always with a smile and a purpose, weaving through the thick, green, spiky grass of the region's sixteen soil-rich provinces and risking his life to confer with "his" provincial chiefs, "his" village elders, and "his" ARVN commanders. It was all one grand adventure, and more than a touch of the consul's devil-may-care aura had rubbed off on the strait-laced Hasty, who was by now an acolyte. The feeling was mutual.

"My young John Wayne," McNamara had affectionately taken to introducing the long and lanky Marine on their inspection tours. The physical image was suspect—out of uniform, the bookish and bespectacled staff sergeant, at six-foot-three and barely 150 pounds dripping wet, was more likely to be mistaken for Ichabod Crane than the Ringo Kid. But Hasty nonetheless took the sobriquet, and its inference, to heart. It reminded him of why he had dropped out of school at age seventeen and chosen the Corps over the other military services in the first place. If you're going to be a bear, his Marine recruiter had told him, be a grizzly. To that point in his life, Steve Hasty had been more of a cub.

Born in Decatur, Georgia, the only boy and the oldest of three children, Hasty and his younger sisters had spent much of their childhood shuttling between his divorced parents' homes in southwest Texas, where his father, Boyette Sr., sold insurance, and Atlanta, where his mother, Pat, worked as a telephone operator. Money was tight in his mother's home, and the young Hasty often found himself being reared by his grandmother. An introverted child, always the new boy at school, he found it difficult to make friends. Instead he passed much of his childhood on long, solitary walks in the woods and escaped into the pages of his beloved history books. After spending a year at an Oklahoma military academy at his father's insistence, he decided that his life's calling was to fight for his country in Vietnam.

He was nearly turned down by the Corps for being too skinny when he enlisted in 1968; he weighed 130 pounds at the time. To his chagrin, by the time he completed boot and basic camps, the Marine presence in the war was being subsumed by the Army. He applied to the Marine Security Guard program with the idea of working his way to Vietnam through the back door. "It's like going around your ass to get to your elbow," he wrote to his father.

After indeed drawing Saigon on his graduation from MSG School, he wangled an assignment with the civic action arm of the U.S.'s MAAC-V (Military Assistance Advisory Command–Vietnam), where he worked with a mixed military-civilian unit building schools in the northwest provinces of Kontum and Pleiku. It wasn't the type of combat action he'd dreamed of. Still, he was serving his country in an active war zone. Because of his MSG status, Hasty was one of the last American troops to vacate Saigon following the signing of the Paris Peace Accords. He yearned to return. He bided his time with the Bangkok MSG detachment until the summer of 1974, when Kean made him the offer to deploy to the brand new consulate in Can Tho. Once there, he immediately sensed an enmity between the freewheeling McNamara and the CIA's regional station chief, an athletic and brush-cut conservative "suit" named Jim Delaney. Delaney, newly arrived from Laos, had no experience in Vietnam, and though McNamara was nominally his superior, the spook's distrust of the American diplomatic corps in general, endemic to the Agency's purview of South Vietnam, and his dislike of McNamara in particular were plainly evident impediments to command unity. Delaney reminded McNamara of the character Alden Pyle in *The Quiet American,* Graham Greene's classic depiction of American naiveté in Vietnam.

Hasty watched as Delaney and McNamara set up and operated separate networks of informants tracking enemy movements throughout the delta, with the intelligence each clique gathered often clashing diametrically. McNamara was convinced that Delaney's people were merely, and literally, selling him what he wanted to hear. The consul also found the CIA man's analytical skills particularly banal. The conflict came to a head in late April when McNamara learned from Colonel George Jacobsen, Ambassador Martin's evacuation coordinator in Saigon, that Delaney was planning a rogue operation. From McNamara's point of view, the CIA in Can Tho had no intention of putting its four Air America choppers at Ambassador Martin's disposal for the Saigon evacuation as McNamara had promised Jacobsen and Martin. The consul suspected that the Agency was instead devising a secret escape for its own operatives directly to the American fleet.

As the feud festered and the country collapsed around them, Hasty instinctively sided with the consul general. Again unlike Ambassador Martin, McNamara treated his MSGs with a bonhomie verging on brotherhood, and to Hasty, loyalty was a two-way street. The Marine also came to admire the diplomat's confidence and competence in the face of what was clearly turning into a disaster for the United States. After overhearing one caustic quarrel between the consul and Delaney's second-in-command regarding the plans for the Air America choppers, Hasty telephoned Kean and reported, "McNamara isn't a guy that can be rolled."

Hasty also placed great faith in McNamara's prescience. The small confines of the rural outpost may have necessitated a more intimate relationship, or perhaps it was merely McNamara's gregarious personality, but the older man was not averse to sharing his political, personal, and strategic thoughts about the state of Vietnam with his young Marine NCOIC. Even prior to the NVA conquest of South Vietnam's northern provinces, he did not hesitate to label Martin's quest for cease-fire negotiations with Hanoi as "pure fantasy." And though McNamara may have clung to a dim hope that the disciplined ARVN units stationed throughout the Mekong Delta, Vietnam's storied rice basket, could be used as a bargaining chip to make the inevitable terms of the final surrender more palatable to the United States, that notion evaporated when he visited Martin after the fall of Da Nang.

In Saigon, McNamara was struck by what he later described to aides as the ambassador's "distracted and faraway gaze." He was one of the only American diplomats in Vietnam who had no prior professional relationship with Martin, although he had met him in Washington when Martin was summoned to testify before Congress. McNamara felt some sympathy for the untenable position in which the ambassador had been placed. In his opinion, the job of pleading for more aid to South Vietnam should have rightly fallen to Henry Kissinger as secretary of state, and he sensed that Martin was being set up as a fall guy.

This empathy, however, did not extend to Martin's staff, one of whom suggested during his visit that when the time came to evacuate Can Tho, he abandon his Vietnamese employees, his mission wardens, the endangered local police officers, and the Amerasian children of American soldiers he had promised to get out. Instead, the aide said, he should concentrate on taking only Can Tho's American contingent to Saigon for airlift. McNamara countered with a one-word response—"Bullshit"—and the aide backed down. Still, on his return to Can Tho, he told Hasty that he found the distressing atmosphere of the capital city "almost poisoned by fear."

"The South will fall, and fall hard," he said one evening as the two shared a bottle of ten-year-old scotch at the consular residence. "We'll be forgotten down here. Our delusions of an air evacuation, much less a negotiated peace, call to mind Chamberlain at Berchtesgaden."

Hasty may have been hazy on the specific geographic reference, but he knew enough about England's appeasement of Hitler to take the general idea. In case he did not, the North Vietnamese drove the point home. By mid-April Can Tho was being shelled intermittently by NVA mortars and heavy artillery off-loaded from the southern tip of the Ho Chi Minh Trail across the Cambodian border, and several vague evacuation plans were in place. One involved a fixed-wing airlift from the small, rutted airfield operated by the Royal Vietnam Air Force on the outskirts of town. McNamara scoffed at the idea. Sure enough, when Hasty visited the base commander to probe for his reaction, it had been short and simple: "You'll be overrun as soon as the first plane lands," he told the American Marine.

A second option—the one McNamara had learned the CIA had no intention of carrying out—was a mass evacuation to Saigon, with the Air America Hueys flying the consulate's thirty or so American employees, the MSG detachment, and as many endangered Vietnamese as possible to Tan Son Nhut. Although the helicopters were originally specced out to carry perhaps eight Americans, the feeling was that once the seats had been removed, perhaps fifteen or so of the smaller Vietnamese could be jammed aboard. This would still mean the Can Tho contingent would need assistance from the Seventh Fleet's larger Marine choppers. Again McNamara merely laughed at the hubris. He maintained that when the South imploded, they could expect no help from Martin, Saigon, or the Seventh Fleet. And certainly not the CIA.

There were also rumors among the Can Tho MSGs that the CIA had amassed a fortune in gold bars, ingots, and coins from banks throughout the delta to prevent the wealth from falling into Communist hands. If true, and given the limited space on their small fleet of aircraft, the Marines felt this certainly altered the CIA's evacuation priorities. But McNamara shot the story down in a meeting that Hasty attended.

"They're not greedy," he said of the spies. "They're merely stupid, and in a few cases cowards. Either way we can't count on them. So let me tell you what we're going to do. We're going to take Saigon's evacuation Plan A under consideration. And then we're going to put together our own Plan B."

The next morning he purchased an old round-bottomed rice barge and two fifty-five-ton military surplus LCMs—landing craft, mechanized—from a local shipping firm, the Alaska Barge and Transport Company. The slab-sided landing craft had been modified for commercial river traffic; each was about fifty feet long with a fourteen-foot beam, and they drew a little over four feet of water. They were ramped at the bow, powered by a pair of strong diesel engines, and their open wells were big enough to carry a tank—or, McNamara guessed, between 100 and 200 people. The barge, the venerable *Delta Queen,* could hold perhaps another 100.

McNamara asked his aide, Walt Heilman, a "gentle bear" of a man in charge of the consulate's maintenance, to oversee the outfitting of the LCMs with makeshift gun pits and concrete collars, and the consulate staff began stockpiling tins of C-rations and jugs of water in preparation for the seventy-mile run down the Bassac River to the South China Sea. That this directly countermanded Martin's orders seemed to bother the consul not a whit, and his insouciance was infectious. Hasty and McNamara even requisitioned an Air America helicopter and flew a secret reconnaissance mission downriver, charting the waterway's bends, narrows, and—aware that the NVA controlled the southern reaches of the river—the most logical sites for an enemy ambush.

The two made for an odd couple of sailors. McNamara had virtually grown up on the water, working summer jobs on tugboats plying the Hudson River and Erie Canal as a teen, serving as a submariner in the North Atlantic during World War II, and called back to active duty from the Naval Reserve as a gunnery officer aboard the cruiser USS *St. Paul* during the Korean conflict. Hasty's familiarity with seafaring stretched not much further than fishing from a rowboat as a boy in Texas and Georgia—although, he proudly informed McNamara, the first book he ever recalled reading, hidden under his bed covers with a flashlight, was Kenneth Dodson's classic World War II naval yarn *Away All Boats.* "No guts, no glory," Hasty had told McNamara on being briefed on the plan.

McNamara merely smiled at the wide-eyed young Marine and put him in charge of collecting firepower for the journey. It was a job Hasty knew how to do. It was the rare American living and working in the delta who did not carry a gun; most were former military of some sort, and many had lived through the trauma of Tet in 1968. Moreover, the stories coming down the river about the deprivations of the Khmer Rouge were making everyone jumpy. Each day since Christmas had brought fewer boats and barges heading into the interior, and as the months progressed, Western civilian contractors and aid workers began to pack up and leave.

Hasty erected roadblocks along the roads to the airfield to "purchase" their weapons with money from a special fund McNamara had set up. The MSGs had soon confiscated a small cache of sidearms, rifles, and even a few M-79 "Blooper" grenade launchers. Good, but not enough. So throughout April, before the two-lane highway that connected Can Tho to Saigon became too dangerous to travel, Hasty also made several overland gun runs in the consul's Ford Bronco.

On one of these journeys he arrived at the DAO just as the dismembered bodies from the ill-fated Operation Babylift were being sorted on the Tan Son Nhut tarmac. He joined in and helped bag the unrecognizable chunks of flesh. On his final run, one week earlier, he'd gotten a late start out of Saigon after he and a fellow MSG had procured a load of M-60 machine guns and three crates of ammunition. Nearing Can Tho around dusk, they spotted a platoon of pajama-clad soldiers emerging from a tree line. Hasty cursed himself for being on the road so close to dark, but he managed to slip the Bronco into a culvert before they were seen. Random sniper fire on these journeys had always been a given. But to see a unit of VC operating openly in the daylight was an omen. His heart pounded as if he were back in Pleiku, and his first instinct was to hide the Bronco, find cover, and open fire. His second instinct was to consider his first instinct insane. They slipped around the VC patrol and drove on south.

Although nowhere in a class with Saigon's "Black Market King," Duane Gevers, Hasty was an inveterate pack rat, and proved an excellent scrounger. When McNamara had given him the go-ahead to start the evacuation process earlier that morning, he'd proudly informed the consul that if it came to it, the bang-bang quotient collected from all his schemes had been sufficient to arm every man, American and Vietnamese, they hoped to take downriver. Now it was time, time for the total American retreat, and as he stood on the quayside in Can Tho loading the weapons and cursing the CIA's perfidy, a bright, swollen sun sent spikes of light through the thick fronds of the coconut palms on the far bank of the Bassac a mile away.

He turned at the noise of a loud engine. McNamara's Ford Bronco screeched to a halt, nearly running him down. The consul was accompanied by three of the CIA's Filipino employees, several of the Agency's local Vietnamese operatives, and one American agent who worked the communications shop in the consulate. The spooks had left them behind too.

It was almost 11 A.M. when Chuck Neil, a civilian news announcer working for the Armed Forces Radio and Television Network in downtown Saigon, received a telephone call from Marine Colonel Alfred Gray at the DAO. Colonel Gray was General Carey's choice to command the regimental landing team of Fleet Marines who would provide security for the helicopter evacuation. The colonel asked Neil how many Americans remained at the station. Neil told him there were four, including his station manager, Ian Turvett.

"You and all Americans," the colonel said, "are ordered to evacuate the station immediately and proceed to the embassy for an evacuation flight."

Neil was dumbfounded. He knew the North Vietnamese were closing in, but he had never really believed it would come to this. He found Turvett, told him it was time, and the two recovered an audiotape cartridge from a safe in Turvett's office. Neil had recorded the tape weeks earlier at the behest of a DAO public affairs officer. The last time he'd seen her alive, she was boarding the doomed Operation Babylift flight. He later heard that when one of the plane's doors blew, she was sucked out.

Neil popped the tape into the station's Gates Automatic Programmer, punched it up to a prearranged setting, and he and Turvett grabbed their personal gear and walked down a back stairway to a van parked in the alley behind the station.

There was no radio in the van. As he, Turvett, and several sound engineers navigated through crowds and checkpoints along Hong Thap Tu Street on the six-block drive to the U.S. Embassy, Neil never heard his own voice proclaim, "The temperature in Saigon is 105 degrees and rising." The announcement was followed by Bing Crosby's rendition of "I'm Dreaming of a White Christmas."

Western civilians throughout the city reacted differently. At the CBS News bureau, a reporter stood, said, "Well, time to go," and led a line of newsmen to a nearby bus pickup point. On the roof of the Hotel Caravelle, another reporter who had been designated as the group leader responsible for Americans shouted, "We're going," and did the same.

Westerners dragging suitcases clogged the hotel hallways on the edge of panic. Foreign reporters unfamiliar with the song, including a segment of Japanese, sensed that something big had occurred, and fell in. Across the city, the reaction of ordinary Vietnamese to what had clearly become an inevitability offered a surreal contrast. In some neighborhoods, children continued to play on the streets and sidewalks amid clusters of old men and women gossiping about the coming regime. In several cases their older sons and daughters had contemplated escape, only to be discouraged by the size of the crowds encircling the U.S. Embassy. Others had weighed the advantages of starting over in a strange country versus adapting to communism, and decided that northern overlords could be no worse than the southern regimes they had lived under. Yet those ordinary Vietnamese who had worked in close proximity to the Americans—hotel and café waiters and bartenders, tailors, taxi drivers, shoeshine boys, and, of course, the B-girls—looked on in astonishment, or incredulity, or outright fear and loathing. If the Americans were leaving, it really was the end. And the beginning of the unknown.

At the embassy, not a single MSG heard the broadcast.

Part III
Escape

There is no reason for Americans to still be there. At four o'clock this morning I find out that nobody is off the ground yet. Now what the hell is going on?
—Henry Kissinger, to CIA Director William Colby
and Chairman of the Joint Chiefs of Staff
General George Brown

One

Saigon, 1200, 29 April 1975

At 12:30 P.M., the first U.S. Navy A-7 Corsair attack jets and U.S. Air Force Phantom fighter jets, dispatched from bases in Thailand, crossed into South Vietnam airspace. Their mission was to provide cover for the initial wave of Marine Sea Stallions, Sea Knights, and Air Force Jolly Green Giants powering up on the deck of the Essex-class aircraft carrier USS *Hancock* and bound for the DAO compound. These squadrons, about thirty-six rescue helicopters, would also deposit a battalion of Fleet Marines as an appropriate show of force to secure the grounds.

Having made the decision to defy the Paris Peace Accords and send in armed troops—in fact, more than fifteen times the fifty allowed by the January 1973 agreement—General Carey resolved to personally oversee the evacuation. Shortly after 1 P.M., he climbed into a Marine Huey and lifted off from the deck of the USS *Blue Ridge*. The flight was an eye-opening experience for him. On approach to Tan Son Nhut, Carey took in the breadth of the enemy's firepower as the NVA continued its ground attack on the flight lines and South Vietnamese aircraft. What surprised him most were the disparate ARVN forces that had coalesced to make what looked, for the moment, to be a successful defensive stand. *To this point, at any rate*, he thought.

Carey's helicopter touched down at the DAO compound not far from where the first buses, crammed with refugees, had begun arriving. He met with his ground commander, Colonel Gray, as well as a small contingent of embassy-based Marines dispatched by Major Kean to accompany the bus drivers; they reported chaos throughout the city. They also told the general to expect many more refugees than the Americans had counted on. Word had spread throughout Saigon that the evacuation would take place primarily from the DAO and the U.S. Embassy. As Jim Kean had warned Juan Valdez, "Common sense says that people in a panic will run to the American flag."

Once on the ground, Carey established an austere command post and waited for the arrival of his Fleet Marines. Some evacuees, including Ambassador Martin's wife, Dorothy, and their poodle, Nit Noy, had already, per General Smith's instructions, been ferried to the fleet in the little Air America Hueys. But it was the big Marine CH-46s and CH-53s that would do the bulk of the work. It was at this command post that Graham Martin reached Carey by telephone.

The ambassador was hesitant to report specific numbers, even downplaying them by a factor of four or five, yet managed to impart to the general that the embassy evacuation had not proceeded according to plan. There were, he said, at the least hundreds of people encamped on the grounds awaiting retrieval. Carey was floored. He was under the impression that the embassy, if not now nearly emptied by buses, soon would be. There had been no planning for any major movements from that location. He wondered again about Martin's mental state. Despite days of numerous requests from officers of the fleet, even up until the last moment it had been impossible to get an accurate refugee estimate from the ambassador. He radioed Admiral Steele and informed him that an immediate adjustment in helicopter priorities was needed.

Across the city, word spread quickly of the Americans fleeing their hotels and gathering at designated bus pickup areas, and the crowd of mostly Vietnamese encircling the embassy had begun to surge against the walls and gates like an incoming tide. Jim Kean ordered Mike Sullivan to make sure that the vehicle and back entrances were closed and locked, and as Sullivan took off at a trot, the major hollered after him, "You tell every man on the gates I don't care if somebody shows up with a black diplomatic passport. They send him 'round front. No one in or out of those gates."

Meanwhile, at the main gate, Westerners were being allowed to pass into the compound without question, while Valdez distributed to his men a list containing the names of Vietnamese and third-country nationals to be "saved." This was, he recognized, a futile gesture. The pandemonium in the street made it impossible to follow any protocol, and how his MSGs were supposed to distinguish between legitimate identification or exit visas and forgeries was anyone's guess. Beyond the embassy walls, in every direction, spires of smoke curled to the slate gray sky from looters' fires, but as Valdez soon learned, at least one of his Marines, Sergeant Greg Hargis, was doing his part.

Valdez was headed from the main gate to the motor pool when he ran across Mike Sullivan and asked him to fuel up the bread truck and square away the weapons inside in preparation for any last-minute pickup runs through the city. Sullivan's response, or lack thereof, momentarily baffled him.

"Hargis, uh, borrowed it," Sullivan finally said. "Personal thing. Said he'd have it back in an hour."

Valdez guessed immediately the nature of Hargis's "personal thing."

"Whores?"

The staff sergeant nodded.

Hargis was a stern-looking Marine whose most distinguishing features were two bushy eyebrows that resembled a single woolly caterpillar crawling across his forehead. He was also one of the security detachment's foremost aficionados of Saigon's night life. He was not a bad guy, Valdez knew. He'd just forgotten to grow up.

Hargis had driven the bread truck to the bars and cafés along Tu Do Street in search of his favorite bar girls, singing "White Christmas" at the top of his lungs. The women, however, were loath to leave. For years, the American and ARVN soldiers had provided them a steady stream of income, with even a little left over to send back to their rural villages. Why should North Vietnamese soldiers be any different?

"Because their commanders will shoot your pimps and lock you up . . . if you're lucky," Hargis told them. There were rumors—false, as it turned out—that after the NVA and VC captured Da Nang, they'd rounded up every woman and girl with painted fingernails and tortured them, pulling the nails out with pliers. As Hargis spread these stories along Tu Do Street, a few of the more intelligent, and older, girls seemed to comprehend the danger of their situation. By the time Hargis was barreling toward Tan Son Nhut, he had two dozen jiggling and sequined "erring sisters" packed into the back of the bread truck, along with one little tailor, an Indian expatriate named Mr. Singh who ran the street-front New York Tailoring shop below the Magic Fingers massage parlor frequented by the MSGs.

Mr. Singh's creations, particularly his finely crafted white safari suits, were a favorite of the Marines. Even the stoic Phil Babel was a regular customer, and he and many of the other MSGs shipped them home by the dozen. The location of Mr. Singh's establishment was also convenient for the ultimate in one-stop shopping. The MSGs were fond of dropping off their dry cleaning with Mr. Singh, continuing upstairs to experience the magic-fingered girls, and picking up their cleaned and pressed clothes on the way out.

Passing though the DAO compound en route to the main terminal, Hargis convinced a U.S. Air Force ground security crew that he would vouch for each woman, and the one man, he carried. "They're all personal friends," he assured the airmen. Inside at the debarkation counter when he was asked to sign as their official sponsor, Hargis did so without hesitation. The MSG did in fact know most of these girls well, and as he watched them board the plane, he had no doubt that they would find work and accommodations faster, and more easily, than any other Vietnamese fleeing the country. Wherever they ended up, he knew, from Thailand to Guam to New Zealand to the United States, their experience would serve them well.

When Hargis returned to the embassy with the bread truck, Valdez was waiting for him in the parking lot.

"Burn unit. Roof. Now." Valdez pretended to be angry, but was secretly delighted that Hargis had rescued Mr. Singh.

Hargis nodded and headed toward the elevator. Then he stopped. "Top, just thought you ought to know something."

He said that during his rescue mission, he'd caught an early warning of the looming bedlam when he'd passed a contingent of ARVN soldiers and Saigon Cowboys setting fire to a warehouse owned by a private American aid agency. Nearby, he said, South Vietnamese soldiers guarding the Presidential Palace had merely looked on passively.

"Only saw for a minute, before a couple of them turned guns on me, and I got the hell out of there. But they had a big bonfire going. You could tell it was going to spread to other buildings. And I could swear they were burning the sacks of food and just carrying off the stuff like televisions and refrigerators. This city's gonna blow all to hell."

Valdez thought about this for a moment. *What the hell was an aid agency doing bringing in televisions and refrigerators?* But he said nothing.

It was not long before Hargis's prediction was borne out. Within moments of his return, a good portion of Saigon's phone lines were cut and gunfire had begun to echo down alleys and streets. Who was doing the shooting, and at whom or what they were shooting, Valdez had no idea. But as more and more American civilians made it inside the embassy walls and relayed the horrible stories, a picture of a desperate city on the brink came into focus.

Gangs of looters roamed the main streets, breaking down doors and smashing windows, cleaning out cartons of liquor and cigarettes from bars and cafés, and assaulting the few Western reporters attempting to cover the chaos. A cameraman for CBS News told of filming a bizarre scene near the Presidential Palace of an unhinged South Vietnamese police captain emptying his .45-caliber sidearm into a stalled taxi. When he saw the cameraman shooting, he turned his gun on the American, but his pistol jammed. He then began chasing the fleeing newsman and beating him over the head with the barrel. And a newspaperman about to be shot by another Vietnamese policeman screaming "American Traitor" saved his life only by producing his Australian passport.

As it became obvious to Saigon residents that the noisy green Japanese buses winding through the city streets were ferrying Americans and select groups of locals to either the U.S. Embassy or the DAO for evacuation, some people grew even more desperate. A British reporter aboard a bus bound for the DAO saw two panicked Vietnamese lawyers in their official court costumes of black robes and white tab collars try to throw themselves in front of his vehicle. And the ABC television correspondent Ken Kashiwahara watched as a Vietnamese man, his face like a clenched fist, ran alongside his bus carrying a baby and pleading to board. At one point, he tripped on the curb and dropped the infant. The passengers who had witnessed this, jolted by the crunch of the bus's rear wheels crushing the baby's bones, screamed at the American Foreign Service officer in the driver's seat to stop. Instead, he floored the accelerator.

There were reports of gunfights breaking out on the city's river docks, where local fishing captains were jettisoning their crews and selling passage to the Seventh Fleet for as much as $12,000. And several Westerners recounted tales of their inexperienced American bus drivers, lost and panicked, careering down narrow side streets sideswiping passing vehicles, upending fruit stands, plowing through soup stalls, and even knocking an infant from its mother's arms. This heedlessness had begun to spur retaliation among even normally placid Saigon citizens, and one DAO-bound rescue bus and its Jeep escort were surrounded and overturned by an angry mob.

Not all Americans exhibited such a disregard for Vietnamese lives. Two State Department officers driving a pair of white-paneled mini-vans exited the embassy on their own in an attempt to retrieve several of their South Vietnamese government counterparts almost certainly destined for prison camps. When they reached their prearranged meeting point, however, the crowd had grown so large that they were forced to turn away elderly women and babies after packing their vans full.

Back in the embassy compound, on the opposite side of the grounds from Valdez at the main gate, Mike Sullivan could sense the disintegration of order outside the walls. And as the stories began to circulate about the flight of his fellow Americans, their ignominiousness as ugly as an exit wound, his resolve to make up for it in some small way only increased.

He formed a squad of MSGs and led them on a sweep of the embassy buildings to round up any Vietnamese employees still at their work stations, divided these survivors into two groups, and escorted them to the vehicle and CRA gates. There he told them to alert the nearest Marine should they spot anyone outside who worked for a U.S. agency. Not long afterward, a local mission warden employee whom Sullivan recognized approached the back vehicle gate holding one end of a rope that trailed behind him. The other end was tied to the wrists of between thirty and forty people. Sullivan was reminded of a kindergarten class out on a field trip. The mission warden told Sullivan that the men, women, and children were his extended family whom he had promised to bring out. The MSG was at a loss.

"You have to get it down to fifteen, maybe ten," Sullivan said.

The man began to weep. He could not make the decision. He begged the Marine to make it for him.

Sullivan hesitated. Finally he said, "Okay, your wife, your own kids. And any babies you want to take."

The Marine turned his back on the scene as the man began his selection. His stomach hurt. *Who the fuck am I to play God like this?*

Two

At the main entrance to the embassy, when a minor miracle did occur and someone brandishing the proper papers or passport was found to match a name on the list, the MSGs pushed open the double gates slightly to allow him—or in a very few instances, her—to pass through. At this, however, the mob would erupt, forcing the gap between gates to widen even more and allowing a trickle of people to steal in before the Marines could push back the crowd and close the gates.

This, finally, was too much for Valdez. He disappeared into the embassy to find Kean and reappeared at the main gate a moment later. "Lock it up!" he hollered.

John Ghilain turned to make sure he had heard correctly. The big corporal from Boston had arrived in Saigon eight months earlier from a deployment at the Brussels Embassy. Although his classmates back in Quantico couldn't believe his good fortune when he'd been tapped at only twenty years old for a Western European capital straight out of MSG School—they were unaware that Ghilain, of Belgian descent, spoke a few words of Flemish—the posting had actually bored him nearly out of his mind. Looking for adventure, he had requested a transfer to South Vietnam. He assumed he'd get a consulate, but his luck held, and he was posted to Saigon. Nothing in Brussels had prepared him for this, and for a moment he faced Valdez with a blank stare.

The NCOIC yelled again. "I said lock it up!"

At that all the Marines snapped to, and as MSGs wound thick chains through the wrought-iron bars and clasped them with padlocks, Valdez motioned for Ghilain to join him.

"Can you hold me?" the top sergeant asked.

Ghilain didn't understand.

"On your shoulders."

Now Ghilain got it. He had lost his helmet, and his thick flaxen hair was matted with sweat across his forehead. "Yes, Top."

"At the gate, then," Valdez said.

The embassy walls were embedded with coiled concertina wire, and thus the only safe place to lift people over was at the nine-foot-high main gate. Valdez grabbed the nearest Marine by the collar of his flak jacket and spun him around. It was Bobby Frain.

"You're checking papers," he said, extending a thick, double-columned register. "They match names on the list, you move them in front of Ghilain. I lift them over."

Valdez climbed up on Big John Ghilain's shoulders and was soon plucking people off the sidewalk as if they were rag dolls. Out on the street, Americans and refugees fought for space in front of the two-headed giant. One American reporter of Japanese descent, afraid he would not be recognized, stood before them hollering, "The Dodgers won the pennant! The Dodgers won the pennant!" Valdez lifted him over. Another refused to be hoisted without his heavy camera equipment. Valdez complied, but "accidentally" dropped and smashed the gear from the top of the wall.

A middle-aged Vietnamese man managed to slip through the crowd and stood face to face with Ghilain. He was dressed up like a well-kept grave. He withdrew a grease-paper bag from the inside pocket of his tattered suit coat, thrust the bag through the bars, and opened it. Ghilain, his hands gripping Valdez's boots, looked inside. The sack was filled with uncut gems. Ghilain thought he saw diamonds among the red, blue, and green stones. Someone elbowed "the jeweler" aside and flashed a handful of shiny gold South African krugerrands. Ghilain recognized them from the depiction of the springbok antelope on the coins.

He yelled to Valdez, "Get rich here, we want, Top."

Valdez ignored him. He was intent on a scene unfolding a few yards to his left, where a young Vietnamese couple edged toward the concrete wall on the fringe of the crowd. The man cleared a path with his elbows, the woman trailing close in his wake. She was carrying a tiny package wrapped in a blue blanket. *No, this cannot be happening.*

At the base of the wall, the woman handed the man the swaddled baby. He swiveled, holding it low to get maximum thrust, and heaved it up. The blanket snagged on the concertina wire. Bobby Frain looked up in shock. He had been one of the MSGs assigned to Tan Son Nhut to tag and bag the remains of the tiny bodies from Operation Babylift. The sight of the infant caught in the barbed wire atop the wall filled him with black memories of those dead children. Before Frain or Valdez or anyone else could react, Major Kean had shimmied up the wall and untangled the baby. He dropped the child back into its father's arms.

Bobby Schlager was on the southern-most end of the vehicle gate. He was approached by an old man on crutches with a face like cracked parchment and teeth like a broken fence. Pinned across the chest of his ancient South Vietnamese Army tunic was a neat row of ribbons and medals. He pressed an envelope, creased and yellowed with age, through the space between the hinge bar and the wall. Inside was a letter, written in English, under the rubric of the U.S. Air Force Officer's Club in Pleiku. It was dated 1967 and signed by a sergeant who'd once supervised the club. With growing incredulity, Schlager read it aloud to Lance Corporal Mike Sweeney, a young MSG standing shoulder to shoulder with him: "Mr. Nha, the bearer of this letter, faithfully served the cause of freedom in the Republic of Vietnam."

The tiny Mr. Nha then produced a toy Texas Rangers badge and tried to hand it to Schlager and Sweeney. He began making circular motions with his right hand. "Wash dishes, club; wash dishes, club." He repeated the phrase over and again.

Schlager was devastated. How long had we been telling these poor souls to fear the terrorist barbarians from the North? Now the Communists were here, and we were abandoning them. He thought of all the South Vietnamese with connections already inside the embassy walls, cordoned off in predesigned sticks near the pool, swigging liquor looted from the CRA bar and grill. Military brass and police officers. Politicians. Draft-age "ghost soldiers" who had bribed their way out of service. They would escape along with the bags they gripped. It was not difficult for Schlager to imagine what was inside that luggage. But this poor, decrepit old man, a loyal veteran who had served his country. *And mine?* No room for him.

With a gentleness he did not know he possessed, Schlager handed the letter back to Mr. Nha and pushed him, soft as starlight, away from the gate. Bobby Schlager had a lot of hard bark on him, but now he felt ashamed. He felt like weeping.

He was not alone. Sergeant Doug Potratz, pulled from his machine-gun post in the Chancery to help with crowd control at the gates, was similarly devastated by the chaos surrounding the embassy complex—despite the fact that he had seen it coming. One night not long ago, he had been posted as Sergeant of the Guard in the lobby of the Marine House when an elderly Chinese man walked in off the street and slapped three thousand U.S. dollars down on the desk. The old man was a local, from the Cholon district that Top had warned them about, and he wore a thin, wispy beard that reminded Potratz of Spanish moss. In halting English, he said that the money was a dowry for any Marine willing to marry his daughter and take her out of the country.

Potratz had smiled at the man, and with great kindness escorted him back to the street. The veteran MSG was used to these types of entreaties, but that night he had been working the post with the newbie Darwin Judge, who took the man's desperation to heart. Judge continued to talk about the incident for days afterward, and the kid's innocence, Potratz thought, was in stark relief to the hardened shell he'd developed during his time in-country.

When Judge had first dropped his gear at the Marine House, Potratz had scanned his personnel file, and Judge's hometown had jumped out at him. Marshalltown, Iowa, was only 330 miles away from the 160-acre farm in Sioux Falls, South Dakota, where Potratz had grown up. The southern states were the backbone of the Corps, and Marines from the upper Midwest, though not exactly rare, were sparse. So Potratz had sought the new man out and a nascent friendship had developed. They shared memories of the customs and habits of their cold corner of the country, comparing county fairs they'd attended and recalling the local television programming they'd watched as children. Potratz did not exactly see himself as a father figure to the new kid, but a kindly uncle would not have been too far off.

Thus the irony. The newbie was now dead, yet it was to Judge that Potratz owed the debt of his life.

Close to a month earlier, on April 4, Potratz had broken the cardinal rule of Marine Security Guard custom and married his Vietnamese girl-friend. The idea behind the marriage ban, as Potratz well knew, was to deter men stationed behind the Iron Curtain from being compromised by female plants. Top Valdez was divorced when he deployed as an MSG, and Staff Sergeant Sullivan was the only noncom Potratz was aware of who had ever been married while posted. But Sullivan was an established veteran who had sought, and been granted, special dispensation when his future wife had followed him to Saigon from his previous posting in Iran.

To Potratz the marriage proscription made sense from a security point of view. But he had fallen in love with a beautiful local girl named Huynh Thi Tot and her lovely three-year-old daughter, Trang. He could not imag-ine leaving them behind. A woman who had openly consorted with a United States Marine would not fare well when the Communists took over. Hoa, as he'd nicknamed his bride—the name meant "Flower" in Vietnamese—would probably be executed and Trang sent to live in an internment camp. So he had made all the visa arrangements, signed all the right adoption papers, and bribed all the right local bureaucrats. A few months earlier, a Vietnamese marriage license had sold for no more than twenty dollars' worth of piasters. Potratz paid two thousand, in American dollars, for his.

He'd kept their wedding secret until Major Kean flew in, although he suspected Valdez, and perhaps even Sullivan, knew of the arrangement. But Kean's arrival was a clear sign that it was time to get Hoa and Trang out of the country. He'd made a clean breast of it to the major, who'd dressed him down and fined him two hundred dollars in a nonjudicial hearing the Marine Corps refers to as "Office Hours." But Kean declined to ship him out.

"You're an idiot," Kean had told him. "But you're a good Marine. And I need good Marines here with me now."

The day after his confession, Potratz arrived at the DAO in civilian clothes accompanied by his new wife and stepdaughter. The place was a mob scene. The family took a position at the end of a long queue that snaked through the gymnasium and out the door to the tennis courts. The line moved slowly, and time was running short. Potratz was beginning to panic, feeling that he might miss his night shift posting—and betray Major Kean's trust—when someone tapped his shoulder from behind. It was Judge. The young Marine guided the three to a desk in the front of the room and pulled aside a harried State Department official who was dividing evacuees into passenger sticks. The two conferred for a moment before Judge turned and handed Potratz two *laissez-passer*s.

"Current cargo manifest two people shy, Sergeant," he said. Judge's broad smile belied the intensity of his piercing blue eyes. "Your wife and daughter are on the next flight out."

Before she and her daughter left, his "Flower" had dug into her suitcase and presented Potratz with a parting gift: a bayonet she'd purchased on the black market. Doug Potratz fingered that bayonet as he watched Judge walking across the Tan Son Nhut tarmac toward an American C-141, lugging Flower's suitcases with both hands and carrying Trang piggyback style. It was the last time he saw Darwin Judge.

His mind was lost in that image, an image he would never forget, when his reverie was interrupted by a scuffle at the front gate. He adjusted his helmet, shouldered his rifle, and took off.

It was the first time MSG Sergeant Kevin Maloney had ventured beyond the wire of the DAO compound since he'd discovered the bodies of Darwin Judge and Charles McMahon. He was tearing along the "Santa Fe Trail" as part of a Jeep escort accompanying three battered buses in search of American citizens and third-country nationals. The most horrendous, terrifying, and exciting experiences of his twenty-two years on earth had all occurred within the past eighteen hours.

Maloney was well aware of the age-old military proverb that no military plan survives first contact with the enemy, and so it was that at every major intersection they had planned to pass through, South Vietnamese soldiers had unfurled giant coils of barbed wire. Maloney and the Marine officer in charge of their "wagon train," Captain Tony Woods, would halt the buses at the roadblocks and cautiously move on ahead to speak to the

ARVNs. Woods was a former Special Forces operator who since February had been a member of General Smith's defense attaché staff to help coordinate the final evacuation. Sometimes after he and Maloney parlayed, the South Vietnamese soldiers would allow the convoy to pass; sometimes they would sneer, pretend they spoke no English, and shoot their rifles into the air. Woods had anticipated the hostility, which is why he had requested that an MSG accompany him. Maloney was familiar with the city's side streets.

It seemed to Maloney that most of the Americans they were sweeping up were journalists. They streamed out the Caravelle, the Continental Palace, the Miramar, the Peninsular, and the Majestic hotels, trailed at each pickup site by ever larger crowds of locals. At one point Woods and Maloney crossed paths with another DAO bus whose progress had been blocked by an abandoned truck. The vehicle was empty, and the Vietnamese driver had fled with the keys. Woods flagged down a passing group of embassy MSGs and asked if any of them knew how to hot-wire a vehicle.

John Stewart, an eighteen-year-old lance corporal, stepped forward hesitantly. "I think I can, Sir," he said in a Texas drawl.

Stewart climbed into the cab, disappeared below the dashboard, and a moment later the engine growled. Woods, whom the Marines had dubbed "The Wagonmaster," was impressed. "Can you drive it too?"

The lance corporal coaxed the truck, gears grinding, out of the street and into an alley.

"Good going, Corporal," Woods said. "Now you're hired."

"For what, Sir?"

"I need a driver for that bus."

With Stewart behind the wheel, the small convoy, expanded by one, continued its circuitous journey through the back streets of Saigon. They were soon full, and at every roadblock and corner, Vietnamese beat on the doors of all four vehicles and tried to climb in through the windows.

When they finally reached the DAO compound, the South Vietnamese Military Police at the main gate raised their guns and refused to let them pass. Woods, interpreter in tow, confronted the MPs and tried to bribe them with American dollars. Midway through the haggling, two, three, four, and then a dozen gunshots erupted toward the rear of the convoy.

Maloney and Stewart, leaping from a bus, pointed their rifles but Woods shouted, "No firing!"

Calmly, he raised Colonel Gray on his handheld. Almost immediately two Cobra gunships materialized over the main gate. The shooting ceased.

Colonel Gray's voice crackled over the radio. "Captain Woods, can you control a close air support mission?"

"I can see, and I can control."

Some of the Vietnamese guards seemed to understand English, including the MP who appeared to Woods to be in charge. The rest merely had to glance at the hovering Cobras with their arrays of rockets, cannon, and miniguns to imagine the outcome of the standoff. The MP commander waived the Americans through. Two of the buses, however, had been disabled by the rifle fire. Their passengers squeezed into the other two or walked past the raised gate. As they did, several of the South Vietnamese guards dropped their weapons and tried to board the working buses or blend in with the Americans and refugees on foot. Maloney saw them, but did nothing.

On Maloney's third downtown run, his Jeep was forced off the road by a two-and-a-half-ton military truck, its bed packed with armed and sullen ARVNs. He felt as if he had been culled from the herd, and it took him a moment to remember he was wearing a South Vietnamese uniform shirt. When his Marine utilities had been bloodied beyond cleaning while collecting the body parts of Judge and McMahon, he'd shed his own shirt and replaced it with the camouflage ARVN blouse he'd found in the barracks. Was that why the South Vietnamese soldiers had waylaid him? He did not stay to discuss it. When the ARVNs leaped from the truck and started toward him, he jumped the curb, floored the Jeep, and throttled down a back alley.

He eluded his pursuers, but once back out on a main thoroughfare, he could not find Captain Woods and the convoy. He decided to make for the embassy. He abandoned the Jeep three blocks from Thong Nhut Boulevard, pulled his helmet low over his forehead, hunched his shoulders, and braced his M-16 across his chest. Feeling as if he was walking point, he bulled his way through the crowd. At the main gate a chorus of American voices screamed, "Drop the gun! Drop the gun!"

Maloney whipped off his helmet. He was nearly face-to-chest with a surprised Valdez, who eyed his South Vietnamese tunic and pulled him over the gate.

"Thanks, Top."

"CRA gate," Valdez said. "We're shorthanded back there."

Three

What, exactly, are we going to do about this?"

It was nearly 2 P.M., and Jim Kean was kicking the great stump of the tamarind tree with his combat boot. About him, several sweating Marines and Seabees had set down their axes and were gulping from jugs of water. Others continued to collect small branches and shavings from the downed tree that would otherwise be sucked into the rotors of the incoming helicopters.

Valdez studied the stump. "Pull it?"

"What I was thinking, too." Kean turned and yelled across the parking lot. "I need a chain and a two-ton truck."

As Kean supervised the stump removal, Valdez glanced up to the high wall of the French Embassy to the south. He could swear the French Legionnaires on the parapets were grinning. *Why not?* he thought. Paris had made its separate peace with Hanoi, even if it had taken a Dien Bien Phu to bring the French to the table. They'd never much cared for the fact that the Americans thought they could do better in this corner of the world. Even the bond between military men was strained, and the MSGs were careful to avoid the bars and cafés frequented by the gendarmes.

If the French were disdainful of American naiveté, however, they saved their greatest contempt for the British. The Brits were Old World, and from the French point of view, they should have known better than to have ever gotten involved in this country. The Brits, although officially neutral during the war, had allied themselves in spirit with the Americans—likely to spite their age-old Continental nemeses, the French were certain. But they had fled Saigon a week ago, and, earlier, while lifting people over the gate, Valdez had watched their embassy across Thong Nhut Boulevard being ransacked while a squad of policemen in white helmets, White Mice, stood by and chattered with equanimity. The Brits had left a giant Union Jack hanging across the main entrance to their building, and Valdez puzzled over this; Americans would never purposefully abandon the flag. Look at the risks Bobby Schlager had taken to retrieve Old Glory from Bien Hoa. Now the remnants of the Union Jack were in tatters, blue and red strips of cloth scattered across the sidewalk and street.

A chill came over Valdez, enveloped him. *Fear? Yes,* he thought. He was frightened. Not at the prospect of a fight, of the major's Alamo. He was prepared for that. It was the fear of not knowing whether it would be the NVA storming full force through the city until they reached the embassy or the bitter ARVNs turning on them. The feeling seemed to crawl over his skin, throbbing in his chest, clogging his throat. This was not the fear of the known in the bush, the leeches and jungle rot and immersion foot and exhaustion. It was the fear of the unknown. *Stop this,* he told himself. *Stop this. Just do your job.* His mind was clogged with too much thinking. *Just do your job.*

He walked the perimeter of the compound, locating and accounting for MSGs at, first, the main gate, and then the vehicle gate. He was heading for the CRA gate, thinking, *Now, if we can just . . .* when the words *Harvest Moon* popped into his mind.

Harvest Moon? Where had that thought come from? Why now? Harvest Moon was the name of an operation the Marines had run near Chu Lai back in 1965. Valdez's AMTRACS, just arrived from Okinawa, were floating in a cargo bay off the beach and preparing to "swim" ashore when word spread that a scout platoon of Marines had been massacred in an NVA ambush. Valdez and his men were ordered out of their tractors and told they were going in as grunts. *Every Marine a rifleman.*

He remembered the dead Marines, strewn about a narrow ravine. By the time he arrived, the fighting was over. It was the first time he'd seen, up close, what bullets and mortars could do. Things you read about, hear about, and then have to see; he could never explain that feeling to anyone back home. All that was left for the dead men was to tag 'em and bag 'em.

The body bags were heavier than he thought they'd be. He was sick to his heart that day.

Harvest Moon. He made the connection. It was the last time he'd felt like this. Afraid.

His mind reeled. This was the reality. Here, now, in Saigon. Like Harvest Moon. Damn Martin. The NVA had given us fair warning; they just wanted us out. But the ambassador had to drag his ass. It had taken the shelling of Tan Son Nhut and the deaths of Judge and McMahon, and Lord knows what else he didn't even know about to force the ambassador to recognize the futility of their situation. Valdez could have strangled the man right now. He unscrewed his canteen cap and took a deep slug of water. *Just do your job. Like a Marine.*

In the narrow walkway between the embassy and vehicle gatehouse, he saw a dog with three legs. It was gulping the dregs from a half-empty C-ration tin. He took a step toward it and crouched.

"C'mere, boy. C'mere." The dog looked up at him, bared its teeth, and limped away. Valdez headed back to the parking lot.

"Top, grab the other end of this chain, willya."

Valdez loped toward Major Kean's side and helped pull out the final, stubborn piece of tree stump.

A slight breeze rose from the surface of the Bassac River as Steve Hasty's gaze angled from the angry South Vietnamese naval commander's patrol boat to the American consul general's wide, welcoming grin. Terry McNamara was leaning on the helmsman's wooden wheel of the lead landing craft and wearing the blue helmet liner the Marines had presented him when they'd shoved off: "Commodore, Can Tho Yacht Club," it read in ragged, yellow painted lettering across the front. The pose he'd adopted reminded Hasty of a scene from a high society movie; a yachting swell indeed, about to welcome guests aboard. All that was missing was a tray of champagne flutes.

"Jesus, ain't that just like him," Hasty said to Sergeant Steve Moore, the MSG standing beside him at the stern of the boat.

The Vietnamese commander's skiff closed the distance across the dung-brown water, and Hasty considered the incongruity of their situation. Just prior to casting off, the local crew of professional sailors and bargemen they had hired to guide them downriver had deserted. This had forced the old seaman McNamara to assume the role of skipper and added to Hasty's list of concerns, which also included the VC, the NVA, pirates, shoals, currents, and mechanical breakdowns, approximately in that order.

Nowhere had he planned on their progress being waylaid by three South Vietnamese patrol boats lobbing shells across their bows and halting them only a few miles from the docks. Yet here they were, three ragtag river craft idling midstream against the swift current, awaiting an unexpected boarding by an armed and dangerous "ally" who might very well be—what?

There was no chance of outrunning them, and Hasty considered the possibilities. Would they scuttle us? Tow us back to Can Tho? Let us proceed to the sea? He did not like the odds of the last. He looked again toward McNamara. The consul general was standing tall at the helm, his helmet liner tilted at a jaunty angle.

Sergeant Moore elbowed Hasty and jerked his chin toward four more South Vietnamese patrol boats approaching from upriver.

"What now?" Moore's voice was barely audible.

Hasty thought hard. In the skiff, the Vietnamese commander's four-man escort had their rifles trained on McNamara. Hasty slowly dug his hand into the burlap sack he was holding where his own M-16 was hidden. He clicked the safety switch off and surreptitiously swiveled the barrel toward the boarding party. He looked about the decks of the two converted landing craft. The afternoon sun was searing, and most of the hundreds of Vietnamese refugees were huddled together beneath small, crude tents fashioned out of ponchos, clothing, and parasols. The last thing McNamara wanted, the last thing the American Marines wanted, was a gunfight. Still.

What would Terry do? He waited for some sign from McNamara. Nothing. He whispered to Moore, "I guess we either grab the guys with the guns if we can. Or we put a couple of bullets in their heads and fight it out with the rest."

Moore reached for his own burlap bag. But now some instinct, a hunch, seized Hasty. McNamara was too cunning for this, he thought. He put a hand on Moore's forearm. "I don't think we have to worry," he said. "The consul got us into this. He'll get us out."

Hasty released the tension from his trigger finger. They had been sitting, waiting, in the middle of the Bassac for two hours. When the original patrol boat stopped them, McNamara had insisted to its captain that he would speak only to his commander. It had been a gutsy demand, but it had worked. In the interim, the consul had asked, and received, permission from the young South Vietnamese Navy officer to transfer to the two LCMs all the refugees who occupied the leaky rice barge. There was more room than he'd foreseen in the landing craft, and the barge was slowing their progress.

Hasty had overseen the midstream relocation, and the South Vietnamese sailors had for some reason appeared pleased to take the old *Delta Queen* in tow as a parting gift. During the transfer, Hasty noticed that the veteran river man who was piloting their second LCM, a local captain who had remained for the adventure when his crew deserted, had seemed none too happy to venture so near to the armed patrol boats. *Probably a smuggler or part-time pirate himself.*

Now, as the South Vietnamese commander stepped aboard, Hasty glanced across the rusting well of his own craft toward his wife, packed into the lee of the boat with her mother, sisters, and brothers. He wondered how she'd adjust to life as a Marine bride. He also wondered how long they would last together. Theirs had been the ultimate marriage of convenience: she and her sister had worked at the American Consulate, more than enough reason for their names to find their way to the enemy's prison camp list, if not its "to-kill" register. He liked her enough—what was "love," after all; Hasty was not certain—and he had vowed that she would never see the inside of a reeducation camp. The rushed wedding had been the gentlemanly thing to do.

Up at the helm, McNamara and the naval commander were engaged in an animated conversation. Though Hasty could not overhear their words, the American consul had his arm draped over the man's shoulders like a long-lost friend. Finally, the two "commodores" shook hands and exchanged salutes, and the Vietnamese's thin, wispy beard blew across his shoulders as he clambered back into his skiff.

One of his guards lingered for a moment, spotted who he was looking for, and jumped into the well. He hugged an old man, his father it turned out, saying good-bye for the last time. Then he rejoined his fellow sailors.

Hasty made his way to the prow, his M-16 still in its burlap sack. McNamara met him with a fulsome smile of white teeth that reminded the Marine of a row of Chiclets.

"The commodore told me he's staying to fight," McNamara said. "Brave man. He's got orders to search all boats for men and boys of combat age." He turned a key, and the landing craft engines reignited with a cough. Hasty glanced about the deck. There was really no need to; he knew they carried at least two dozen male refugees who fit that description.

"I thought this might happen," McNamara said. "Which is why I reminded the dear commodore how relieved I was two weeks ago when I helped his wife, children, and several cousins get to Saigon and out of the country on a cargo plane to Guam."

McNamara looked away from Hasty and spun the wheel. "I'd say we have a good four hours before we hit the sea. Get everything squared away. Distribute the weapons to the men who know how to fire one."

He jutted his chin toward the river banks closing in up ahead. "We might need them."

The muddy current, a sticky broth, ran swiftly downstream as the river narrowed. Hasty surveyed the thick monsoon clouds enfolding the swampy banks on either side of the Bassac far downriver. *River of Poems*, my ass, he thought, recalling the waterway's local name, and he had just begun to relax when out of the corner of his eye he caught the metallic glint.

He hollered, "Everybody down!" at the precise moment the machine-gun bullets sluiced a choppy path across the water.

[Left] Lance Corporal Darwin Judge of Marshalltown, Iowa. *Courtesy of the Fall of Saigon Association*

[Right] Lance Corporal Charles McMahon of Woburn, Massachusetts. He and Corporal Judge were the last two American military personnel killed in South Vietnam, on April 29, 1975. *Courtesy of the Fall of Saigon Association*

[Above] Major James Kean, a Vietnam combat veteran, was the officer sent to command the last contingent of Marines in Saigon. *Courtesy of John Ghilain*

[Left] Master Sgt. Juan Valdez, who had served a previous combat tour in-country, was the noncommissioned officer in charge of the Marine Security Guards at the U.S. Embassy. *Courtesy of Juan Valdez*

Staff Sgt. Mike Sullivan (middle) and Master Sergeant Valdez greet guests at the Marine Corps Ball in Saigon in November 1974. *Courtesy of Steve Schuller*

The Saigon Marines softball team. Back row: Marvin Garrett, Cpl. David Wilkie, and Cpl. Walter Sweeney. Middle row: Cpl. Manny Bispo, Sgt. Kenneth Geagley Jr., Sgt. Steve Schuller, Sgt. Halstead Murray, and Cpl. Duane Gevers. Front row: Cpl. Randy Smith, Sgt. Robert Frain, and Cpl. Steve Bauer. *Courtesy of Juan Valdez*

Marine helicopter pilot Capt. Gerry Berry flew his CH-46 Sea Knight for almost twenty continuous hours during Operation Frequent Wind, the final evacuation of Saigon. *Courtesy of Gerry Berry*

With unflagging humor and courage, Francis "Terry" McNamara, the American consul in Can Tho, led a flotilla of Americans and more than 300 Vietnamese civilians downriver to the sea. His helmet is inscribed "Commodore, Can Tho Yacht Club." *Courtesy of Cary Kassebaum*

Sgt. Boyette "Steve" Hasty, ranking Marine Security Guard at the Can Tho consulate, manning an M-60 machine gun as the flotilla navigates the Bassac River under enemy fire. *Courtesy of Cary Kassebaum*

Ambassador Graham Martin discusses the deteriorating situation in South Vietnam with President Gerald Ford (not pictured). After meeting with the president, Martin returned to Saigon for the last time. *Courtesy of the Gerald Ford Presidential Library*

General Van Tien Dung, seen earlier in his military career, led the North Vietnamese forces during the Ho Chi Minh campaign, which resulted in the fall of Saigon. *Courtesy of Bettman/Corbis*

President Gerald Ford (left) and Secretary of State Henry Kissinger (right) discuss the implementation of a massive helicopter evacuation of Saigon on April 29, 1975. The administration officials present are (l to r) John Marsh, Max Friedersdorf, Frank Zarb, Donald Rumsfeld, Vice President Nelson Rockefeller, Alan Greenspan, and Dick Cheney. *Courtesy of the Gerald R. Ford Library*

The U.S. Embassy in Saigon before the siege of the city by General Dung began. *Courtesy of Juan Valdez*

Major James Kean (right) oversees the preparation of the "burn barrels" that would destroy reams of official documents and hundreds of thousands of dollars in cash during Saigon's final hours. *Courtesy of Juan Valdez*

A Marine observes an evacuation helicopter landing at the Defense Attaché's Office compound adjacent to the Tan Son Nhut Airport in Saigon. *Photo by Dirck Halstead*

For 36 years, this photo has been mistakenly believed by many to be of the last helicopter out of Saigon atop the roof of the U.S. Embassy. It is, in fact, a CIA chopper preparing to ascend from a nearby building the day before the actual final evacuation. *Courtesy of Bettman/Corbis*

A squad of Marines forms a phalanx inside the U.S. Embassy grounds as thousands of desperate South Vietnamese soldiers and civilians mass outside the gates on the afternoon of April 29, 1975. *Courtesy of Steve Schuller*

The last Marines left in Saigon on the U.S. Embassy roof prepare their weapons for an "Alamo" assault. *Courtesy of John Ghilain*

Thousands of South Vietnamese refugees, fearing execution and imprisonment by the conquering North Vietnamese, paid enormous sums to be evacuated by fishing trawlers and other boats. *Courtesy of Stuart Herrington*

Cpl. Steve Bauer (right), speaking with one of the helicopter pilots, spent much of the last twelve hours on the embassy roof guiding the choppers in for a landing. *Courtesy of Steve Schuller*

As Operation Frequent Wind continued, Vietnamese civilians were hurriedly crammed onto Marine and Air Force helicopters that landed within the U.S. Embassy compound. *Courtesy of Stuart Herrington*

Race against time: As the North Vietnamese encircled Saigon, the number of Marines left at the embassy dwindled until Major Kean (left, in golf shirt, facing camera) would be left with only ten men under his command. *Courtesy of Juan Valdez*

Swift 22, the last helicopter dispatched to Saigon from the United States Seventh Fleet, approaches the roof of the embassy soon after dawn on April 30. *Courtesy of Juan Valdez*

he last Marines to leave aigon were (some hidden om view) Major James Kean, gt. Juan Valdez, Sgt. Michael ullivan, Sgt. Phillip Babel, gt. Terry Bennington, Sgt. obert Frain, Sgt. Duane evers, Sgt. Steve Schuller, gt. Robert Schlager, Cpl. teve Bauer, and Cpl. David orman. *Courtesy of Juan aldez*

Sgt. Terry Bennington and Cpl. Steve Bauer arrive safely on the USS *Blue Ridge* early on the morning of April 30. *Courtesy of Mike Sullivan*

A North Vietnamese tank carrying celebrating NVA soldiers weaves through the streets of Saigon as General Dung's forces take over on April 30. *Courtesy of Bettman/Corbis*

Four

The first wave of Fleet Marines disembarked at the DAO from six CH-53s at six minutes past 3 P.M. The troops—the first of four rifle companies and an 81-millimeter mortar platoon, over 800 men in total—were met by an angry General Carey, who demanded to know what had taken the helicopters so long. He was told by a platoon commander that there had been a mix-up between the Marine and Air Force flight controllers. For the Marines, the designated launch hour, or L-Hour, signified the time they would reach the landing zone. To the Air Force, it meant the time they were wheels up from the fleet. Carey's already mottled face turned from red to crimson as he fanned out the Marines to preassigned sectors. They wasted no time establishing a security zone to protect the nearly 400 Americans and over 4,000 Vietnamese and third-country nationals already being formed into sticks, units of anywhere from twenty-five to fifty evacuees, depending on the aircraft's size and power.

Despite the initial delay in the helicopter arrivals, the evacuation was soon proceeding smoothly. The choppers were guided to the compound's designated landing zones by Marine air traffic controllers on the ground waving signal paddles of various colors that allowed them to coordinate with descending pilots. There were three pickup points: in the parking lot, on the baseball field, and on the tennis courts. When the helicopters touched down, the sticks of evacuees were escorted from the staging areas to the flight ramps. Families huddled together, locking arms, afraid of being separated. Bending beneath the deafening rotor blades before trundling up the tailgates, they looked as if they were bowing to the rescue Birds.

"No baggage! No baggage!" the Marines hollered over and again as piles of suitcases, duffel bags, and rucksacks began to grow into a small range of hills.

As the choppers filled, however, General Carey and Colonel Gray became alarmed by reports of the increasing number of sullen ARVN troops, airborne and regular army, roaming the edges of the DAO compound watching their window of escape rapidly closing. The two Marine officers knew—and knew that the ARVNs knew—that when the NVA and VC entered the city in full force, uniformed South Vietnamese soldiers would be their first targets. At one point, a skirmish erupted when a small unit of ARVN charged the Marine perimeter, shooting wildly. The Fleet Marines drove them back by firing over the heads and took no casualties.

On another occasion, four South Vietnamese soldiers spotted one of the embassy MSGs, Sergeant Ted Murray, patrolling a ditch that ran parallel to the chain-link fence that separated the American compound from the airport. Armed and agitated, they approached Murray and began yelling through the fence in English.

"American coward!"

"Why are you abandoning us?"

"What happened to your promises?"

Murray did not dare raise his M-16 rifle, even when one of the ARVNs produced a pair of wire cutters and began severing the chain links. He was at wit's end—he agreed with everything they said—until two more MSGs and a half-dozen Fleet Marines appeared from behind a barracks building. There was no tense standoff. The ARVNs merely stared with contempt, pocketed the wire cutters, and walked away as if daring the Americans to start something.

By now the leading edge of the rain squalls Gerry Berry had spotted two hours earlier had formed a curtain falling across the eastern edge of Saigon, and the first wave of Marine pilots departing the DAO compound with full loads, including Berry and his squadron, reported poor-to-zero visibility. Seventh Fleet air traffic controllers, distracted to exasperation by the constant approach of South Vietnamese helicopters buzzing American ships in search of sanctuary, tracked the storm clouds on radar while simultaneously remaining alert for American craft straying out of the two predetermined corridors in and out of the city.

The Michigan corridor, at 6,500 feet, was reserved for in-bound aircraft; the Ohio corridor, at 5,500 feet, for outbound. One pilot heard the names of these states repeated so often through his headset that he was reminded of listening to a Big Ten football game on the radio. Soon enough, both pilots and air traffic controllers knew, the monsoon clouds would force their aircraft below the flight corridors and down into range of small-arms fire and rocket-propelled grenades.

At about half past the hour, the first outbound helicopters crossed paths with the second wave of inbound choppers ferrying the remainder of the Marine security battalion. When the returning pilots reached the sea and reported "Feet Wet" to fleet air traffic controllers, they were directed to helipads on designated ships across the wide swath of the South China Sea. At 3:40 P.M., U.S. Marine Corps pilots safely delivered the first evacuees from Operation Frequent Wind to the waiting ships of the Seventh Fleet.

Sixty miles away, a light drizzle began to fall on the embassy compound. Up on the roof, Steve Schuller stuck out his tongue and caught the first few drops of rain. He had not been off the roof in ninety-six hours, and the days and nights had begun to run together to form one long, wearying routine: shoveling, watching the shelling, cleaning his gun, more shoveling. Schuller had no idea what day it was, much less the date. Only the hot chow for breakfast and the distraction of seeing the tamarind tree come down had broken the routine. As he lifted his shovel yet again to the open lid of a burn barrel, he felt two great hands clap his shoulders. Tiny flutes of powdery ash burst from his T-shirt.

"Grab some sleep." It was Valdez. The NCOIC seemed to have an internal clock that monitored his MSGs' energy levels, and he had been performing these "sleep patrols" for several days.

Without a word Schuller began shuffling toward the bedroll he'd

153

stashed in the lee of the incinerator room. Valdez, his arms still clamped on Schuller's shoulders, instead steered him toward the stairwell.

"Elevator," the NCOIC said. "Cot in my office. I'll wake you when I need you."

Schuller weaved into a lift and rode it to the ground floor. The old cot in Valdez's room off the lobby was flush against the wall. Its green canvas was frayed and spotted with strange dark stains. Soda pop? Piss? Blood? He was so tired he did not care. He looked at his watch. *Just thirty minutes,* he told himself. He collapsed to the canvas and unconsciously played with the safety on his M-16. He had fired the rifle only once in anger during his thirteen months in Saigon. The previous summer, the night at Ambassador Martin's residence. The scene ran through his head.

A firefight in the cemetery across the street. The Red Alert reaction alarm signal crackling over his handheld radio, the first such bulletin he had ever heard. The PSUs pouring into the ambassador's Japanese garden. The bullets suddenly pinging off the front gate and *thrup-thrupping* into the sandbags piled at either end of the driveway. Schuller had leaped down from the lone guard tower and squatted next to John Ghilain behind one of those piles. Charlie was shooting at them. At him.

As per Valdez's standing orders, neither Schuller nor Ghilain had returned fire until the PSUs opened up, fanning their automatic weapons across the cemetery. Schuller shouldered his M-16 and waited for a muzzle flash. He saw one erupt from behind a tiny crypt. He took aim and ripped off half a magazine. He did not know if he hit anyone. The sniping slackened, but the PSUs kept firing for the next twenty minutes. Schuller thought it pointless.

The next morning at sunrise, he'd swept the acres of tombstone-pocked sawgrass with his binoculars. Not a soul. Staff Sergeant Sullivan had once told him about the crazy tool the NVA and VC used back during the war to deny the Americans their precious body counts—a kind of meat hook attached to a long pole. After a firefight, Sullivan said, they would reach out from behind cover to drag their dead and wounded back into tunnels. No better place for a spidery network of tunnels than a graveyard, Schuller thought.

Now as he lay his rifle on the floor beneath Valdez's filthy cot, the thought crossed his mind that the enemy might be tunneling under the embassy at this very moment. He saw a gecko scurry across the stucco ceiling above him and watched as it was joined by another, and then a third. A nest. He laughed to himself. Little buggers had slipped through the most heavily guarded U.S. Embassy in the world. If they could do it, why not Charlie?

He could not take his eyes off the mottled brown lizards criss-crossing the ceiling. He thought of the movie *The Exorcist*. The little girl with the spinning head. What brought that on? Were there geckos in that movie? He couldn't remember. *Get it out of your mind*, he told himself. *C'mon, grab just a couple minutes of rack time.* But the geckos continued cavorting, and Schuller continued to stare, transfixed.

Hell with this. Too weird. His boots smacked the floor. He lifted his rifle and trudged out of the guard room, still dog-tired. Terry Bennington, speeding down the corridor, nearly ran him down.

"Top says you, me, riot control, vehicle gate," Bennington said.

From the edge of the parking lot, Jim Kean watched the helicopters overfly the embassy. He knew they were headed toward the DAO. What he did not know was if anyone out on the ships realized that thousands of Vietnamese refugees and hundreds of Americans, including his MSG detachment, had never made it out to Dodge City. He had no idea Ambassador Martin had already spoken to General Carey.

Kean loped inside the embassy and took the stairs two at a time to Wolfgang Lehmann's office. The room was empty. He picked up Lehmann's telephone and was patched through to Colonel Gray at the DAO. As Kean suspected, Gray told him that General Carey and Admiral Steele had been under the impression until just hours ago that all but a skeleton staff had been extracted from the embassy by bus and convoyed to the DAO. General Carey had scheduled only two airlifts for the embassy, to accommodate the ambassador and a small remaining Marine guard.

"I need choppers here, lots of them," Kean said. He told Gray that in addition to the embassy staff, his Marines, and the thousand-plus refugees already inside the walls, he was receiving estimates that there could be as many as 10,000 Vietnamese surrounding the compound. Moreover, he said, South Vietnamese military sources had passed word to the CIA that the crowd was interlaced with VC assassination squads and NVA demolition teams. And then there was Snepp's warning of the 6 P.M. shelling, no longer a secret to anyone in the compound. How much more could go wrong? Who else would he be responsible for putting in danger? He hesitated, and juggled the odds in his mind before speaking his next thought.

"Things are getting out of hand," he finally told Gray. "I also need Fleet Marines, or we're going to lose control."

Kean hung up and took an elevator to the roof. He found Valdez outside the incinerator room.

"Choppers on their way," he said. Both men peered over the edge at the parking lot. "Fifty-threes down there . . ." Kean swiveled to check the helipad atop the incinerator room, ". . . 46s up here. Assembly line. Like a train station."

Kean paused. "Oh, shit," he said.

Valdez looked up and followed his gaze. The major was staring at the embassy radio tower, a 300-foot steel needle piercing the dull, gray sky. Four heavy steel cables guyed the tower to the roof, and several thinner fiberglass power cables stretched taut from the tip of the structure and across the parking lot below. They would interfere with any helicopter descent.

"Those wires live?" Kean said.

Valdez had no idea, and there were no electronic technicians left at the embassy to tell him. "Fifty-fifty," he said.

"Well, let's see if . . ." Valdez stopped the major midsentence. He pointed to Sergeant Gregory Hargis climbing the metal structure, bolt cutters in hand. Steve Bauer was right behind. Mike Sullivan stood at the base of the tower directing them.

"Guess we'll know in a minute," Valdez said. He wondered if Hargis was trying to atone for his stunt with the hookers.

"Kill himself if those wires are live," Kean said.

Valdez did not answer.

Hargis reached the tower's midpoint and, with Bauer steadying him, cut the first cable. At that exact moment, the steel incinerator room door slammed shut behind them with a loud bang. Kean and Valdez flinched and turned. Bobby Frain stared back at them, his white teeth gleaming beneath the soot and ash that powdered his face.

"You do that on purpose?"

"Top, you think I'm that kind of guy?" Frain's grin broadened. Kean said nothing.

A moment later, the last of the severed cables whipped down to the roof deck. Kean inspected Hargis's "work." Exactly what he needed. He turned to ask Valdez who the crazy MSG was, but the NCOIC was already headed back down to the front gate.

Five

It had been only thirty minutes since he'd watched Greg Hargis cut the radio tower wires, and already Juan Valdez's back and shoulders were barking like whipped dogs. He had returned from the roof to rejoin John Ghilain at the front gate, and between them they'd hoisted at least another two dozen people into the compound. British journalists, Korean diplomats, Japanese photographers, Vietnamese with the correct papers. It was like moving meat. Now he and Ghilain were slouched on the marble floor of the embassy lobby as Ambassador Martin exited the elevator and strode purposefully toward the front door. To Valdez, the diplomat resembled nothing so much as a wounded man trying to convince his fellow soldiers that he was fit for duty.

Valdez rose and followed him. The ambassador's bulletproof limousine awaited him. The car had become something of a hobbyhorse for Martin. It was several years old—hardly a vehicle befitting the American proconsul in Vietnam—and several months earlier, he had put in a requisition for a replacement. He'd become livid on discovering that the new Cadillac he had ordered was, at the last minute, diverted to the U.S. ambassador in Tel Aviv. As word spread among the MSGs about the destination of Martin's new car, it became a metaphor of America's intentions in Vietnam. They suspected it sent the same message to Martin.

Outside, Martin walked past the hole where the tamarind tree stump had been without giving it a second glance, and waited for a bodyguard to open the vehicle's back door.

"Think he's going?" Valdez said.

"The residence," one of Martin's PSUs said. "To pack up."

The NCOIC eyed the frenzied crowd still buffeting the vehicle gate. He was dumbstruck—he had seen this image somewhere before. It dawned on him. The Hungarian tapestry he'd packed away in his lost steamer trunk. The siege of Budapest.

"He's crazy," Valdez said under his breath.

The armored Chevrolet rolled forward perhaps ten feet before Major Kean appeared from nowhere, stepped into its path, and threw up his arms. The car stopped, the back door flew open, and Martin climbed out slowly, his long legs employed in the fashion of a praying mantis, lifted extraordinarily high with each step as if they were feelers.

"Sir, with all due respect," Kean said, "there is no way in hell you are going to drive that car out of here. I recommend that you move back upstairs until . . ."

Martin slammed the door, glared, and raised his index finger, cutting off any more conversation. Kean envisioned his next posting in Alaska. *If I make it out of here alive.*

"In that case, I am going to walk once more to my quarters," Martin said. There was a hint of the old steel in his voice. "I shall walk freely in this city."

Martin disappeared back into the embassy. Valdez and Kean exchanged glances.

"Round up a squad," Kean said.

The dark corridor was cramped and hot, and Terry Bennington had to crane on his tiptoes to see over the scrum of the ambassador's PSU that had assembled quickly. He eyed Martin's head bodyguard, a black giant of a staff sergeant named Clemon Segura, and as was his nature wondered if he could take him. Segura had a good seven inches and at least 100 pounds on the five-foot-six-inch, 130-pound squad leader. But Bennington had dropped larger men.

On Major Kean's orders, Bennington and a half-dozen MSGs had positioned themselves several feet from a secret entrance the Seabees had cut into the southernmost wall that the American Embassy shared with the

French Embassy. Bennington watched as Kean made one final attempt to convince Martin it was too dangerous to leave the compound, on foot or otherwise. Everyone in attendance, including Kean, knew he would lose the argument. But the major felt it was worth the effort, if for nothing other than form's sake.

Bennington glanced from the ambassador, whose sallow face had turned red with anger, and up to Valdez standing beside him.

"How long you give it?" Valdez whispered.

"Minute," Bennington said.

"Thirty seconds," Valdez said. "He's really pissed."

Kean had already given Bennington and his men their orders. When the ambassador stole through to the French Embassy and exited to the street, they were to form a human corridor. They would accompany Martin and his bodyguards out onto the street to ensure he had slipped past the masses now flooding the block and then haul their butts back to their posts on the vehicle gate. If there was trouble—or, Lord forbid, shooting—the PSUs would hustle Martin back into the embassy compound while Bennington's squad provided cover.

"Hey, Top, you smell that?" Bennington said.

Valdez sniffed the air. He looked puzzled. "What?"

"Exactly." Bennington laughed. "Been in-country nine months, and today's the first time I never, ever had the stink of nuoc mam up my nose. If nobody's cooking out there, things must really be the shit."

Valdez said nothing. Bennington, the NCOIC thought, was one of the oddest ducks to have ever been deployed as a Marine security guard. He was a soldier's soldier for certain, a top-notch physical specimen despite being as skinny as a willow branch. And there was no one Valdez would rather have next to him in a foxhole, or in an AMTRAC for that matter. But how Bennington had wound up drawing embassy duty was beyond Valdez's ken.

He had seen the twenty-one-year-old Bennington's personnel records, of course. The Marine had scored high in all his physical and aptitude exams, but his education was spotty—he hadn't even obtained his high school diploma until prodded into a correspondence course by his company commander back in basic training. And though there was little in the file about Bennington's life prior to the Corps, the scuttlebutt around the detachment was that his childhood had been straight out of Dickens.

Bennington was the second of three sons born a year apart to a poor farming family on the Ohio bank of the Ohio River. He was four years old when his mother gathered her three young boys in the living room, turned on the gas in the kitchen stove, and went into her bedroom and shot herself. Neighbors heard the gunshot and rescued the youngsters before the small house blew up.

Bennington's father was an alcoholic, and after the tragedy, he was nowhere to be found. It was left to his grandfather to claim custody of the boys. Not long afterward, his grandfather "rented" all three out to separate area farms. The potato farmer to whom Bennington was leased worked him dawn to dusk in the fields, housed him in a dirt-floor shack, and beat him so mercilessly that he was subject to sudden nosebleeds for the rest of his life. Two years later, when his father took the pledge of abstinence and then remarried, he came to reclaim his sons. By then young Terry was nearly feral. Despite a loving stepmother who spared no effort to show him affection, he ran away from his new home so often that neighbors learned to be on the lookout. When they did snatch him off the street, they often bathed and fed him before returning him to his family. The experience scarred the boy, leaving him hurt, confused, and perpetually angry.

From kindergarten on, he fought with older, tougher boys every day, and despite his stepmother's attempts to redirect his life—to control his anger and assuage his fears—he grew up relying on his fists. By the age of twelve, he too, like his father, had developed a taste for whiskey. When he did attend school, which was not often, it was frequently with a searing hangover.

He quit high school midway through his junior year and moved to an island in the Ohio River midway between Ohio and the West Virginia panhandle city of Wheeling. There he earned a meager living working on a boat dock by day for two dollars an hour and boxing for hat money in a makeshift ring by night. Craft was not his specialty; he was a vicious puncher, and when someone once asked him what part of the face he aimed for, his quick answer was, "All the way through to the back of the head." But one night he drank too much and beat up a black man in a local saloon, and when the man and his friends returned with shotguns, the seventeen-year-old Bennington decided it was as good a time as any to move on. He settled in Wheeling.

He had no intention of joining the Marine Corps, or any other military service for that matter, until one day when he and a buddy poked their heads into a Marine recruiting center in downtown Wheeling. The noncom in charge showed interest in Bennington's friend, but shooed the hollow-cheeked, undersized "runt" away.

"How come him and not me?"

The Marine eyed the teenager up and down. "Because I don't think you can take it."

Bennington could not let the challenge pass, and by the summer of 1971 he was beginning his two-year hitch in boot camp on Parris Island in South Carolina. The island was overrun with Marine veterans sporting Vietnam combat badges and commendations on their dress blues. Bennington had a vague idea that there was a war going on, but he had no idea where Vietnam was. Ohio, West Virginia, and now South Carolina were the breadth of his exposure to the world.

He made sergeant nineteen days shy of the end of his first tour with an artillery unit and happily extended for another two years. For the first time in his life, he felt he was a part of something on this earth that wasn't going to beat him down. The Marine Corps had become the family he never had, and like so many others in the Saigon MSG detachment, serendipity intervened in the form of his company commander who had once deployed to a Marine security post. The officer wrote to Bennington's high school principal and set up a tutorial correspondence course. He also recommended his "favorite hillbilly" for Marine Security Guard School at Henderson Hall, where Bennington thrived.

Upon his graduation Bennington did not even fill out his "dream sheet," so thrilled was he to be going anywhere overseas. In July 1974, after an eighteen-month posting at the U.S. Consulate in Hamburg, West Germany, he drew Saigon as his next assignment.

Mike Sullivan was the detachment's NCOIC when Bennington arrived, and though Bennington liked and respected the staff sergeant, it was not until Juan Valdez took over that for the first time in his life he was star-struck. Valdez, he thought, was everything a Marine was supposed to be—"broad as a house and as steady as she goes." Many of the young MSGs were in awe of the top sergeant's physical presence—even the twenty-one-year-old Corporal Dave Norman, one of the few men in the detachment with combat experience in Vietnam, admitted to being a bit overwhelmed by the "Frito Bandito"'s larger-than-life countenance—but Bennington in particular followed Valdez's lead like a puppy dog. The NCOIC, true to his soft spot for strays, saw potential in the grunt Marine and made him a squad leader.

In his first few months in-country, Bennington treated Saigon as one big party. Steve Schuller became his best friend, and together the two competed with a ferocity in every venue, from physical fitness tests at the DAO and shooting drills at Boomtown Beach to raising hell on Tu Do Street—and, of course, to taking the most whacks at the tamarind tree. When the tenor of the besieged city began to change and its population swelled to nearly 4 million people, he and Schuller often sat on the roofs of, first, the Marine House, and then the embassy, gazing with dismay as the city's once gorgeous side streets and alleys swelled with what looked like hobo camps filled with frightened refugees from the northern provinces carrying their lives on their backs.

Neither thought the situation—whatever the hell the situation was—would end well. Now Bennington only wished Schuller, who was still manning the vehicle gate, was here to see the ambassador's head explode as he twitched with naked impatience as a "mere" Marine major tried to tell him what he could and could not do in "his city."

To the surprise of no one, Martin finally cut off Kean's argument with a regal wave of his hand. He had decided that it would attract less attention if he traveled with only two of his bodyguards, the staff sergeants Colin Broussard and James Daisey. The PSU squad leader, Staff Sergeant Segura, protested. He had to go also. But Martin convinced him that the sight of a snow-haired Caucasian man strolling down Thong Nhut Boulevard in the company of a large, muscular black man did not serve the interests of subtlety.

Martin, Daisey, and Broussard exited the French Embassy unnoticed through an unobtrusive pedestrian gate and walked the four long blocks to his residence. The ambassador's brisk gait returned for the first time in weeks; to Broussard and Daisey, toting heavy submachine guns and hurrying to keep up, walking freely once more in Saigon seemed to invigorate the sick, tired man. A block from the residence, a motorcycle carrying two armed young Cowboys—Daisey judged them ARVN deserters—skidded to a halt before the small entourage. Broussard stepped in front of the ambassador and Daisey jumped in front of Broussard and leveled his submachine gun. The two Cowboys sped off.

When the trio reached the residence, two MSG sentries still stationed at the gate escorted them into the small compound, and Martin entered his house for the last time. He gathered all his classified material and piled it next to the cryptographic machine in his private communications room, a walk-in vault secured by a safe-like door the Marines referred to as the "Small Bubble Room." The house seemed freighted by fonder, older memories, and it was decorated with expensive souvenirs from Martin's previous postings around the world. Yet when he finally exited, the ambassador was carrying nothing more than an overnight bag and a few small keepsakes, including a treasured porcelain antique model of a Chinese pagoda he had received in Bangkok as a gift. As Daisey toted the diplomat's belongings to the driveway, he turned to Broussard with a questioning look.

"We walking with all this?"

"Garage," said Broussard, tossing him a ring of keys.

The MSGs were amazed when Daisey retrieved Martin's backup car from beneath a dusty tarp. They did not know a second armored car even existed. The vintage black Oldsmobile 88 had belonged to Ellsworth Bunker, the previous U.S. ambassador to Saigon, and while Daisey raised the hood and attached battery cables from a portable power cell, Broussard went back inside and laid thermite grenades around the cryptographic machine in the walk-in vault.

The machinery was melting from the pyrotechnic incendiary devices' 4,500-degree heat by the time the Oldsmobile, with Broussard behind the wheel, rolled through the residence gates and out on to Dien Bien Phu Street. Behind them, also ablaze, was Martin's prized grand piano. He had ordered it burned out of spite and frustration.

The traveling party encountered no resistance for three blocks, but as it edged through the teeming streets closer to the embassy, someone in the crowd recognized the small American flag, which Martin had refused to remove from the whippy antenna. Daisey lay his body across the ambassador's, and the two MSGs squeezed in nearly on top of him as stones and rocks pelted the bulletproof windows. A man jumped atop the hood and battered the shatterproof windshield with a two-by-four, and more people with sticks and boards joined in. The car was beginning to rock.

Broussard had had enough. He took a sharp left and screeched up to the gates of the French Embassy.

When Martin entered the building, he presented the model pagoda to the French ambassador and asked after any progress in a last-minute deal with the North. The PSUs could not understand the Frenchman's exact reply, but they understood from Martin's slumped shoulders that it had not been what he had hoped to hear.

It was hot and close in the small corridor, made hotter and closer by the concrete dust thrown up by the Seabees' jackhammers and sledges. The wall separating the U.S. and French embassies was three feet thick, and the hole through which Martin had slipped back inside was being expanded to fit the contours of a heavy steel door the Navy construction crew had welded together from plating stored in the maintenance room of the CRA.

Bobby Schlager watched as the makeshift door was wedged into the opening and fresh concrete was poured around it. "Think the ambassador's plan is to get us through there when it comes to it?" he said.

The Seabees attached the hinges and swung the door open and closed several times before it slammed shut with a resounding clang.

"Don't know," said Mike Sullivan. He wiped his face with a dirty kerchief. "But wouldn't count on it. My guess is it only opens from the Frenchy side."

Six

It was nearly 6 P.M. when the last of the rescue buses straggled into the DAO compound. The Marine Sea Knights and Sea Stallions setting down and lifting off had been joined by ten Air Force Jolly Green Giants deployed from the USS *Midway* and bases in Thailand, and the conveyor belt operation was making quick work of the dwindling evacuees. As their numbers decreased, so too did the size of the security zone, and the Fleet Marines and fifteen MSGs consolidated their positions by pulling back into tighter and tighter perimeters. In the occasional lull between takeoffs, Marines constantly walked among the anxious Vietnamese to assure them that more inbound helicopters were on the way. Among them was Captain Tony Woods, the "Wagonmaster." It was his Jeep that had been lifted off the downtown street and flipped over by a mob.

With the evacuation running so smoothly General Carey had time to consider Major Kean's request for more security at the embassy. Mindful of any further military provocations toward General Dung and the NVA, which he knew to be monitoring all American movements around Saigon, he decided to ask permission from the Joint Chiefs in Washington. Given the go-ahead, he ordered the first platoon of what would eventually total 130 Fleet Marines extracted from the DAO and ferried to the embassy.

Jim Kean, on the embassy roof, was the first to hear the washboard thumping of the helicopter rotors in the distance. A moment later he spotted a squadron of four Sea Knights banking hard over the Presidential Palace and lining up in formation for successive descents. Soon the lead chopper bounced in on its rear wheels, and the first test of the rooftop

166

helipad to bear the weight of a 46 was a success. The lead squad of the first-response Sparrow Hawk assault team, consisting of about forty Marines, began to disembark. Kean took note of their eager pink faces and starched combat fatigues. They were well armed and dressed in full 782 gear: packs, ponchos, and ammunition belts. As they converged outside the incinerator-room stairwell he ordered the young first lieutenant in charge, Brice Thompson-Powers, to assemble his men in the courtyard below.

He noted that Thompson-Powers did not look old enough to apply for a driver's license and thought of Darwin Judge and Charles McMahon and the too many other American boys who had returned home from Vietnam in a box. *For what?* His eyes wandered beyond the Fleet Marines, beyond the parapets, to the teeming crowds packing the streets around the embassy in every direction. *For this.* He wiped the impression from his mind.

A moment later, near the embassy's front doors, Kean stood before the assemblage knowing that he must have appeared a strange sight. He wore a custom-made leather shoulder holster—holding his personal Colt Gold Cup pistol—strapped over his filthy striped golf shirt. His hands were nearly black with soaked-in gun oil that gave off the faint aroma of bananas, and his clothes were spattered with dirt, grease, snot, and sweat. It was as if Bob Hope, on one of his USO tours, had mysteriously been trapped in the evacuation of Saigon. One of the embassy secretaries had allowed him to use her apartment for a shower. Kean tried to remember how long ago. Three days? Four? No matter. He eyeballed the infantrymen in their crisp, clean camouflage and jerked a thumb over his shoulder toward the refugees gathered by the swimming pool in the CRA. They had been using the pool as a bathroom since the night before, and it had become a fetid stinkhole.

"Our first job is to get these people out safe," he said. "Our second job is to defend United States personnel and property."

He looked hard at the young platoon leader before nodding toward Valdez. "Top, here, will show you what we're thinking."

With that Kean turned the meeting over to his NCOIC, who unfolded a map of the embassy compound across the top of a low concrete abutment and indicated to the lieutenant and his squad leaders the locations of all

167

embassy gates, various choke points on the premises, and the sites where Kean had ordered machine-gun emplacements.

The platoon leader ran his index finger over the paper. He appeared most impressed with the gun preparations. "Clear fields of fire from all mounts," he said. "Nice, Top."

Valdez smiled inwardly. *Pup. Hell you think we've been doing here?*

He also allowed himself an appreciative thought for the squad leader, Sergeant Phil Babel, and how handy his alleged by-the-book rigidity had come in. Before they had moved out of the Marine House, Valdez had put the former infantryman in charge of the refresher courses on disassembling and reassembling the M-60s. And once they'd billeted inside the embassy compound, he'd instructed Babel to hold regular weapons classes at what came to be referred to as "Babel's Stables" in the CRA. Babel had even helped draw up the perimeter maps the Fleet Marines were studying.

"Yes," he said to the platoon leader. "But don't forget, the machine guns are for Charlie. The others, we're here to get them out." He swept his eyes across the platoon, staring hard at the squad leaders. "Not to shoot them."

The huddle broke up, and Valdez led the newcomers to their positions. Mike Sullivan, meanwhile, had already cordoned off four groups of refugees, each consisting of twenty to twenty-five people, and was herding them up the stairs to the roof for boarding on the empty CH-46s.

At the vehicle entrance at the north end of the compound, Steve Schuller sensed that the crowd beyond the wall was rapidly turning into a mob. He looked out on this strange new world through the wrought-iron grille of the double gates and simmered with anger and frustration. He watched a small unit of renegade ARVN soldiers trample a family of six in an effort to reach the entrance, and yearned to bolt onto Mac Dinh Chi Street and personally butt-stroke each of them to the sidewalk.

"Our fuckin' allies," he said to Terry Bennington. His voice oozed sarcasm.

Bennington, standing beside Schuller, opened his mouth as if to answer, but the words clutched in his throat. He had nothing to add.

Most MSGs considered the Marine Security Guard handbook chloroform in print, but Schuller had scrutinized the vast fabric of the thick volume cover to cover. Yet as hard as he tried, he could find no crack, no fissure, in which to weave in his own design today. He was resigned to the fact that his only function in life, right here and right now, was to protect American personnel and property at any cost—even if it meant watching innocent civilians beaten down on the street.

Yet something still nagged. The poor souls on the other side of the gate bars were merely frightened papa-sans and mama-sans clinging as fast to their children as they were to their hopes—families to whom the United States had made a promise. They'd bet their lives on that promise, and now they were going to lose. He was haunted by their pleading eyes.

A moment later, both he and Bennington spotted a tall, thin American elbowing his way across the sidewalk. The man was waving his blue American passport book high above his head and shouting, although Schuller could not make out the words. A phalanx of Fleet Marines swung the gate open a crack and pushed outward in a V formation, allowing just enough space for the American to slip past.

Or try to. Vietnamese men and women of all sizes and ages clung to the man's arms, his legs, his clothing, attempting to follow him through the opening. One Fleet Marine butt-stroked a middle-aged woman with his rifle. Another tossed a tear gas grenade into the multitude. Schuller blanched. *What the hell was going on?* This wasn't what he had signed up for. Something, he knew, was bad wrong here.

Now two more Americans, women—*reporters?*—appeared on the fringe of the pulsating mass. Again the gate opened a crack, and this time two Fleet Marines "swam" through the crowd, yanked the females by their shoulders and hair, and began to walk them backward toward the compound. Schuller anchored the far right side of the V, the last of four Marines on that side of the gate.

Suddenly he felt his knees buckle. The heat, he told himself. The rain had stopped, but the atmosphere was heavy with a dense, sticky humidity. Heat and no sleep. He was so hot in this damn flak jacket. And his helmet was crushing his head. He gasped for a breath. *Get it together, Steve. Get it together.* He fought it. But he was so damn hot. Unloose his flak jacket. One little buckle wouldn't matter, he told himself. Get some air on his heavy chest. He reached down to undo a latch; just one latch, get some air. The crowd surging in front of him now was a wavy, hypnotic knot of color moving in slow motion. He willed himself not to pass out as he reached down for his flak jacket. Just one buckle.

"Schuller! Schuller! Dammnit, Steve. Behind you. Watch out!"

He thought he recognized Terry Bennington's voice. It was as if Bennington were shouting to him from underwater. *Be right with you. First, just one little buckle. Get some air. So damn hot.*

"Steve!

He saw the glint of metal and followed it back to its source. An ARVN soldier, still in uniform, his rifle pointed. At the tip of the barrel, a bayonet. The soldier was on him now, lunging.

Oh, fuck. It's over. I'm screwed.

He felt the steel point glide between his ribs. He was no longer hot, or tired, or woozy. He was wide awake, as if he had been jolted by electricity. Then, tender oblivion. He doubled over, and before he slumped to his knees, he saw Bennington butt-stroke the ARVN under his chin. The man's rifle sailed through the air and his head flew so far back with such speed that Schuller thought it might come off. He felt two sets of hands slip beneath his armpits.

"Inside. Get him inside." Bennington again. The voice sharp now. Crisp. "Inside, Steve, get you fixed up."

Bennington and a young Marine in camouflage dragged him to a bench in the shadow of a storeroom building.

"Find a medic," Bennington said. Schuller could not make out who he was talking to.

"No, no bother," Schuller said. He poked his right index finger into the wound. It disappeared to his second knuckle. It stung, but it wouldn't kill him. *It ain't bad. It ain't bad. It ain't bad.* Just as long as he stopped the bleeding.

He unlatched his flak jacket—finally!—and tore off a strip from his T-shirt. He unscrewed the cap from his canteen, soaked the dirty rag, balled it up, and plugged it into the hole in his side.

"Women get in?" he said.

Bennington nodded.

"Kill the guy that did me?"

"Dunno. Maybe." *Our fuckin' allies*, Bennington thought.

Rocket fire from the rushes on the south bank of the Bassac River followed the machine-gun bursts. The explosives sailed over the two landing craft as Steve Hasty blasted back at the muzzle flashes with an M-79 grenade-firing "Blooper" gun. Then he dived flat on his stomach and swiveled an M-60 machine gun toward the shore. He hollered to his Marines to open up. The instructions were unnecessary. The thick vegetation along the river bank was already shredding in a shower of rifle fire.

Terry McNamara steered the lead LCM as near to the north bank as he could without grounding it. The South Vietnamese river pilot kept the second boat close on his stern. McNamara had seen the jet black rocket clearly, and its red-tail fireball passing above with a loud hiss brought back memories of Korea. The cruiser he'd served on had traded shells with a squad of Chinese T-34 tanks during the evacuation of the survivors from the Chosin Reservoir. It was the only running land-sea gunfight of the war. Now he had two, in two separate wars, under his belt. A moment later, all was quiet. McNamara told Hasty he suspected the lull would not last long.

No one had been wounded, and neither vessel had been hit. *A good thing*, Hasty thought. The LCMs' armor and concrete bumpers would repel small arms fire, but if a rocket or rocket-propelled grenade had made contact with their flimsy slab siding, the result would have been like tossing a stick of dynamite into a trash can. The brief firefight, however, had certainly alerted any VC or NVA troops downriver that they were coming. About a mile ahead, the Bassac narrowed dramatically and then broke into several slender channels that wove through an archipelago of small wooded islands. This was where the NVA, infiltrating from Cambodia, made river crossings. When Hasty and McNamara had taken the CIA helicopter to scout their escape route, they had agreed that it was from these choke points where an enemy ambush was most likely.

"What now?" Hasty ducked at the sound of a sniper's report, answered by a fusillade of rifle fire from the landing craft. McNamara did not flinch. "North channel? Looks the widest."

171

"Also most likely where they'd be waiting for us." McNamara pointed to a dark, jagged wall of clouds scudding toward them from the southeast. "We'll make for the weather."

Within moments, both boats were engulfed in what seemed like murky night, and rumbling thunder ushered in torrents of rain so thick that Hasty, his bush hat pulled low and still huddled behind the M-60, could not see his hand held at arm's length. "You know where we're going?" he hollered.

"North channel," McNamara said. "You said it looks the widest."

The barrage of water masked them from the enemy positions on the shore, and the roar of wind combined with the force of the downpour roiling the river to muffle the hum of the boat engines. They sailed blind through the storm, letting the swift current take them for ninety minutes. When the rain squall passed, when they could once again see the banks of the Bassac, they were through the channel, the islands behind them, the broad river open before them. They were making over twelve knots an hour.

It was early evening when General Dung received a radio message from one of his division commanders camped in the suburbs west of Saigon. His subordinate reported that National Liberation Front troops—Vietcong—had captured the nearby town of Cu Chi. Moreover, the VC commander had strolled into the local post office, placed a call to an operator in Saigon's central telephone exchange, and brazenly pumped her for information regarding the disposition of ARVN troops and Saigon police.

Finally, Dung was told, when VC scouts had entered the headquarters of the ARVN division commander stationed in Cu Chi, they had found it deserted, although cups of coffee resting on a large map table were still warm. As the scouts left the building, local residents had led them to the division commander hiding in a rice field. He was now in NVA custody.

Seven

Steve Schuller was back on the embassy roof. His bayonet wound was throbbing. He had cleaned it with rubbing alcohol and was poking a somewhat cleaner rag into the gash when he spotted the first squad of Marine CH-53s banking west off the Saigon River and heading toward the embassy.

For the past week while working the burn squad he'd watched the little blue, gray, and silver Air America Hueys darting and hovering like dragonflies over the helipad atop the CIA living quarters at the Duc Hotel a few blocks away. The Agency was operating on its own agenda and had already flown out hundreds of people, both Americans and Vietnamese. Earlier this afternoon, he'd even spotted one of their little Hueys landing atop the Pittman Apartments about a half-mile away on Gia Long Street. He hadn't even known there was a landing zone on the roof of that ten-story building, which had been taken over by the U.S. Agency for International Development, which everyone suspected was an Agency front. The pilot must have been a crackerjack to have put his aircraft down on an area no larger than a two-car garage, and then all hell had broken loose as an American standing on the helipad began tossing the little Vietnamese into the Bird like he was throwing darts. Finally the helicopter had lifted off, leaving a lot of them behind with the same American—no room for him inside, Schuller supposed—standing precariously on one skid.

Every once in a while over the past day or so, one of those Air America pilots, perhaps new contractors, had become confused by the similarity of the city's rooftop LZs and strayed into embassy space, only to be warned off by the MSGs. One in particular had come close enough for Schuller to see the frozen Asian faces of what he assumed to be Agency operatives from somewhere up north. Da Nang perhaps; maybe Quang Tri. The pilot had ignored radio calls to back away, and the RSO, Marvin Garrett, had directed the MSGs to shoot it off the roof if its skids so much as touched down on embassy property. The pilot flew off at the last moment, averting disaster. Schuller wondered who in the detachment would have actually obeyed the command.

Now as the CH-53s approached, he was surprised by their size. Accustomed to the little Hueys, he had forgotten how large a chopper the Sea Stallion was. With the tamarind stump gone and its branches dragged off, the parking lot was now ready to take the big Birds, and Major Kean had ordered a squad of Marines to circulate among the evacuees and separate them into sticks of sixty to seventy people. His plan was to lead the separate sticks from the CRA compound to the parking lot as each helicopter set down.

The Sea Stallion squad leader descended first. As he dropped below the roof line, the steady drone of rotor blades, augmented by the shriek of turbine engines, increased tenfold, and the blades kicked up so much wash that Schuller had to buckle his helmet chin strap. Halfway to the ground, the pilot nipped the branches of another, smaller tamarind tree off to the side of the parking lot, and several of the Fleet Marines mistook the sound of the snapping wood for gunshots. They assumed firing positions and the pandemonium rose as Marine squad leaders barking orders tried to outshout the cacophony of the whirring chopper blades and the screaming refugees. Kean, who had seen and heard what happened, ran from the parking lot through the compound screaming, "Hold fire! Hold fire!"

When order was restored, the helicopters resumed their descents at tenminute intervals. They found the top of the vertical tunnel, slowed their forward progress, hovered for an instant, and one at a time made the dizzying seventy-foot drop as if hurtling down an elevator chute. Schuller watched Kean waving what looked like two large Ping-Pong paddles to guide them in and realized they were flying more on feel than on skill. If they strayed ten feet or so in any direction on the descent, the rotors would whirl into either the side of the embassy building or the wall separating it from the

CRA compound. Not only would we have one dead Bird, Schuller thought, but also one dead LZ. If a helicopter crashed in the parking lot, there was nothing with which to move it, and thus no more choppers coming in.

Tracer bullets, meanwhile, were flying over the roof from all directions—the hidden NVA firing from the tree line north of the embassy and ARVN deserters with nothing left to lose taking potshots just for the hell of it. Once on the ground, the pilot would gear down as Kean and Mike Sullivan hurried the sticks up the ramp. Despite the CH-53's official troop-transport capacity of fifty-five, those specifications had been made with Americans in mind, and Kean stuffed as many as seventy of the smaller and lighter Vietnamese into each load. He tried to keep families together and even allowed each person to carry on one small bag.

Some of the better-dressed evacuees tried to pull rank and argue their way into taking larger suitcases aboard. Steve Bauer, charged with keeping the sticks moving, even got into a wrestling match with a Korean diplomat attempting to board with a small steamer trunk. Kean and Sullivan stepped between them and offered the man a choice: leave or remain with your contraband. As at the DAO, the luggage was soon piled high around the parking lot LZ. But with less space here at the embassy, Kean had to get rid of it. He ordered it thrown into the swimming pool.

Schuller thought the helo flyers' skills breathtaking—not only in their ability to descend into such a small opening but particularly to lift off. Once the craft was packed tight, each pilot would raise it a foot or so, testing his weight to ensure he could actually get the machine off the ground. More often than not, this was the case—although a few had to discharge passengers—and then Kean would stuff two or three more bodies aboard. On one load, Schuller counted eighty-three of the tiny Vietnamese piling into an aircraft.

Then, instead of performing a chopper's normal translational ascent—the Bird's nose dipping forward as it rose on an angle—the pilots shot straight up, their rotors shuddering and whining as they clawed the air for lift. One Air Force Jolly Green Giant did not have the power to lift vertically, and Kean emptied it of most passengers and told the pilot not to come back. An hour or so into the operation, a couple of snipers—good ones by Schuller's evaluation—began dinking the choppers from an apartment building across Thong Nhut Boulevard. Kean found the young Lieutenant Thompson-Powers of the Fleet Marines and ordered him to send a squad of his men over the walls and into the building. The sniping ceased and they returned thirty minutes later. Kean never asked the lieutenant what happened.

So engrossed was Schuller by the choreography above and below him that he did not hear Valdez approaching. The NCOIC tapped him on the helmet and eyed the new rag covering his wound. It was already soaked with blood. A packed helicopter ascended so near it nearly blew them over.

"Probably sending some NVA sappers out to the fleet on one of these," Valdez said.

Schuller waited for it; he knew it was coming.

"Listen, we're gonna get you downstairs. Get out on one of these. See a fleet medic."

Of course, the thought of leaving before the rest of the detachment had crossed Schuller's mind. He had mixed emotions. He wanted out; he had no idea if the bayonet had nicked an important organ. Moreover, Charlie was coming, lots of Charlies. The MSGs, even with the Fleet Marine reinforcements, were outmanned and outgunned, and it wasn't going to be pretty. On the other hand, fly out now? Over this little cut? The wound surely wouldn't prevent him from firing a rifle or even a machine gun. He thought of all the trips he'd taken to the consulates, of all the imaginary sniper positions he'd staked out. Well, he had the perfect position now, and he didn't even have to go anywhere. They would come to him.

"No way, Top." He turned instinctively, as if hiding his wound would change Valdez's mind. "No way. I go out with everyone else."

Valdez opened his mouth, and for an instant Schuller was certain he was about to order him away. Instead he turned and walked toward the stairwell.

There was less than an hour of daylight left before the sun disappeared over the western horizon. The whirring of the big CH-53 rotors drowned out all sounds. Jim Kean leaned into the cockpit as the pilot yelled a question: "How many left?"

"At least a thousand."

"Fleet not gonna like that."

Kean shrugged.

"I might be the last for a while," the pilot said. "Deciding out there whether to fly after dark."

Kean knew that even Marine pilots needed downtime. There was nothing he could say. He loaded the helicopter, watched it rise from the chute, and once it had cleared the roof, saw the pilot jam his throttle forward as the helicopter bucked and curved out of sight, following the contours of the Saigon River. He headed into the embassy and found the ambassador in his office. He realized, with some embarrassment, that he must have smelled as ripe as the inside of a leper, but Martin did not seem to notice. The lines in his haggard face resembled the veins in a marble statue.

"Should we strike the colors?" Martin said.

Each night at sundown, in accordance with law and custom, the American flag was lowered from the courtyard staff. Kean considered the mass of people surrounding the embassy.

"In view of the situation, I'd hold off," he said. His voice was hoarse and cracking. "You've got a lot of people out there who might see that flag come down and figure it's the very end. I'd wait until after dark."

Martin flicked his head imperceptibly. Kean took the signal for agreement. He wheeled and headed back downstairs.

Frank Snepp sat in the sixth-floor reception area leading to Tom Polgar's suite and stared at the wall clock hanging above a secretary's desk. It was 5:58 P.M. In the next room, CIA officers were wielding sledges, hammering communications equipment into shapeless hunks of metal. Snepp wondered if that would even be necessary.

The intelligence warning Snepp had received regarding the 6 P.M. bombardment had set off a frantic afternoon-long round of phone calls, visits, and negotiations among Polgar, Big Minh, and Hanoi, all with the intent of assuring the North that the Americans were moving as quickly as possible to vacate the city. But General Dung was the wild card, and no one was certain of his intentions.

Snepp was trying, with little luck, to convince himself that Dung had called off his "shattering barrage," or at least postponed it, when the minute hand of the clock struck six. At that precise moment, an explosion resounded like an ear-splitting basso organ chord through the building. Snepp ran to the nearest window and looked down. A Volkswagen camper parked across the street on Thong Nhut Boulevard was in flames. Someone had dropped a lighted match into its gas tank.

Snepp had no idea that, with the Politburo's approval, Dung had decided to give the Americans until dawn on April 30 to get out. The NVA general knew that Ambassador Martin and President Minh, against all sanity, continued to inquire about a negotiated settlement. Martin had even suggested sending representatives to Hanoi. *What fools,* Dung thought.

General Carey watched the western sky purple to the color of a mussel shell before turning a sooty black. He thought of his original orders; the evacuation of Saigon was supposed to be completed by now. Two of the three landing zones at the DAO—the parking lot and the tennis courts—were equipped with lights, but not nearly enough to guide a chopper in. He ordered the lights to be augmented by cars and trucks set in a ring around the landing zones, their headlights ablaze. Moreover, as night fell, the helicopter pilots reported an increase in the many fires raging in and around the airport as a result of the NVA's continuing advance. But he had no other recourse. There were still hundreds of people to get out.

When even the vehicle headlights proved inadequate, a Marine officer with a strobe light took up position on the roof of the DAO headquarters building and began flashing beacons to the incoming Birds. But the strobe was itself an invitation to enemy sharpshooters, and small arms fire poured into his position. So constant was the concentrated gunfire that after a few minutes, the strobe light gambit was abandoned in favor of the more dangerous technique of talking the pilots in through the darkness by radio. This appeared to work, and by 6:30 P.M., most of the Marines forming a defensive perimeter along with a few civilian stragglers were withdrawn to the DAO's main headquarters building to await the final flights.

Meanwhile, Major Kean was informed by General Carey that as soon as the DAO evacuation was completed, the embassy would begin receiving double doses of flights: CH-46s off the roof and CH-53s out of the parking lot. But as the twilight shadows lengthened, helicopter pilots descending into the embassy compound also began encountering difficulties with visibility. The last few to make it in to the parking lot landing zone told Kean that the Task Force 76 commander, Admiral Whitmire, had ordered all CH-53 evacuations to cease at complete dark. They might be able to get in and out off the roof, but there was no way they could chance a blind vertical descent to the parking lot.

Kean thought fast and arrived at the same conclusion as the Marines at Dodge City. He asked a CH-53 pilot to relay the message that he would have the parking lot lit up like Broadway and ordered Sullivan to take a squad of MSGs to round up and fuel every vehicle remaining in the compound. Within ten minutes, the parking lot landing zone, already marked with luminescent paint, was encircled by glowing headlights. Kean took a moment to consider his MSGs. After so many weeks of meticulous planning for any possible evacuation contingency and with so many lives at stake, it was his Marines, when all had fallen apart, who had done what Marines always do—improvise.

By now, the remainder of the Fleet Marine contingent had been choppered over to the embassy, and Kean put them to work alongside the MSGs trying to control the ever-growing, and ever-panicky, crowds gathered at the gates. In the brief lulls between Sea Stallion landings in the parking lot, the major moved to the center of the ring of light so all the Fleet Marines could see him. Most of them did not know who he was, and he told his MSGs and Lieutenant Thompson-Powers's men to pass word that the man with the three-day growth in the short-sleeved Arnold Palmer golf shirt was in charge.

As complete darkness encompassed the compound, tracer fire increased, and the helicopter pilots were ordered to fly without lights as a new rooftop landing scheme was devised. As they hovered on approach, the helo crews were told to blink their landing lights in a set sequence of short flashes. These would be answered by guiding lights from Marines in the parking lot and on the rooftop helipad. Kean decided he would handle the parking lot descents and traded his Ping-Pong paddles for a set of flashlights.

He summoned Valdez and told the NCOIC to tap someone on the roof to do the same. Valdez thought of Steve Schuller and Dave Norman.

Eight

Sixty miles away, somewhere over the South China Sea, the Marine CH-46 Sea Knight, call sign Swift 14, skimmed the water at 110 knots. Its crew chief, Corporal Stephen Wills, cupped the microphone of the aircraft's internal intercom and hollered over the roar of the twin rotors to his first mechanic, Corporal Richard Scott.

"Careful what you wish for," he said. "Just might get it."

Wills's stony humor went unanswered. Scott, staring out from his port gunner's window and entranced by the fireworks display of heat lightning and artillery detonating over the mainland, barely stirred. Wills shrugged as the joke fell flat, fondled the trigger guard of his own 50-caliber heavy machine gun, and returned to monitoring the floating carpet of desperate sampans, barges, and fishing smacks bobbing atop the shallow sea beneath the helicopter's skids.

For the previous six days Wills, Scott, and the rest of their flight squadron's crews had squatted in the Number One Spot—first to fly—on the deck of the aircraft carrier USS *Hancock* awaiting the start of Operation Frequent Wind. Earlier this morning, they had finally received word that it was on, and that they were going in—all, that is, except for Swift 14, which had drawn the short straw and been tasked with overwater search-and-rescue duty. Since then Swift 14 had been flying "angel runs" on an orbit point, or constant loop, between the *Hancock* and the Vung Tau peninsula. The abrupt change of plan had come as a blow to Wills.

A lean, long, and cocky cowboy born and raised in Missoula, Montana, in his brief Marine career the twenty-three-year-old Wills had but one goal: to fly into Vietnam. He was a third-generation Marine, with an older brother who had served as a grunt in "the Nam" and had regaled the teen-aged Wills with war stories. As soon as he had graduated from high school in 1971 Wills had enlisted. But though it was prior to the Paris Peace Accords, it was still too late for him to get his boots muddy in Southeast Asia. Since then he had not been shy about sharing his disappointment or telling anyone who would listen about his itch to match his older brother's combat exploits.

He had, in fact, volunteered for Marine aviation duty precisely because he guessed that American helicopters would be the first units to be deployed to any new war zone or, should the Lord listen to his prayers, if hostilities resumed in Vietnam. And when his squadron, Marine Medium Helicopter 164, had deployed from California to Japan three months earlier, that dream appeared closer than ever. Scuttlebutt had it that the Corps was sending helicopters in-country to block the NVA streaming south from the Central Highlands.

Wills had studied the history of the Vietnam War, and he'd made sure to keep on top of the news coming out of Saigon. He could not believe that in the end the United States would cut and run from its promises to an ally. When the Marines returned—and Steve Wills was certain that they would—he expected his unit to be in the vanguard. On the morning his Sea Knight had set down on the tarmac at Futenma Air Station in Okinawa, Wills's sergeant major had even told him, "Things are happening, they're losing everything, and we're going back in." The hectic night-and-day training pace his squadron was put through thereafter only cemented his hunch.

While in Okinawa, Wills had also somehow found time to finish his noncommissioned officer studies and pass his final exam. Although teased often about his resemblance to the freckle-faced kid named Timmy on the old *Lassie* TV show, he took the razzing in good nature. There was, however, a muted steel to his blue eyes that belied the country-cousin persona, and he was devastated when he learned at his NCOS graduation ceremony that his squadron had left him behind when it was abruptly ordered to scramble from Japan to the *Hancock* by way of Subic Bay in the Philippines. He managed to hitch a ride on a C-130 transport plane to Subic and arrived a day after his unit. But in the brief amount of time he had been absent, "his" CH-46 had been reassigned to another crew chief. He was not happy when he hit the carrier deck only to be escorted by his maintenance chief to his new helicopter. Swift 14 looked like a bucket of bolts.

"What the hell's wrong with that Bird?" he'd asked the chief.

"Well, nuthin', except that the engines keep dropping off line."

"You mean, just quitting in flight?"

"Yup."

Wills spent the next three weeks, eighteen hours a day, haunting the *Hancock*'s maintenance shops for spare parts. He'd scrounged new engines, new rotor heads, and new bearings, but the first time he started Swift 14, it shot a fifteen-foot fireball out of its tail pipe and emptied its fuel tanks across the Hancock's deck to a chorus of curses and raised middle fingers from the seamen who had to clean up the mess. Wills was called before the *Hancock*'s captain to explain. If he had known the identity of the chopper's previous crew chief, he would have keelhauled him. How any Marine airman could leave such a beautiful machine as a Sea Knight in such awful condition was a mystery.

But, finally, on April 12, the day before the evacuation of Phnom Penh, he and Swift 14's crew completed their first successful test flight. Wills was jubilant when he reported to his maintenance chief.

"We got her up."

"Will she stay up?" the chief said.

It had taken seventeen days to find out.

Since just after dawn, Wills and the mechanic, Scott, had been flying continuous SAR orbits, nearly twelve straight hours of flight time interrupted only by regular hot refuelings—that is, taking on fuel without shutting down the engines. Both men were exhausted. *Be careful what you wish for.* For about the last half of that period of time, Swift 14 had been piloted and copiloted by Captain William Nystul and First Lieutenant Michael Shea. Nystul was a former fixed-wing instructor at the Naval Aviation Training Command at Pensacola who had only recently finished his CH-46 schooling, and Shea was a CH-53 pilot by trade. The two officers, brand new to the squadron, had relieved the aircraft's original pilots and swapped into the cockpit around midday.

Now, peering out the starboard crew door and watching the thunderheads blacken the few remaining stars in the sky, Wills's thoughts drifted to those earlier "drivers," no doubt down in the *Hancock*'s air-conditioned galley right now, wolfing down sandwiches and drinking cold soft drinks. This, he knew, went with the territory. Pilots came and went on Marine Corps helicopters, but the aircraft's care and feeding, from maintenance to logs, was entirely the responsibility of the crew chief, who "owned" his helicopter much as a civilian owned his car. Any pilot might fly the vehicle, and during missions the officers in the cockpit served as the aircraft's ranking commanders. But a crew chief was in sole charge of the cabin, even to the point of being allowed to overrule any decision he deemed hazardous to the craft or crew. The bottom line was, where Swift 14 flew, Wills flew. Always and every day. Even if she was a dog.

As the day had worn on, the monotony had been occasionally broken when Swift 14 had been asked to ferry sticks of refugees, predominantly Vietnamese civilians, from the *Hancock* to American troop transports farther out to sea. On one such milk run, they had just off-loaded twenty or so civilians on the deck of the USS *Blue Ridge* when Wills was overcome by a feeling of sadness. To a youngster from Montana, these poor souls appeared nothing so much as frightened and lost, without expressions in their eyes, as if coming from no past and having no future. He tried to imagine the families when they ended up in some stinking tent city, well beyond the far edge of their world. It was unreal, and as he tried to wipe the dark thoughts from his mind, Captain Nystul announced that they were launching immediately without topping off the gas bags.

"Small aircraft crash just aft of the ship," the pilot shouted over the intercom, and Wills could sense the adrenaline rush in his voice. They were up and gone from the *Blue Ridge* within seconds, and as Nystul hovered over the crash site—a Royal Vietnamese Air Force Huey had gone down trying to reach the American ship—Wills readied the aircraft's hoist while the mechanic, Scott, opened the "hellhole" in the helicopter's floor.

"Ready back here," he told the pilots. "See three personnel in the water. Lowering the hoist." He was as excited as the captain. It was the most action they'd had all day.

Of the three Vietnamese men clawing to get out of the sinking Huey,

Wills could make out blood pouring from the heads of two. When the horse collar attached to his hoist hit the water, all three lunged for it. A Navy photographer who had jumped aboard Swift 14 from the *Blue Ridge* to film the rescue elbowed Wills aside to get a better view, and the crew chief body-blocked him back in time to see the man who wasn't bleeding slip the horse collar under his arm pits. As he was being lifted, Wills spotted one of the bleeding men slide under the surface.

"Man under," he yelled to Nystul. "I'm jumping in, Sir."

"Send Scott. We need you on that hoist, Chief."

"Scott can't swim, Sir," Wills said.

But by now, it was moot. Wills and Scott pulled the unscathed Vietnamese into the helicopter at the same time a small Navy launch from the *Blue Ridge* began circling the two remaining swimmers. Swift 14 dropped the survivor and the Navy photographer on the *Blue Ridge*, topped off its tanks, and was released to return to his SAR orbit points. Wills never knew what became of the two men in the water.

Once the sun had set over the Gulf of Thailand, Swift 14's refugee hops were discontinued, and the combination of darkness and the low cloud cover made the search-and-rescue loops more dangerous. The evacuation flights from the DAO and the embassy had picked up, and the American choppers returning from Saigon were flying without lights even over the sea on the off chance an NVA gunboat might be lurking near the coast. Moreover, the panic-stricken Vietnamese pilots running low on fuel were attempting to land on American ships in any manner possible, even if it meant directly on top of ill-lit refueling Marine helicopters. Since dusk, Swift 14 had avoided half a dozen midair collisions with various South Vietnamese aircraft, and as the night wore on, they had made three more hover-and-hoists over ditched Vietnamese helicopters, each more dangerous than the last. Wills could sense that his Bird's pilots were tired and on edge.

A bit after dark, when a frenzied South Vietnamese Huey nearly pancaked them as they refueled without lights on the *Hancock,* the mechanic Scott told Wills that the entire scene reminded him of "a crazed nest of hornets, zipping this way and that, looking for something to sting."

"I assume you're telling me we're the stingees," Wells said.

"Keep your bug spray handy, is all I'm saying."

Wills had laughed at the joke, but some unnameable dread continued to grow in his gut as he listened—and occasionally joined in over the intercom—as the two pilots cursed their lack of relief.

Terry McNamara, Steve Hasty and five U.S. Marines, three dozen or so American civilians, a handful of Filipinos, and nearly 300 Vietnamese refugees, many with mouths agape, stared at the large waves cresting and breaking on the reefs beyond the Bassac River delta. Far to the west, a thin sliver of pink sky was barely visible over the flat, green, endless rice paddies of the Cau Mau peninsula.

"No rescue ship?" Steve Hasty did not know why he had formed the sentence as a question. It was not. "Those waves'll break us."

McNamara, still at the helm, checked his watch—it was nearly 7 P.M.—and picked up the radio transmitter. He broadcast a Mayday on the Seventh Fleet's emergency bandwidth. There was no response.

Since the firefight near the islands, they had progressed to the sea without incident. Several times their little flotilla had been approached by motorized sampans. Local fishermen? Pirates? It did not matter. On each occasion Hasty had ordered his Marines to stand, rifles and "Bloopers" pointed. Each time the sampans turned away.

Now they had made it, but where was the U.S. Navy? During his final visit to Saigon, McNamara had conferred with a Navy liaison stationed at the DAO and informed him of his plan to sail down the Bassac. The Navy man had promised that a rescue ship would be standing by off the mouth of the river waiting for them. *Jesus Christ,* the consul thought now, recalling years of naval service spanning two wars. *You'd think they'd come through for one of their own.*

He made a half-turn toward Hasty, standing beside him at the helm. "I think they forgot about us," he said.

Then he turned fully and waited for the second landing craft to pull alongside. When it was near enough, he hollered loud enough for all to hear, "That ship is out there somewhere. Don't worry. They haven't forgotten us. We'll find it, or they'll find us. Soon."

Neither Hasty nor McNamara was aware that hours earlier, when the

Air America helicopters stationed in Can Tho had alit on the deck of the transport dock ship USS *Vancouver* and discharged their CIA passengers, the Seventh Fleet's Admiral Steele was under the impression that these refugees were the entire Can Tho consulate staff.

While Hasty used a boat hook to hoist the American flag in the stern of the lead craft, MSG Sergeant John Kirchner walked to the bow and affixed the large consulate flag—a white "C" encircled by thirteen white stars on a blue background—to a railing. McNamara steered southeast and headed for the largest of the breaks in the reef. He laughed to himself. *Taking to sea in a flat-bottomed LCM.* Yet with flags whipping, engines coughing, and passengers bouncing, both boats made it past the perilous surf line without damage. Within moments, the tide had carried them far enough from the coast to be beyond the artillery range. Hasty, who could still smell the thick, sweet aroma from the vast expanse of mangrove swamps that blanketed the shore, estimated the distance at two miles. Despite having managed the successful reef crossing, the flat-keeled river boats continued to rock dangerously in the heavy swell.

"Vessels may or may not stand open water for long," McNamara told Hasty. He looked toward the mainland. "But nothing back there for us except a long march to a prison camp."

With that McNamara instinctively glanced down at the stanchion holding the ship's instruments. Two brackets encircled an empty space where a compass should have been. The cloud cover was too heavy to steer by the stars—if, in fact, McNamara had remembered how. He wasn't certain, but at least they were close enough to shore to make a rough guess as to direction. Somewhere beyond the mangroves, tracer fire and artillery explosions lit up the night sky. The Americans guessed it was an ARVN base camp under attack.

"I think we set a southern course and hope for the best," McNamara said. "That's where our ship will be coming from. Keep on the radio. Fire off a flare every thirty minutes or so. How many do we have?"

Hasty knelt and opened the crate at his feet. "Couple dozen."

"More than enough," said McNamara. "Won't even get through them all before they pick us up. If not, we have enough fuel to make it to the Philippines."

Hasty was not certain if the American consul was joking. The closest Philippine island was 700 miles away.

The incandescent orange muzzle flashes delineating the tree line between Saigon and Bien Hoa were the only lights Steve Schuller could see. He lay flat on his back atop the concrete helipad, the heat from the furnaces beneath nearly baking him alive. To the southwest, he could hear the whirring rotors of the CH-46 as it followed the winding Saigon River up from the sea before banking hard to port toward the embassy rooftop. When the helicopter was nearly on top of him, no more than 100 feet above, he cupped his left hand around the green bulb in the flashlight and blinked it three times. The pilot responded with three short flashes of his landing lights before descending like a shot amid a whirling funnel of dust and dirt.

Schuller rolled to the edge of the helipad and covered his eyes and ears. He wondered if this would be the occasion when the pilot miscalculated and missed the landing zone or, worse, caught the edge of it and crashed down on them all. Schuller and his fellow MSG, Dave Norman, the former infantry grunt who had served in Saigon prior to the signing of the Paris Accords, had been shanghaied by Top Valdez into acting as rooftop air traffic controllers after the Fleet Marine officer who had been flown in to handle the job slipped and tumbled the fifteen feet from the helipad onto the roof. He'd landed on his head amid a brace of unlit burn barrels. While he was being med-evaced out, Valdez had handed the two MSGs flashlights with red and green bulbs and given them a crash course in flight control.

Norman had taken the first rotation, and one of the first helicopters he'd guided in had descended with its spotlights on. Norman was bathed in a sea of white, totally exposed and ducking heavy ground fire. When the Sea Knight powered down, he'd grabbed the intercom from the crew chief and told the pilot the next time he came in lit up like that, he would personally shoot out his lights. Now it was Schuller's turn, and the irony was not lost on him. He was fairly certain that Valdez had no knowledge of his previous experience at—and deliberately flunking out of—Marine flight school. Just the luck of the draw. As the Sea Knight's tires thudded down a few yards away, he remained low. During the previous landing, the on button on his flashlight had stuck, and before he could cover the bulb, he'd taken a torrent of sniper fire.

He didn't know how the pilots did it. Bullets whizzing. Flying blind. Three little flashlight flashes. And suddenly they were touching down right on the bull's-eye, the luminous "H." He was close enough to see the multiple bullet holes in every helicopter. The pilots never shut down the engines, only geared the twin rotors down to idle. As soon as the wheels hit the rooftop, Norman led the next stick of refugees, mixed with embassy staff, from the inside stairwell. They raced out through the incinerator room and up the outside steps that climbed to the helipad. The Marines had soon figured out that on average, two of the smaller Vietnamese could be jammed into the CH-46s for every one American it was built to carry.

Steve Bauer stood on the roof of the two-story generator building in the northwest corner of the compound and lowered an aluminum ladder down to the roof of the adjacent mission warden station outside the embassy wall. Someone on Martin's staff—no one was certain exactly who—had promised the mission wardens that their families could jump to the front of the evacuation line if they themselves remained to assist with crowd control inside and outside the gates until the last helicopters arrived. It was the only leverage the Americans had.

Earlier in the day, Bauer had noticed a throng of angry mission wardens descend on the main gate demanding their back pay. The State Department had withheld the final cash payments to these poor men, most of them former South Vietnamese military, as a ruse to keep them working as the city fell apart. When it became obvious that the cash was not forthcoming from the Americans—in fact, most of it was being burned on the roof—many had deserted their posts, rightfully in Bauer's opinion. It had since fallen to the few remaining to help the MSGs keep some fragile order.

Now the mission wardens' families had gathered on the roof of the station, and Bauer and a squad of Fleet Marines were pulling them up. When one mission warden attempted to scale the ladder, the Marines shook it violently, and Bauer repeated the warning at the top of his lungs: "Just women and children."

When all the families were safely inside the embassy walls, the mission warden in charge climbed the ladder to speak to the Marines. "My men will continue to work outside, in the streets," he said. Even through his thickly accented English, Bauer could hear the futility in the man's voice. "But I want to reiterate—when the time comes, you must promise to take them out. You must not leave them. Do I have your word?"

Bauer looked around. The other Marines were all staring at him. Reluctantly he stepped forward. "Tonight then," he said. "On our signal. A flare. Have all your men assembled right here, and we'll drop the ladder. We'll see you then."

The mission warden captain hesitated. He performed what to Bauer seemed like a small bow. "I will have my men here," he said. "But you will not see me again. I am staying. This is my country."

Bauer was overwhelmed. He had become inured to the sight of the spineless Vietnamese authorities—military, political, police—clawing over each other to flee. Yet here was a true patriot, a man undoubtedly destined for a prisoner of war camp at best, the gallows or a firing squad at worst. Yet he was making the ultimate sacrifice for his beliefs, for his patriotism. Bauer was speechless. It was what he would have done, he thought. It was what he may yet have to do. He reached out and shook the man's smaller but steady hand.

It was 9:30 A.M. on April 29 in Washington, the business day well underway, when Secretary of State Kissinger telephoned President Ford as he was preparing to receive King Hussein of Jordan. Kissinger informed the president that the civilian evacuation of the DAO had been successfully completed. Ford detected an edge to Kissinger's voice. He asked about the embassy.

"I suggest we order Ambassador Martin to wrap it up and get his ass out of there," Kissinger said.

"Yes," the president said. "Yes."

He then asked Kissinger to look over a draft of the speech about South Vietnam he planned to deliver later to a national television audience. Ford was to announce that all American personnel had been evacuated safely from the country.

"Of course, Mr. President," Kissinger said. "As soon as I speak to Martin."

Nine

Graham Martin, alone in his office, alone in his life, hung up the telephone and considered the finality of his circumstance. Henry Kissinger, his accent more guttural this morning than Martin had ever heard it, wanted him out. Now. Gone from a dying country that not only no longer needed him but no longer wanted him. A country that by dawn would likely cease to exist. He would be the last U.S. ambassador to the Republic of Vietnam, a footnote—contemptible? laughable?—when the history of the Vietnam War was written. He had failed, and the thought of General Dung sitting in this very chair, perhaps as early as tomorrow, ate at his insides.

His door was ajar, and from somewhere down the corridor he could hear the sound of clinking glasses. He knew no one would enter, no one would offer him a final drink. He would refuse, at any rate. His body was in revolt, Manichaean, the spirit imprisoned in the flesh. His stomach lurched, and his hands trembled, and he could not remember the last time he had eaten. He lit a cigarette and moved from behind his desk, crossed the room, and shut the door. One of Kissinger's sentences stuck in his mind. The consequences of his capture by the Communists, the secretary had told him, would be "catastrophic." *As catastrophic as the consequence of abandoning an ally?* The enormity of the betrayal was staggering. But he had said nothing. Was he a coward? A fool? No, merely a defeated and diminished man. He remembered a line from *King Lear*, once, in what seemed another lifetime, his favorite of Shakespeare plays. "Wilt break my heart?" the old king had asked. Indeed. Lear had lost a daughter. He had lost a country.

He noticed the stacks of folders and notebooks piled on the floor in a corner of the office. Those back-channel cables from Washington, he thought, they will tell the true story. He recrossed the room and plucked one at random. Dated April 18, Kissinger had written, "I must ask you to reduce total American presence to the level of 1,100 by COB [close of business] Tuesday. This is the number of people whom we estimate can be evacuated in one helo lift. I know that this decision will come as a blow to you."

Another, from April 22: "You may think I am perpetually harassing you. However, when you get back here you will find that the record shows that I defended you and your approach without exception."

And another, from April 26: "I may have an odd way of showing it, but you have my full support."

Martin could not help but laugh at this last. *Said the spider to the fly.* The laugh made him cough violently, and he returned to his desk and stubbed out his cigarette. There he picked up one final cable that had arrived this morning and added it to the pile in the corner. "We have studied your request to keep a small staff behind and the President insists on total evacuation." Kissinger had signed it with "Warm regards."

Martin needed some air.

Jim Kean spotted the ambassador pacing near the swimming pool. He was so pale he looked like daylight would kill him. Martin told the major that he was attempting to take a head count of the remaining Vietnamese. He'd just gotten off the phone with General Carey at the DAO, he added, who had none-too-subtly accused him of underplaying the evacuee numbers when they'd spoken earlier in the afternoon.

"We've still got well over one thousand people to get out of here," Kean said. He wondered if the number was closer to double that.

"Then we've got another dilemma," Martin said. *Naturally*, the major thought. *Never one crisis at a time.*

The ambassador told Kean that the problem, specifically, was the Army Captain Stuart Herrington, the intelligence officer attached to the dormant MIA negotiations team who earlier that day had arrived from the DAO via convoy along with two of his colleagues, Army officers Colonel John Madison and Lieutenant Colonel Harry Summers. Herrington, Martin said, had been informing the incoming chopper pilots that the Vietnamese refugees were an unending stream into the compound that would never be plugged. The pilots in turn had reported this to their commanding officers on the Seventh Fleet, and Admiral Steele on his flagship, the light cruiser USS *Oklahoma City,* and Admiral Gayler in Hawaii were threatening to refocus the entire operation in favor of evacuating only the remaining Americans.

"Look around," Martin said. "We've got this under control. But Herrington's telling the pilots that each time they land that there will always be two thousand more refugees to get out, no matter how many trips they schedule."

There was no need for Kean to look around. He considered that Herrington might well be correct—that they might indeed never stanch the flow of people America had vowed to help escape. Herrington, he knew, had no secret agenda. He was merely reporting what he saw, or thought he saw. But Kean's opinion of Martin was turning. The ambassador may have erred on the side of thinking that the singular force of his personality would see this mess through to the end. But at least he was taking the reins and running with them when no one else appeared to want to. It crossed Kean's mind whether, say, the nuclear evacuation plans for New York, or Los Angeles, or even Washington, D.C., included second-hand buses carrying people out of a panicked city while small helicopters descended onto rooftops and makeshift landing zones. He bet they did. *And how did they think that would work out?*

At any rate, he decided, even with a clearer head, such bureaucratic infighting was well beyond his pay grade. Yet standing there with an anxious look on his face, the ambassador was obviously awaiting some kind of positive response from the Marine major. Kean was at a loss for words. As he tried to compose a suitable reply, an aide ran up to Martin and whispered something into his ear.

Martin listened, nodded, and before turning to head back inside, laid a soft hand on Kean's shoulder. "You're doing a good job," he said.

The major, fighting off exhaustion, found Valdez by the vehicle gate. "They want the old man out. Now."

"He won't go, you know."

"I know."

It was 10:20 P.M., and the most recent CH-53 pilot to set down in the compound had told Kean that someone in the Navy chain of command had ordered all evacuation operations to cease by 11:30. Both Marines recognized that there was no way they could clear the embassy grounds in seventy minutes.

"Just keep them moving, Top," Kean said, and followed the ambassador's path into the embassy. On his way to his office, he passed a knot of civilians gathered in the conference room next to Wolfgang Lehmann's office. State Department employees. Aide workers. A few reporters. Some were singing along to a radio playing rock and roll, and liquor bottles and glasses littered the desks. Kean had heard that the embassy stored more than $10,000 worth of wines and spirits in the cellar for formal receptions and dinners. He wondered how much was left.

In the vestibule leading to Martin's office, a secretary had left a small makeup mirror on her desk, and Kean unconsciously picked it up. He was so weary he began to have a fantasy that if he looked in the glass, he would not see a reflection. He pushed the crazy thought from his mind, took a deep breath, knocked, and walked in. Martin was seated behind his large desk. The major did not mention the drunken farewell party playing out down the hallway. Better, he thought, to stick to the business at hand. He told Martin about the 11:30 deadline.

"Mr. Ambassador, I am certain that you can use your influence to extend the helicopter sorties."

"How many people left?"

In the last thirty minutes, Kean knew that at least three more Sea Stallions had landed and departed. "Maybe less than a thousand by now," he said. He hoped he was in the ballpark.

"I will see what I can do," Martin said with a finality that Kean took as a dismissal.

Ten minutes later, back in the parking lot, Kean was flagged down by one of the ambassador's aides. They conferred for a moment as Valdez watched. The aide disappeared back into the embassy as the major told Valdez that the evacuation flights would continue to be flown past the 11:30 deadline. He shook his head with some admiration for Martin: *There's still a few teeth left in the old lion.*

The official U.S. presence at the DAO's compound in Saigon, once the massive hub of America's entanglement in Southeast Asia, ended at precisely 10:50 P.M. when General Carey accompanied the final platoon of Fleet Marines and the last of Jim Kean's U.S. Embassy MSGs up the ramp of the CH-53 idling in the compound's tennis court. A few moments earlier, when General Smith and the remnant of his staff had also stepped into the belly of a CH-53 Sea Stallion, his operations officer, seated across from him, had begun to weep. Smith understood. It had been the saddest day of his life.

Another squadron of helicopters hovered high overhead, waiting to pick up the small demolition team left behind to destroy the compound's communications equipment, computer data banks, satellite spotting station, thousands of paper files, and the remainder of the $7 million in paper money the Americans had been burning since early morning. When these tasks were complete, the team would activate the timed explosive charges that, as a last American gesture, would blow up the buildings.

The evacuation from the DAO had lasted eight hours and involved over fifty Marine Corps and U.S. Air Force helicopters. A total of 395 Americans and nearly 4,500 South Vietnamese and third-country nationals had been taken out. Despite what the operation signified, Carey took pride in the fact that not one evacuee, not any of his Marines, had been killed or wounded.

As one of the last Sea Knights ascended, MSG Ted Murray, seated beside the helicopter's door gunner, peered down at the sprawling complex. The blinding white thermite flames, eerily silent, were already beginning to sprout across the compound like fiery mushrooms. Beyond the chain-link fence where he'd encountered the disgruntled ARVNs with the wire cutters, where they had taunted him as a coward, where the pit in Murray's stomach had suddenly felt bottomless, he could see NVA tanks moving in an orderly column across the Tan Son Nhut flight lines.

He imagined he could hear through the mad whirl of air the clank of their treads.

At a few minutes past 11 P.M., with his search-and-rescue CH-46 Sea Knight, Swift 14, again drawing down to its last thirty minutes of fuel, Captain William Nystul radioed the USS *Hancock* for clearance to land. The pilot was given permission by the ship's air traffic controller and the aircraft, gearing down to eighty knots, circled for a downwind approach toward the carrier. The ship's superstructure had just come into sharp contrast with the surrounding sea when the chopper's crew chief, Corporal Steve Wills, caught a glimpse of a bright-white pinhole light out of the corner of his eye. He spun aft and spotted a South Vietnamese Huey running up their tail. It was no more than ninety feet away and closing.

"Hard right!" he screamed over the intercom. "Hard right!"

Nystul veered and threw the Bird into a dive. Wills's stomach rose to his throat, and through the crew door he felt the Huey's rotor wash buffet him. The little helicopter missed clipping Swift 14's tail by mere yards. After Nystul reset Swift 14's course for the *Hancock,* not a man on board uttered a word for several moments. Finally, in a voice that could scour a stove, the pilot Nystul said, "Somebody's gonna die up here tonight."

Wills and the chopper's mechanic, Corporal Richard Scott, exchanged glances. It was a good ten minutes before Wills again heard someone speak. Again it was Nystul. "Am I cleared for a left turn?"

The request took Wills by surprise. The *Hancock* was dead ahead. Fearing another collision, he leaped from the starboard crew door to Scott's port-side gunner's window and thrust his head into the night air. All clear. The carrier was close. What was the pilot talking about?

"You're clear," Wills said into the intercom. "You're clear." The crew chief had no idea what was happening.

At that, an unfamiliar voice broke into Swift 14's frequency: "Pick it up! Pick it up! Pick it up!"

Who the hell is that? It was not Captain Nystul, Wills knew, and it lacked Lieutenant Shea's distinctive Texas twang. He jumped back across the cabin to the crew door. His mind reeled. Could it have been the *Han-*

cock's landing signal officer breaking into their frequency, warning them of yet another bogie intruding on their airspace? A chopper he hadn't seen? He looked out the crew door again. Again, nothing but pitch-black sky. Something was very wrong. He did not know what.

"Brace yourself," he hollered to Scott. It was never clear what happened.

The last thing Steve Wills saw before they hit the water was the bright yellow flash of Swift 14's Hard Initial Lights, which signified a crash landing. It was as if a flash grenade had exploded in the helo. It was the first time he'd ever seen the crash lights come on. He never heard the anguished whine of buckling metal as his Bird dumped into the sea.

Wills had no idea how much time had elapsed when he awoke below the surface of the South China Sea. He instinctively tried to gulp air. Salt water poured down his throat. He reached down with his left hand to pull the tab on his safety belt to inflate the left side of his airmen's life preserver. But his belt was not there; neither was his radio or pistol. He felt the serrated edge of a large bone punched through his jumpsuit. His tibia. He ran his fingers over his torso. He was sliced open from his left hip to just under his left armpit.

He held his breath and moved his right hand down the right side of his body. He could feel that his right hip had dislocated from its socket, but the other life preserver tab was dangling from the shredded remnants of his belt. He yanked the tab, and half of the compressed-air preserver inflated under his right armpit and over his right shoulder. It lifted him to the surface, but he was floating cockeyed. Gasping for air, he took a deep breath before a wave pushed him back under. Again the life preserver buoyed him to the surface. The water was warm, he knew he was bleeding, and the thought of sharks crossed his mind.

He swiveled his head, searching for Swift 14. She was gone. Without a trace. Just disappeared. He made out the lights from the nearby *Hancock*'s wheelhouse, and then, far above him, a searchlight sweeping the waves. There was a faint sound. Not the ocean. Different. Human. It was the mechanic Rich Scott's voice.

"I can't swim. I can't swim."

It was like a distorted echo, something heard in a dream. Wills's water survival training kicked in automatically. With his left hand he grabbed the pen flares attached to his safety vest and shot off two. He tried to swim toward Scott's voice. He couldn't move his legs. He heard the mechanic again. "I can't swim."

This time the sound was farther away. The current must have been pulling them apart.

Wills sucked as much air as he could into his lungs and screamed: "Scottie, my legs are broke. I can't move. Can you get to me!"

"I can't swim."

"Pop your life preserver!"

Now a searchlight above was descending, the oval contour of the beam growing larger, and Scott was also firing his pen flares. Wills recognized the outline of a helicopter—a small, single-rotor SH-3 Navy rescue Bird. It hovered above them, midway between Wills and Scott. Scott was shooting his flares right at the chopper. Wills watched as the Navy pilot took evasive action and dodged the tiny artillery.

"Scottie, you gotta quit doing that," he shouted. Yet inwardly, for some odd reason, he found Scott's action hilarious. *Old Scottie, gonna make sure they see him or else he's gonna shoot 'em down himself.*

He yelled again. "Scott! They see us. Quit shooting!"

And with that, the Navy Bird was gone. The searchlight receded into the black night and disappeared.

"No problem, Scottie," Wills hollered. He felt as if he was trying to convince himself. "Probably didn't have a hoist on board. They know where we are."

Wills patted himself down again. His body felt as if it had been crushed in a trash compactor. "Scottie, I can't find my strobe. You got one? Light her up. Light her up."

From fifty yards away Wills saw the beam of a miniature strobe light shoot from the sea and zigzag across the sky. It instantly settled on the underside of a descending CH-53. Wills shot another pen flare. With as much effort as he could muster, he reached down to his boot and located his own strobe light. He locked it on the chopper. The Sea Stallion headed toward him, its landing lights illuminating the sea around him. Mistake. The chopper settled over him, and its heavy rotor wash pushed him below the surface. He felt like a plastic slip bobber being dragged to the bottom by a huge fish.

He fought to the surface, his legs screaming in pain. He spotted the CH-53 again, this time dragging a horse-collar hoist toward him. As it closed on his position, the rotor wash pushed him under once more. He cupped the strobe beam with his palm so the chopper crew could not see him. He could drown on his own, he didn't need their help. He blacked out.

When Wills awoke, the CH-53 was gone, replaced by a smaller CH-46 hovering some distance away. He guessed it was over Scott. He watched in disbelief as it plopped into the sea, its skids and wheels disappearing below the surface. Four hands reached out. They grabbed Scott by the horse collar and pulled him aboard. Wills shone his strobe at the chopper. It darted like a horsefly and water-taxied toward him nose-down.

Jesus! CH-46s don't float. No, no, no, he cried. The crazy sonofabitch driving the Bird was either a fool or a hero. Maybe both.

Wills struggled against the Sea Knight's rotor wash, but managed to keep the right side of his face above the surface. The CH-46 was almost on top of him now. In his semiconscious state, he was not sure if these things he suddenly saw before his eyes were human hands. He reached out, and they clutched at him. He was floating on his belly. Now the helicopter's crew chief was pulling him through the aircraft's crew door. His shattered thigh bone caught on the bottom cowling and tore through more of his flesh. He screamed in pain, let go, and shoved off back into the sea.

Steve Wills knew he was losing too much blood. He did not care about sharks anymore. He checked his watch. He guessed he'd been in the water for close to thirty minutes. He would lose consciousness again soon, he realized—this time, perhaps, for good. The CH-46 water taxied in a huge semicircle, and he summoned all his strength. He rolled over onto his back. His leg felt like it was on fire. He threw out his arms again, and again he made contact with the crew chief, who yanked him in through the crew door.

He lay on his back in the cabin, panting, nearly submersed in a foot of salt water. The South China Sea poured in through the crew door. He heard the helicopter's emergency throttles whine and scream. He could feel the entire aircraft shudder against the pull of the sea. There was no way they would get airborne against that kind of weight.

Wills awoke as the chopper hit the deck of the USS *Hancock* with a hard jolt. He was facing the cockpit. The pilot and copilot were still strapped in, seated in water up to their knees. They turned to give him the thumbs-up. Water poured from the helicopter onto the carrier's deck. He heard a voice say, "Jesus, looks like a surfacing sub."

He wanted to ask after Nystul and Shea, after his Bird. But before the words could come, someone jabbed him with a syringe of morphine. He found out only later that the bodies of his pilot and copilot rested seventy-five feet beneath the surface of the South China Sea, never to be recovered.

Part IV
"Round Eyes Only"

LADY ACE IS NOT TO PICK UP ANY MORE PAX UNTIL HE HAS AGAIN RELAYED THE PRESIDENTIAL ORDER TO THE AMBASSADOR. THE ORDER IS THAT THERE ARE ONLY 20 ACFT (AIRCRAFT FLIGHTS) REMAINING AND ONLY AMERICANS ARE TO BE EVACUATED.

—U.S. National Security Agency transmission transcript,
secretly recorded and classified Top Secret

One

Saigon, 2400, 29 April 1975

Steve Schuller scratched the thick growth on his chin and watched bleary-eyed from the edge of the rooftop as the DAO collapsed in on itself like a dying star. The detonations were six miles away, but the entire embassy compound seemed to shake. The MSGs surrounding him were well beyond enthusiasm at the fireworks display.

"Thermite?" he said.

Mike Sullivan shook his head. "Barrels of the stuff won't do that. C-4, I guess."

"Us, too?" Schuller peered over the parapet. The U.S. Consulate building, the CRA structures, and the French villa were dark. But lights blazed from every floor of the embassy. By now the sniping had become routine. Schuller, like everyone else on the roof, was accustomed to monkey-walking in a crouch.

"Bubble Room, is all," Sullivan said. "Don't have enough charge to blow this whole building. Don't think the ambassador would let it happen anyway."

Schuller was barely listening. He looked at Sullivan. *Huh?* His mind was as dull as his wound was sharp, and he had forgotten his own question. It hit him, for the first time, that this was the end. The downtown bars, cafés, and hotels, empty. The CIA apartment building up the road, empty; there had not been an Air America helicopter lifting off from its roof since dusk. Now, the Defense Attaché's Office, empty. And destroyed. Rubble.

They were it. A few score MSGs and a hundred or so Fleet Marines. Against . . . Who? What? How many? He had no idea. If Frank Snepp's intelligence was correct, there were 150,000 angry North Vietnamese soldiers converging on them. He thought again of his many trips up-country. Of becoming a sniper with Marine Recon. Who had he been kidding? Himself, he guessed.

Behind and above the MSGs, on the raised helipad, CH-46s were still regularly setting down at ten-minute intervals. Dave Norman was up on the landing zone with the pair of colored flashlights, taking his turn guiding them in. As far as Schuller could tell, most of his detachment and nearly all of the Fleet Marines remained downstairs, on the gates and walls, still sealing off the compound. The people on the streets were tired now, their energy spent. But they would not leave—not while there was still a chance of getting out. Schuller noticed that it was the Army colonels, Madison and Summers, along with Captain Herrington, who seemed to have taken charge of the refugees packing the stairwell. Since the three Army officers had convoyed over to the embassy from Dodge City the previous morning, they had spent most of the past twenty-four hours circulating through the mass of refugees, promising them that no one would be left behind. Herrington had even told the final stick in line that he would be accompanying them on the chopper that flew them out. Now, as each Bird set down on the roof, they would herd a group of forty or so out through the incinerator room and up the outside staircase. Like squeezing toothpaste from a tube. They all assumed that the evacuation would continue through daybreak. Major Kean, down in the parking lot, knew better.

Kean too had felt the DAO imploding at about the same time one of the CH-53 pilots informed him that the latest rumor out on the fleet had the entire evacuation terminating soon, albeit temporarily, for "administrative restrictions."

"Administrative restrictions?"

The pilot translated into plain English. "Everybody's over their max flight time."

"And the people still here? Us?"

The Sea Stallion pilot shrugged. "Dunno, Major. I'm sure there's a plan . . ." His voice trailed off.

The packed CH-53 lifted off, and Kean's mind seemed to fold over on itself. It didn't make sense. *The same guys have flown so many sorties in and out they could do it with their eyes closed.* Did the ambassador know about this? General Carey? How could anyone possibly . . . His thoughts were interrupted by Valdez's voice.

"Moment, Major?"

Kean spun. "Top?

Valdez pointed with his chin. "By the pool. Situation. The Koreans."

Several times throughout the late afternoon and evening, the MSGs forming up sticks had come to Kean complaining about the "Korean problem." Between the Korean ambassador and his secretary, embassy workers, a couple of military attachés, and some of their families, there were close to a hundred of them. They had arrived in the American compound a day late and, particularly with the higher-ups, an attitude. A few had tried to shove their way through the Vietnamese to the front of the evacuation line. When the Marines had stopped them, they'd made a show of waving their diplomatic passports. A couple had also made some loud threats when they saw American reporters being allowed into the Chancery building. There was a reason the boisterous South Koreans were known as the Irish of the Orient, and during one altercation, Valdez had to physically restrain Big John Ghilain from breaking one of the more obnoxious men over his knee.

Earlier, after securing Wolfgang Lehmann's permission, Kean had explained to them that this was a first-come, first-serve operation and that they'd been the last to the party. They'd get out, he promised. After everyone else. They had sulked and stomped off. The major had not given them a second thought until this moment.

"Let's go," he said now, and he and Valdez hurried across the parking lot toward the CRA compound. They found a half-dozen South Korean men passed out at the base of the low wall fronting the embassy's cash liquor store. Half-full bottles of wine and spirits rolled at their feet. The store's thick windows were smashed.

"Broke in; looted the place," said Valdez.

Kean shot him a look.

"Not them alone," Valdez said. "But they were part of it, or at least arrived soon after." He nudged one of the sleeping Koreans with his boot. "Not moving. What do you think?"

"Their ambassador?" Kean said.

"Flown out already."

Kean heard another CH-46 approaching the roof. He decided that he had about had his fill of diplomats in general, and South Korean diplomats in particular.

"Leave 'em," he said. "We'll wake them up later."

Henry Kissinger appeared more agitated than usual as he stood before a knot of reporters in the austere White House briefing room. After a brief preamble about the state of the Saigon evacuation—"running smoothly . . . no casualties"—he reached the point of the briefing. The North Vietnamese, he said, were guilty of perfidy by "changing signals" within the last forty-eight hours.

"Until two days ago we thought a negotiated settlement was highly probable," he said. "But they switched to the military option."

Some of the reporters may have even believed him. In any case, that was the position he was presenting to the American public: *Not our fault.* Any other truth could be damned.

When the secretary finished his statement, someone asked a question about Ambassador Martin. When had he departed the embassy? The reporters were surprised when Kissinger hesitated. Wasn't the secretary of state the ambassador's direct boss? Hadn't Martin been ordered out?

Kissinger fidgeted and cleared his throat. "Ambassador Martin remains at the embassy in Saigon," he said. "We expect him to be evacuated momentarily. Thank you." He turned and left.

After Kissinger exited the dais, a few of the newsmen noted an irony. Just thirty months earlier, on the secretary's return from Paris, he had stood at the same rostrum and announced his greatest triumph: "Peace is at hand."

By 1 A.M. the vectoring helicopter pilots were having difficulty making out the now-dimming headlights with which Kean had encircled the parking lot. Worse, false rumors were spreading among the chopper crews that the NVA had attacked the embassy compound and that the Chancery building was on fire. Earlier in the day, General Dung's artillery had shelled the giant ARVN ammunition dump at Long Binh on the outskirts of the city, and the pilots overflying the conflagration had been forced to skirt the billowing gouts of flames and black smoke. Now the last Americans to depart the DAO had overpassed the embassy and, on reaching the fleet, reported accounts of similar flames and smoke shooting from its roof. One pilot hazarded that these were actually burn barrels belching fire. Nonetheless, flights were waved off while tactics and strategy were rethought in the war room of the command-and-control ship USS *Blue Ridge,* which was the flagship of Task Force 76.

Dazed by mind-numbing fatigue, it took the Marines at the embassy some moments to realize that the *whap-whap-whap* of the helicopter rotors was no longer beating against their eardrums. Had the evacuation operation ended with hundreds of people still within the embassy compound? No one seemed to know. Out on the USS *Blue Ridge,* General Carey finally arrived from the DAO after a brief stop on the USS *Midway.* Once his own helicopter had powered down on the deck, he too noticed the absence of the sound of choppers in the night sky. He was confused when he reached the war room and confronted Task Force 76's Admiral Whitmire.

Whitmire told him that on orders from "Washington," he had grounded all flights out of concern for flight safety. There were concerns about the pilots flying at night, particularly in the deteriorating weather conditions—a line of heavy thunderstorms had moved into the flight path between the fleet and Saigon. This meant pilots could no longer rely on line-of-sight calculations to find their ships. Moreover, with the NVA creeping relentlessly closer, the low-flying choppers were more vulnerable to enemy fire. Those considerations aside, there was also the six-and-a-half-hour envelope mandated by the Naval Aviation Tactical Operations Procedures flight safety manual for any one twenty-four-hour period, and nearly every helo pilot had been in the air for almost twice that long. Dangerous instrument landings by exhausted pilots were only inviting catastrophe. Flights, Whitmire said finally, were to resume at dawn.

Carey tried to hold his temper. *On orders from Washington? Overriding officers on the scene? Who in Washington. George-Fucking-Washington?* Instead, in a calm voice, he noted to Whitmire that by the time the pilots completed their mandatory rest time and got back in the air, the only soldiers left to greet them in Saigon would belong to General Dung. Carey, himself a veteran aviator, knew what his men could do, and that was keep flying to complete their mission. As a series of increasingly recriminatory phone calls flew off the USS *Blue Ridge,* the lonely MSG outpost in Saigon, searching the sky, had no notion that this "cock-up" had gone all the way to Hawaii.

It was there, in Pearl Harbor, that the commander in chief of the Pacific Fleet, Admiral Maurice Weisner, learned from the Seventh Fleet commander, Admiral Steele, that the evacuation had been temporarily halted. A furious Lieutenant General Lou Wilson, commanding general of the Fleet Marine Corps and a hard-bitten Medal of Honor recipient, telephoned the admirals Weisner and Gayler.

"I cannot understand this!" Wilson told them each in succession in a Mississippi accent so thick if flowed like syrup. "There is no such thing as Marines not evacuating other Marines."

Meanwhile, Carey's contentions had already persuaded Whitmire by the time Wilson's orders to resume flights reached the USS *Blue Ridge.* Pilots were summoned from ready rooms, chow lines, and bunks across a plethora of ships and ordered back up in the air. And though the Air Force Jolly Green Giants never did launch again, by half past the hour, the first Marine squadrons began to ascend from decks. Dawn, and all that it implied, was four hours away.

After so many hours of engine roar and beating rotors, the stone quiet combined with a sort of mass exhaustion to produce an eerie stillness in the streets surrounding the embassy. The drizzle had stopped, leaving in its place a heavy mist that formed halos around the dimming vehicle headlights. The humming murmur beyond the walls, interrupted regularly by the *crump-crump* of artillery falling somewhere to the north, were the only sounds. Marines throughout the compound relaxed tense muscles for the first time in twelve hours, and Bobby Schlager and Duane Gevers, their backs slumped against the wrought-iron bars of the main gate, took advantage of the moment of tranquility to squat for a smoke.

They had barely inhaled their deep first drags when a high-pitched shriek cut the thick air. They whipped around and saw a slip of a girl contorting her body like an acrobat's as she slithered through the concertina wire atop the wall near the gate. Even the crowd on the street fell silent and seemed to hold its collective breath. The girl was barefoot and carefully picked her way past the thick shards of broken glass embedded in the top of the wall. When she had made it to the inside edge, she turned to face Thong Nhut Boulevard. Gevers pegged her at no more than ten years old, although you could never tell with the Vietnamese, and it seemed to the MSG that she was searching the crowd for someone. *Maybe to wave good-bye one last time?*

But she could not locate whomever it was she was looking for. She turned back toward the compound, standing with her knees barely bent. Her dirt-splotched legs, as slender as a Barbie doll's, were shaking. A tear rolled down her cheek, then another, and then a torrent. She was afraid of the jump. The terrified look on her face was heart-rending. Before anyone else could react, a burly Fleet Marine dropped his weapon, scaled the wall, cradled the waif in his thick arms, and leaped back down. He carried her to the pool area, brushed a strand of lank hair from her forehead, and deposited her with an obviously bewildered Vietnamese family. He turned and left without a word.

Back at the gate, Gevers caught his eye.

"Got one at home just like her," the Marine said. The Black Market King nodded.

Two

As the hours passed, hope faded, and the smell of vomit rose on the two LSTs bobbing along the South China Sea. Soft whimpers emanated from the clusters of seasick families huddled against the cold wind blowing through the boats' wells, and it did not take a seaman—and Steve Hasty was far from one—to recognize that the pitch and roll of the offshore swell had increased dramatically since they'd left the river delta.

Two hours earlier, Terry McNamara had lashed the craft together after confiding to Hasty that he did not expect any rescue ship to appear out of the night. No one had answered their Mayday calls, the low cloud cover muted the few remaining orange flares, and a light rain had begun to fall. McNamara estimated that they were making seven or eight knots sailing south against the tide and tried to calculate the time to the nearest safe landfall, which he reckoned to be the Vung Tau peninsula. He could not, and his mask of self-assurance was becoming harder to keep up with each passing moment.

Hasty was bone weary from nearly seven hours of standing beside McNamara at the helm. He could only imagine how the consul general, nearly twenty-five years his senior, was holding up. He was about to suggest that they turn with a tide that might bring them closer to land when, at just past 2 A.M., he spotted the mass of lights. At first he could not tell whether they came from shore or sea.

"See that?"

McNamara nodded, and at the same moment one of the Americans on the second landing craft shouted. The boat's Vietnamese pilot, an experienced mariner, was certain that the glare came from a sizable ship. If it was sizable, McNamara knew, that meant it was American. He spun the wooden wheel. "Okay," he said, "let's give it a try. Fire off whatever flares we have."

Hasty lit off two flares and watched the orange trails arc through the night sky and disappear into the clouds. Three hundred passengers stood in the rolling craft and awaited a response. There was none.

"Suppose we'll just go introduce ourselves." A buoyancy had returned to McNamara's voice.

It took nearly sixty minutes, but McNamara could now clearly make out the superstructure of an anchored freighter. When the merchant marine ship SS *Pioneer Contender* hove closer into view, he recognized the red, white, and blue bands painted on her stack. But something was wrong. Foreign sailors leaning over the railing of the big white freighter were waving wildly, warning them away.

"They think we're Chinese pirates," someone yelled from the other boat.

McNamara drew up to the ship and scraped his tiny landing craft against its rusting prow. At the sound of the grinding metal, another row of heads appeared above. Hasty recognized them as U.S. Marines. He cupped his hand to his chapped lips and hollered, "Americans! Americans!"

A moment later, rope slings fell from the sky. McNamara felt his knees go weak. He had been standing at the wheel for fourteen hours, operating on pure adrenaline, and now the strength seemed to drain from his body as if he had sprouted holes. He felt as though he had aged ten years.

The SS *Pioneer Contender,* a private merchant ship on loan to the U.S. Military Sealift Command, had been trawling the waters of the southern tip of Vietnam for boat people for three days, and its crew included a platoon of U.S. Fleet Marines. As the Can Tho "pirate fleet" tied on, the Fleet Marine platoon commander leaned over the rail and shouted for everyone to toss their weapons into the sea. It was too dark for him to make out who occupied the tiny boats. Hasty, his hands still cupped about his mouth, was quick to reply.

"We are United States Marines, and we come aboard with our weapons or we do not come aboard."

McNamara nearly laughed out loud at his young John Wayne.

McNamara and Hasty were two of the first hoisted up to the ship's deck. They were stunned to learn that the SS *Pioneer Contender* was, in fact, not waiting for them. It had merely stumbled on them, as it were, while awaiting CIA Air America helicopters ferrying deserting ARVN officers and soldiers from the Delta, on orders from the Can Tho station chief, Jim Delaney. McNamara had no idea that such an operation had been planned and executed. *The Agency,* McNamara thought, *was screwing us to the very end.* He and Hasty were further confounded when the commander of the Fleet Marine platoon told them that he had spotted their flares hours ago, but that the freighter's civilian captain, under the impression from Seventh Fleet radio transmissions that all of the Can Tho Consulate's staff and refugees had landed earlier on the USS *Vancouver,* had chosen to disregard them, believing the flares to be nothing more than artillery fire from shore by an ARVN unit making a last stand.

In a private conversation with the platoon commander, Hasty also learned that the SS *Pioneer Contender* had taken part in the evacuation of Da Nang. This was why, the Fleet Marine said, its captain and his Filipino crew were leery of allowing armed men to board. The MSG remembered the stories he had heard about Da Nang, and understood. In any event, any anger he felt at the perceived insult was long gone, and all he wanted to do was sleep. But there was work to be done. He folded his five MSGs into the Fleet Marine unit as both landing craft were emptied and tied up to the SS *Pioneer Contender.* The American civilians were boarded first, and then entire families of exhausted refugees were winched up to the deck on giant shrimp nets.

McNamara meanwhile went searching for a radio to contact the Seventh Fleet. He found one in the captain's quarters, and after stating his position and situation, he returned to the deck and spotted a stretcher in the outdoor well of the freighter. He was about to collapse into it when he was summoned to the captain's wheelhouse. He emerged twenty minutes later with a can of Miller High Life in his hand and a grim look on his face. Picking through the bodies splayed about the deck, he found Staff Sergeant Hasty dousing himself with cold water from a borrowed canteen. The consul nodded toward the two landing craft tied up to the merchant ship.

"My mistake never teaching you how to drive an LCM," he said.

Hasty's face betrayed not so much disbelief as confusion. McNamara handed him the can of beer. "The Navy may need those landing craft for use off the Vung Tau beaches. I'm looking for volunteers."

"Hear that?"

Master Sergeant Juan Valdez glanced from Major Kean to the sky and then to his watch. It was 2:15 A.M., and two Marine CH-46s were vectoring over the embassy. Kean was already crouched on the helipad when the first Sea Knight descended. He ran to the cockpit and the pilot leaned out his window and shouted.

"Nineteen more flights behind me, sir. That's it."

The major took a mental head count. There were at least another 850 evacuees scattered around the compound, not counting the 200 or so Marines—the fleet contingent and his own MSGs—as well as a few remaining American civilians and other service members. With the DAO evacuated and Colonel Gray having joined General Carey aboard the USS *Blue Ridge*, Kean was now the United States' lead—and, it was increasingly likely, last—ground force commander in Vietnam. And he had a problem. More than 1,000 people did not divide into twenty helicopters. He knew there was no use arguing with the helo pilot. He would do the best he could.

After the two Sea Knights were loaded with refugees and sent off, Kean found one of Martin's aides. "What's this about only eighteen more choppers?"

"Ambassador's been on with Washington," the aide said. "They think we were dicking around with them, letting all kinds of people inside and promising everyone we'll get them out. Somebody wanted a concrete number."

"Why twenty?"

The aide shrugged, and added, "Ambassador wants all the remaining evacuees pulled into the parking lot LZ." The MSGs and Fleet Marines, he continued, were to form a perimeter around the landing zone below, with a minimal presence on the gates.

"He thinks pulling everyone into the parking lot might stop them from coming over the walls."

Fat chance, thought Jim Kean. He cocked an ear and looked to the sky. Two more helicopters were coming in.

At 3:30 A.M., General Carey received a flash message from the White House. President Ford had grown tired of his polite requests being ignored, and his orders were succinct. He had honored the ambassador's entreaty for twenty more refugee flights, and now he wanted Martin out. Immediately. Moreover, no more Vietnamese were to be evacuated. Carey was surprised by the latter directive, but had anticipated the former. Before the call from Washington had come in, he had pulled aside one of his best flyers and informed him that on his next sortie into Saigon, he was to take out the ambassador. Thus even as Carey discussed the presidential directive with Admiral Whitmire in the war room of the USS *Blue Ridge,* Captain Gerry Berry, piloting the CH-46 Lady Ace 09, was swooping his Bird onto the embassy's rooftop helipad.

Berry and his wingman, Captain Claus Schagut, had flown thirty-two round trips into Saigon and back in the fifteen hours since they'd lifted off from the deck of the USS *Dubuque.* They had long since discovered why the *Dubuque* had broken off from the main body of the fleet—it had been ordered to steam around the southern coast of Vietnam and into the Gulf of Thailand to serve as a refueling depot for the hundreds of South Vietnamese helicopter pilots making their way to American bases in Thailand. Berry and Schagut had thereafter spent the day, night, and now early morning hopscotching below the heavy cloud cover between the DAO, the embassy, and from one landing deck to another through rain squalls and small arms fire.

They had set down on the USS *Midway,* the USS *Hancock,* the USS *Duluth,* and the USS *Okinawa,* remaining only long enough to load and disgorge refugees and refuel—except for once, around 10 P.M., when they had powered off on the deck of a ship for a ten-minute rotor check. Berry was so exhausted that he could not immediately recall the ship's name, but he remembered that someone had passed sandwiches and water in through the window and crew door. Then they were back in the air. Their weariness had become a running joke among the crews.

In the day's confusion, and with their parent command sailing far to the west out of landing range, Berry and Schagut had slipped through the cracks of Admiral Whitmire's across-the-board shutdown, although the other set of helicopters in Berry's squadron had not been so lucky. Around dusk he had been separated from the two wayward Sea Knights, which were ferrying a strategic landing force of Fleet Marines for emergency use. When the emergency force was deemed unnecessary and called back to the fleet, the two choppers landed on a carrier—again, Berry was not certain which one—where a flight commander had examined their logs. He ordered them idle for crew rest, and Berry had not seen them since.

In fact, although Berry was never officially informed of the shutdown while he and Schagut remained in the air, over the past couple of hours it had occurred to him that traffic between Saigon and the fleet had thinned noticeably. First the CH-53s had disappeared from the sky. Then the other CH-46s. Then their Cobra gunship support. Finally, all radio chatter had ceased. He also had no idea that back in Honolulu, General Wilson was in the process of announcing to reporters anxious for news of the evacuation that "Marine pilots don't get tired." In any case, it did not bother Berry so much that they were still flying; what vexed him was that others were not.

Since before midnight, he and Schagut had been in and out of the embassy so often that they were by now familiar with the faces of Kean and the various MSGs acting as air traffic controllers on the roof. And each time they'd hovered over the landing zone, they noticed that the throngs on the ground surrounding the compound had appeared to have grown exponentially. It struck Berry that the embassy had become a bottomless pit, and he realized early on that there was no way all of those people were getting out. The idea of their fate, and the stain on America's honor, had at first enraged him. That emotion had soon enough given over to a sort of depression. He remembered the hundreds of combat and rescue sorties he'd flown so many years earlier in defense of a country, an ally, now disintegrating. This was, he thought, the beginning of the end—the end of an era as well as a long day. *Operation Snatch,* his crew had taken to calling the ambassador's retrieval. They were as tired as he was.

Now, as his tires touched down on the rooftop helipad, he allowed himself an audible sigh of relief. He was greeted by the same skinny MSG sergeant, Terry Bennington, whom he had met on his last descent. This time, however, as Bennington approached his chopper's rear ramp, Berry ordered his crew chief to keep it closed. Bennington stood perplexed for a moment before knocking on the glass. The crew chief pointed toward the cockpit, and Bennington ran to the front of the Bird.

"Orders, direct from General Carey," Berry hollered to him above the rotors. "Ambassador must leave. No one else loads."

Bennington nodded, backed away from the helicopter, and on his handheld Motorola raised the head of Martin's PSU team, Staff Sergeant Clemon Segura. He spoke for a moment, and as he walked back toward the cockpit, Berry could read the look on his face.

"The ambassador says, 'No.' He's not going."

The pilot hesitated. Who was a Marine captain to argue with a U.S. ambassador? Bennington saw Berry say something into his intercom, and a second later the ramp dropped. Thirty-odd Vietnamese and a few American civilians were assisted up the clamshell before Bennington waved the Bird off. *That was strange,* the MSG thought.

Forty minutes later, as Lady Ace 09 sat silently on the flight deck of the USS *Blue Ridge* without the ambassador, its rotor blades sagging from their own weight, General Carey approached the cockpit and personally ordered Berry back to the embassy to retrieve Martin. The rain lashed into Berry's face through the open cockpit window as the general delivered the orders in the same calm, if determined, voice with which he had spoken to Admiral Whitmire. Berry's legs, arms, and shoulders ached, and for a moment he feared that the vapors from the aircraft fuel pumping through the hose at the base of his Bird would make him nauseous. *And what if Martin again refuses?*

He knew better than to ask the question aloud. He was a Marine, expected to employ a variation, any variation, of the Corps' overriding concept of freedom within discipline. He would just have to figure out a way on his own. He glanced from his copilot to his crew as Lady Ace 09 lurched from the deck of the amphibious command ship. The fuselage vibrated and the roar of the rotors increased so that the only voices that could be heard came from their headset radios.

Forty minutes later, Berry again touched down on the embassy roof, Schagut hovering above. This time Bennington walked straight to the cockpit window. Berry grabbed a grease pencil from his pocket and quickly began to write on the frayed and creased laminated card on the clipboard strapped to his leg. When Bennington peered inside, the pilot pointed to the grease-penciled note. It read, "Ambassador Will Depart With Me. Now." Next he extracted the piece of paper and mouthed, "Direct from President Ford."

Bennington raised Jim Kean on his walkie-talkie and relayed the message. Kean reached the roof and, anticipating Martin's reaction, advised Berry that he needed confirmation. Doubting that his grease pencil and scrap paper gambit would work on the major, Berry asked his crew chief to hand Kean a headset. General Carey was on the other end. The general told Kean that the order to evacuate the ambassador had come directly from the president, adding that Kean was to pull back all his men from the compound and into the embassy building. "All remaining lifts," Carey added, "will be limited to U.S. and amphibious personnel."

There was no doubt in Kean's mind what this meant. He chose his next words carefully. Just as Berry was loath to overrule an ambassador, a Marine major questioning a Marine brigadier general, however respectfully, was still dicey business. He also suspected that their conversation was being broadcast in the war room of the USS *Blue Ridge* for Admiral Whitmire and his staff to hear. He himself had already disobeyed an ambassadorial order when he'd refused to pull the Marines back from the compound's perimeter.

"General, my Marines are on the wall, and then there's the front door of the embassy," he began. "Between my Marines and that front door are some four hundred refugees still awaiting evacuation. I want you to understand clearly that when I pull my Marines back to the embassy, those people will be left behind."

There was a moment of silence before Carey's voice crackled over the air. "And I want you, Major, to understand that the president of the United States directs."

"Yes, sir," Kean said.

With that, Kean ran down the three flights of stairs to the ambassador's office. Martin's door was closed. He had been sequestered with his top aides for the past thirty minutes, sitting at his desk beneath the framed, autographed photos of Franklin Delano Roosevelt and Richard Nixon. Kean knocked and entered without waiting for a response. He explained the situation on the roof. He was not sure what to expect. It was common knowledge that Martin had given due consideration to staying past the end, to slipping into the French Embassy in the hope of initiating new talks with the North once General Dung captured Saigon.

But Carey's command still rang in his ears. It was now his job to follow orders and remove Martin from the premises. One way or another. He was horrified at the prospect of having to drag the old man to the roof kicking and screaming. But he would if it proved necessary. Once Frequent Wind was put into effect, the evacuation of Saigon had fallen under military provenance. Ambassador Martin remained the U.S. president's personal representative to South Vietnam. But the Marine Corps, in the person of Jim Kean, was now in charge.

As Kean waited for an answer, PSU Staff Sergeant Segura joined the group, which included Wolfgang Lehmann and Ken Moorefield. The thirty-one-year-old Moorefield, fiercely loyal to the embattled ambassador, had in some ways replaced the son that Graham and Dorothy Martin had lost several years before in an automobile accident. He was a West Point graduate who had been seriously wounded in the delta region a decade earlier and now, as a civilian, held the position of special assistant to the ambassador. Lehmann asked Kean to leave the room. The major backed out hesitantly and said, "I'll be right outside, Ambassador. Again, your helicopter is waiting."

"We'll just need a minute," Lehmann said, and closed the door behind him.

It was clear to Moorefield, Lehmann, and Segura that Martin had nothing left to give. Moorefield, fighting his own exhaustion after spending the past twenty-four hours collecting Vietnamese civilians, uttered five words: "Sir, it's time to go."

Martin's reply was barely audible. "Looks like this is it."

And with that, Segura stepped forward and helped Martin out of his chair.

Martin stepped into the corridor outside his office a moment later carrying his briefcase, a vinyl suit bag, and a small gym bag. The gym bag was open, and Kean noticed an old copy of *Stars and Stripes* folded neatly atop his personal gear.

Martin, Lehmann, Moorefield, and Segura met Tom Polgar near the elevator. While they waited, two more State Department aides joined the group. Together they ascended to the sixth floor and walked onto the roof. As a dazed, hunched Martin shuffled toward the helicopter, one of his bodyguards handed him the folded embassy colors. As promised, Kean had lowered the flag from the staff after dark. Kean was gone by the time Martin received the flag; he was already taking the stairs back down to the parking lot. The ambassador stepped into the awaiting Sea Knight.

Gerry Berry powered up the chopper and lifted off from the embassy roof. He slid his radio handset from its cradle and glanced over his shoulder to make sure the ambassador was properly strapped in amid the sweating, jostling bodies. A sudden thought froze him: at least he hoped that sickly old man *was* the ambassador; he had never seen so much as a photograph of the man. For the first time since he'd taken the throttle on the deck of the USS *Dubuque* nearly seventeen hours earlier, his pulse raced like a trip hammer: What if his ruse had been trumped? He glanced down at the piece of scrap paper jammed into his knee pad, crumpled it into a ball, and wiped clean the grease-penciled "presidential order" with the back of the same sweaty hand that held the handset. Then he raised the radio transmitter close to his mouth.

"Tiger! Tiger! Tiger!" A click of tension was audible in Berry's voice. His throat was dry. "The Tiger is out of his cage."

It was 4:58 A.M., April 30, 1975. With that transmission, nearly twenty-five years of American diplomatic presence in Indochina ended unceremoniously. As Lady Ace 09 gained altitude, Berry could make out the North Vietnamese units moving in on a pitch-dark Saigon from every direction, closing the circle. Inside the dark bubble, the two pilots stole quick glances at each other in between monitoring the altimeter and the pitch-and-roll indicator, their faces glowing green and red from the lights on the instrument panel. Outside, the roads to the four horizons were lit by the headlights of tanks and military vehicles. Berry also noticed that the rain had stopped, and high, wispy clouds scudded between the stars. When he reached the Saigon River, tracer rounds flew past his cockpit window, while farther to the north, expanding black circles, like gloating puddles of oil, limned the dun-colored storm clouds. *Antiaircraft?* His intercom buzzed, and his crew chief, who must have also noticed the bursts, told him that the flare pistol issued to all helo crews to divert heat-seeking missiles was jammed.

"Lose it," Berry said. "Out the window." *As if that little tinsel shooter will stop a SAM.* "I don't want that thing blowing up inside here."

Now, below them, they were nearly over a procession of NVA vehicles, and the dirt and grit thrown up by their tires rose in neat rows of eddies, as if swirling brown pinwheels were heralding the Communist arrival. Berry marveled at the rock-steady methodology of the enemy, at the placid pace of their triumph. It was as if they were savoring their entrance into the city. And why should they not? Their war was over; they had won. Saigon's luminous baroque architecture would soon darken with enemy tanks and artillery, followed by thousands of ground troops. Like an eclipse of the sun, he thought.

As the aircraft cleared the coast, Berry looked over his shoulder one last time at the forlorn ambassador. His windblown shock of white hair resembled a sheaf of sun-baked hay as he stared out the portside gunner's window. It seemed to Berry as if he could read the old man's mind. He had overseen the evacuation of every American civilian who wanted to get out of Saigon at the cost of two Marine security guard lives. He had even taken out more Vietnamese than anyone thought possible. He had nothing to apologize for. Except . . .

We could have taken out those last four hundred, Martin told himself. *We could have gotten out more.*

Berry could watch no longer. He turned back and saw the great body of stone-gray water not far ahead.

Barely thirty minutes elapsed between Lady Ace 09's rooftop ascent and the buzz of the field telephone in General Dung's bunker. The caller was one of Dung's spies in the Minh administration, informing him that Martin had fled. Like his radio operators monitoring the American wavelengths, the general had suspected from his first reading of the hastily transcribed helicopter transmission just who in fact the mysterious "Tiger" was.

Good riddance to the "medicine man," Dung thought. The U.S. ambassador had kept false vigil next to a gravely ill child, a South Vietnamese government that until today had continued to nurture the illusion that the Americans were a reliable and loyal master. First Thieu, the vile politician, bloody criminal, and miserable traitor, and now Martin, his vice-regal mandarin, had beaten their pitiful retreats. To the Communist general, Martin's shameful, middle-of-the-night departure was an appropriate conclusion to thirty years of U.S. imperialism in Vietnam.

He allowed himself a moment to ponder, and enjoy, the astounding occasion. For the first time in history, the U.S. military machine had been vanquished, and was now vanished. He was proud of the part he had played. But his work, he knew, was not finished. His forces were poised on the edges of Saigon, ready for a final attack that represented, in his words, "a divine hammer held aloft."

A colonel rushed into the room with another intercepted transmission and interrupted his reverie. U.S. Marines, he said, were still on the ground at the American embassy.

The radio squawked in the cockpit of Lady Ace 09. It was the USS *Blue Ridge*'s air traffic controller. Other ships were closer, but Berry was ordered to make for the fleet command-and-control ship. The South China Sea was churned by the monsoon, but the landing on the USS *Blue Ridge* was smooth. Berry had barely set his helicopter down when someone threw on all of the ship's deck lights. He was momentarily blinded. When he regained his vision, he spotted General Carey and Admiral Whitmire racing toward his Sea Knight. His stomach tightened in anticipation. What if he had indeed evacuated the wrong man?

The clamshell was lowered, and Berry's anxiety rose as he watched the general and the admiral standing at the stern of his chopper wearing confused—*confounded?*—expressions on their faces. Then he saw the old man exiting through the gunner's door, Carey and Whitmire rushing to meet him.

The exhausted pilot was unbuckling his safety belt when, over the intercom, his crew chief's voice broke in.

"We going back in for those Marines?"

Three

Despite his radio conversation with General Carey, Jim Kean had not quite given up on the arrival of more rescue helicopters. He had been assembling a stick of Vietnamese near the parking lot when the ambassador evacuated, but after Berry's CH-46 lifted off he waited in vain for another. When after twenty minutes none arrived, he told the Vietnamese not to move and walked toward the embassy's front door, where he spotted Mike Sullivan hunched beside a low wall.

"Ambassador?"

Sullivan lit a cigarette. "Gone, sir. Took the flag with him."

Kean squatted next to the sergeant, who offered him a smoke. Kean shook his head, found his last Cuban cigar in his pocket, and lit it.

"Took Marvin Garrett with him too," Sullivan said. "Heard he was shitfaced. Had to carry him on."

The two exchanged weary smiles. As they sat silently amid the blue tobacco haze, Kean saw one of the U.S. Army officers, Colonel John Madison, walking toward them.

"No more CH-53s," Kean said. The big Sea Stallions were finished with their embassy runs. His voice was hoarse from fatigue and grit. "Just Americans now. Roof."

Madison stopped in his tracks. He waved toward the 400 or so Vietnamese still inside the compound. "We made a commitment. Six more Birds is all. This is doable."

Kean was unmoved and too spent for niceties. He stubbed out the cigar, shoved the half-smoked nub in his pocket, and shrugged.

"I'll refuse to leave without them," Madison said. "I'm going to see the ambassador."

"Then you'll need a chopper, sir," Kean said, making it clear that more talk was futile. He spotted Juan Valdez exiting the embassy's front door.

"Time to button up, Top," he said. "Everybody off the walls. Picket lines. Three rings."

Valdez stared hard at Kean. He could guess immediately why the Army colonel was so pissed off. He turned to take in the miserable Vietnamese still staged near the swimming pool. Some were sitting on their luggage, others standing obediently in their prearranged sticks. He wondered if the drunken Koreans were among them. He sensed that the departure of the last few helicopters from the roof had raised some inchoate fear among the crowds on the streets, the ARVN deserters in particular, and the MSGs and the Fleet Marines were once again leaning their shoulders into the wrought-iron bars. Oddly, the refugees inside the compound remained as complacent as a flock of sheep.

"Nobody else?" Valdez finally said. It was more of a plea than a question.

"Round eyes only," Kean said. Two Seabees trotted out of the embassy to inform the major that they had completed the dismantling of the Bubble Room. Everything left was set to blow. Valdez eyed the Navy men. The largest looked as if he had just shaved with a blowtorch.

"Men with the buses?" Kean said.

Valdez motioned toward the PSU staff sergeants, Dwight McDonald and Steve Johnson. He had just posted them at the main gate. A few hours earlier, just after midnight, the two had been among several Marines who had volunteered to accompany vehicles leaving the embassy to make a final sweep of the downtown pickup points in search of American stragglers. The effort had fallen into chaos almost immediately. The two buses had started out along the designated "trails" but soon turned to back roads to avoid the furious congestion caused by hundreds of thousands of people jamming the streets, including thousands of ARVNs. When the vehicles did manage to arrive at a designated site, it was either empty or clogged with frantic locals fighting and trampling each other to board. They saw no Americans and took on as many Vietnamese as possible. At the Newport Pier on the Saigon River, the Vietnamese bus drivers had deserted, and Fleet Marines who did not know the city had taken over behind the wheel.

McDonald, riding shotgun, was attempting to lead the small convoy through poorly lit alleys, Johnson trailing in an open Jeep, when they were stopped at a police checkpoint. Johnson was suddenly jolted by M-16 rifle fire. An ARVN soldier had appeared from nowhere and was standing beside him, emptying a magazine into the air. At least Johnson presumed it was a South Vietnamese soldier. Truth be told, he was not certain tonight who might be ARVN, who might be NVA, and who might be Vietcong. His heart pumped adrenaline so fast he did not immediately feel his right leg burning. He jumped up in the Jeep and brushed the hot rifle casings from his thigh as McDonald ran up to see what was happening. Nearing the embassy, the buses had made it through the vehicle gate, but the Jeep was surrounded. The two had abandoned it and run a gantlet through the crowd, picking up Phil Babel's tai kwon do instructor and his family along the way. Now Johnson was leaning into the main gate at the embassy compound with a good portion of his right leg exposed, his pants leg having been burned off.

"Last one got in five minutes ago, sir," Valdez said. "All PSUs and MSGs accounted for."

"Good. I'll send Sullivan to the back. Tell him to secure the rear door and watch for a star cluster."

Valdez took one last look at the forlorn 400 before he and Kean sprinted off in opposite directions, the major weaving in and among the MSG squad leaders and the young Fleet Marine lieutenants, the master sergeant loping toward the first of the four machine-gun nests about to be abandoned.

"On my signal we will withdraw calmly in a semicircle toward the embassy front door," Kean told each squad leader. "No running, no shouting."

Moments later, someone fired a flare gun that lifted a five-point radius into the night sky. The star cluster. Sullivan led the Fleet Marines to the front of the embassy where they mixed with the MSGs. They formed up, as casually as possible, in three concentric half-moons of about fifteen men each. These were fronted by a six-man picket line of Valdez, Schlager,

Schuller, Norman, Bennington, and Bauer. The 400 or so Vietnamese compacted into sticks stretching from the parking lot to the swimming pool area began to stir as the entire mass of Marines edged slowly backward toward the Chancery's three-inch-thick mahogany double doors.

For one haunting moment, it seemed as if events were transpiring in slow motion. A dead calm fell over the clamor at the embassy gates. The Vietnamese stared blankly at the American troops as the innermost perimeter, its flanks collapsing in on itself, backed into the lobby. Perhaps half of the Marines in the second perimeter had made it inside before a giant roar drowned out even the sounds of artillery falling on the city's outskirts.

"Here they come!" someone shouted, and the front gates gave way like matchsticks. People poured into the compound from Thong Nhut Boulevard and Mac Dinh Nhut Street. Rifle reports rang out. On orders from Kean, the Marines did not return fire, instead crouching and swinging the butts of their M-16s at the encroaching mass.

"That Charlie shooting at us?" said Bauer.

Bennington was bent over next to him. "Them or pissed-off ARVN."

"Take Charlie," said Bauer just as a wiry Vietnamese man squeezed past him and made a run for the elevator. Bauer tackled him from behind, lifted him with one hand, and tossed him back through the door.

The crowd was close to overwhelming the Americans when the huge Seabee chief petty officer lofted one of the three eight-foot steel beams used to bar the Chancery's mahogany double doors. He hefted the pipe, five inches in diameter, to his shoulders like a yoked oxen and dashed out into the courtyard in front of the Marines. He began spinning. The foyer echoed with screams and the dull thuds of steel smashing flesh.

Kean was at the door pulling men inside when one of the Fleet Marine lieutenants hollered, "Tear gas, Major?"

Kean barely looked at him. The Marines had no gas masks. "No, El-Tee. Just get your men in." His voice was so calm he could have been ordering chow.

Bennington and Schlager grabbed Bauer by the back of his collar and yanked him under the Seabee's swinging steel bar. He landed on his butt on the lobby's marble floor. And then it was done. The Seabee was the last man in. The Marines slammed shut the double doors, and the Navy man bolted it with his beam. Inside the lobby, Kean pressed a button to electronically lower a chain-link hand grenade screen that dropped from the ceiling. It fell halfway to the floor and stopped, its gears grinding and its motor stalled.

The hell with this. He hollered, "Everybody upstairs."

Valdez led a squad of MSGs over to the two elevators, rode them to the sixth floor, locked their power off, and threw the keys down the shafts. As the main body started for the stairwell, Sullivan stopped to pick up his PRC-25 radio—the cumbersome, twenty-five-pound "Prick 25" he'd been toting on his back since nightfall. As he lifted it onto his shoulders, he was startled to see four American civilians, three men and a woman, huddled on a bench in a far corner. He thought all of the State Department employees were long gone.

"Time to go, folks."

"We're staying," one of the men said.

The staff sergeant stared at him, puzzled. "You realize the next people through this door are likely either pissed-off ARVN or NVA."

"We're press," the woman said. "The story here is just beginning."

"Have it your way. Good-bye and good luck."

Sullivan took a few steps toward the last of the MSGs sweeping up the stairwell and paused. Should he order the reporters to come with him? He didn't think they had any idea of the gravity of their situation. He also didn't think he had the authority. He had his own men to watch over. He took off at a trot.

There were accordion grill gates on the second and fourth landings. The MSGs closed and padlocked them, but not before another small squad led by Dave Norman broke off for the fourth-floor Bubble Room to set the timers on the thermite grenades.

John Ghilain was one of the last MSGs to make it to the roof. On Sullivan's orders, he had detoured to the makeshift office off the lobby to pick up a sea bag containing the detachment's passports and record books. He found them where Sullivan said he would, threw the bag over his shoulder, and headed up the stairs while Marines waited to lock the grill gates behind him. When he reached the small stairwell landing leading from the incinerator room to the roof, he was stopped by an Army colonel he did not recognize.

"No personal effects," the colonel said.

"Colonel, my assistant NCOIC ordered me to bring this. It's our medical and dental records, pay records and vouchers. Our passports and Marine ID cards."

"No personal effects."

Ghilain dropped the bag. *Fuckin' Army. More deadwood than a fire hazard.*

With the outside perimeter abandoned, it was now a race against time—and more concretely, a race against whoever would be next to storm up the embassy stairs. There was no lock on the steel door that led from the stairwell, past the still-glowing incinerators, and onto the roof. Valdez, Sullivan, and Steve Bauer tipped over a stack of heavy wall lockers near the furnaces, dragged them out through the door, and slammed it shut behind them. They piled the lockers in front of the entrance and buttressed the blockade with two cylindrical fire extinguishers on wheels, each as big as a large man. As they wedged the fire extinguishers against the entrance Kean found the young Lieutenant Thompson-Powers amid the Fleet Marines.

"Lieutenant, get your men into sticks," he said. "Twenty each. Packs off. Leave them. Keep your weapons. Your men off first."

He had already done the math. After Martin's departure, the last of the State Department employees and most of the Fleet Marines had been lifted out while he'd been working the parking lot. There were about sixty Marines and a few scattered men from other services in various states of dishevelment scattered about the rooftop. Kean studied his weary MSGs. He was reminded of a photo he once saw of Pancho Villa's raiders. The incoming helos were reporting numerous firefights throughout the city, as well as intense small arms fire directed at the aircraft from a copse of trees not far outside the embassy wall on the northeast corner of the compound. Who was shooting at the Americans, no one knew, which only set nerves more on edge. *If any more of my men wind up leaving here in a body bag,*

Kean vowed, *someone back in the States will pay.* He looked to the young lieutenant.

"I figure it'll take three, maybe four runs at most," he said.

Steve Schuller noticed a pile of discarded Fleet Marine gear stacked at the foot of the outdoor staircase leading to the helipad. He moved toward it in a crouch and began picking through it in hopes of finding a cleaner shirt. His own was bloody and sticky. He forgot himself for a moment and stood straight up. Small arms fire ricocheted off a cornice a few feet from his head.

"Jesus Christ, stay down," Terry Bennington yelled.

But Schuller was now curious. He crawled several paces and lifted his head above the parapet. Thong Nhut Boulevard resembled a bumper car track. Furious men and boys, many of them drunk, had jump-started the abandoned American vehicles and crashed them into each other up and down its three long blocks. Directly beneath him, the two-ton mission warden fire truck had been driven through the embassy's mahogany doors, smashing them off their hinges. Vietnamese were pouring through the gap. This, however, was not what fascinated, and frightened, Schuller most.

"Bennington, check this out."

The sergeant edged over; Schuller pointed. All about the street, small knots of armed ARVN soldiers were doffing their uniforms. Some remained in their skivvies, while others shanghaied civilians and forced them to strip at gunpoint and hand over their clothes. The ARVNs weren't stupid. Reports had been trickling into Saigon for some time of the Cambodian killing fields run by Pol Pot and his Khmer Rouge. Royal Cambodian Army soldiers had been the first to be executed. Why should the North Vietnamese act any different?

"Believe that?" Schuller said.

But Bennington was focused on the area near the swimming pool, where the outdoor lights still blazed. Schuller followed his gaze. The pool itself was a discolored swamp of luggage, confiscated weapons, and human excrement. Incredibly, some people were drinking the water. More incongruous were the Vietnamese refugees surrounding it, the last of the "endangered list" allowed into the compound. They remained queued up in their squared sticks, awaiting a rescue that would never arrive. Even the local mission wardens, the firemen in the bright yellow coats who had been promised freedom in return for staying to the end in case there was a chopper crash, remained at their posts. Still believing the promise. Convinced that the United States of America would not abandon them.

Not far away, on the roof of the mission warden outpost, a few men in their distinctive jackets stared forlornly up to the embassy roof. Schuller and Bennington could see the ladder used to save their families lying across the roof of the adjacent generator building.

"Shit," Schuller said.

"Yeah," Bennington said.

Top Valdez and Steve Bauer leaned against the fire extinguishers and wiped sweat from their faces.

"You got this, now," the NCOIC said, and dug into his pack. He extracted three gas grenades. Unlike standard Marine-issue explosive or concussive grenades, these contained settings that allowed them to be either tossed or sprayed like mace once their pins were pulled.

"I want you to walk back and forth in front of this door," Valdez said. "Like standing official sentry. Rifle at your chest. They'll be able to see you from that little window. Gun might make 'em think twice. Maybe buy us some time."

Valdez handed Bauer the gas grenades. "Use them if you have to."

The top sergeant left Bauer alone and joined Major Kean at the edge of the rooftop. The Saigon River was at low tide, and the putrid stink of rotting vegetation commixing with the spires of smoke from the looted, burning buildings across the city lent the air the look, smell, and feel of Hell's kitchen. Kean leaned over the parapet and elbowed Valdez. Below them, a few stalwart young men were attempting to scale the rocket screen. One even made it as far as the second story before falling. "Jesus, like spiders," Valdez said.

Four

"So where are they?" Mike Sullivan's eyes darted from the empty night sky to the stick of Fleet Marines ringing the helipad.

"Refueling." Major Kean was pacing the roof. He glanced at his watch: 0510. The sun would be showing itself soon. "They're coming. They're coming."

Disparate visions of the long war danced through Kean's mind. Fire Support Base Ryder. Sandy Kempner blown to bits by a mine. The firefight on the causeway. Shot in the butt, of all places. But he no longer felt like a fighting Marine. He was a fireman now, an exhausted fireman. The blaze was out, and he and his men were dead tired. Yet for all he knew, it could flame up again at any moment. Then it would become a massacre. He eyed the dense grove of cinnamon trees where, a day earlier, Mike Sullivan had spotted the VC, setting up mortars. *Jesus.* He didn't know much about the art form, but if he were not living this nightmare, he could imagine it as the outline for an opera. He glanced once more at the Vietnamese by the swimming pool. He was ashamed.

He remembered a letter he'd written to Rosanne when he'd first arrived in-country, nine years earlier. He knew then, even as a green lieutenant humping the bush, that America's aims in Vietnam were somehow *off,* and he'd told his wife so. The war was nothing like he'd expected. He'd deployed convinced he was helping to win over hearts and minds, so that the South Vietnamese could determine their own destiny. He'd soon enough discovered the folly of that.

There was an incident in particular that he'd ached to share with

231

Rosanne. It stood, he felt, as a metaphor for the U.S. involvement in Southeast Asia. His platoon had been out on patrol when they'd come across an old mama-san villager with a festering, gangrenous thumb. She had treated it by smearing it with cow manure and encasing it in a banana leaf. His platoon's corpsman washed and anesthetized the wound, cut away much of the dead skin, and wrapped it in a gauze bandage. Three days later Kean and his men were backtracking through the same village when the woman waved them over to her hut. She smiled, offered them coffee beans, showed them her thumb—smeared with cow manure and encased in a banana leaf.

"All they want is to live in peace and for us and the North Vietnamese and the French and the politicians in Saigon to all go away," he wrote. "We're just mucking up their rice paddies and pissing off their water buffalos."

Kean's Marines had never lost a fight the entire time he'd been in Vietnam. Now his country had lost the war. He wondered what they'd learn back home from this debacle. Would they in fact learn anything at all? Stay the hell out of some country's civil war next time. Maybe.

Out of the corner of his eye, he saw the Fleet Marine platoon leader pacing the edge of the helipad. He was reminded of his sons. He knew at that moment that he would count himself a failure as a father if they grew up wanting to fight in wars. He prayed he was strong enough to teach them another way. To be a great carpenter. To write a great novel. Anything but pick up a gun.

General Carey paced the deck of the USS *Blue Ridge* and read the cable in disbelief. Somewhere along the line—no one knew where, or who would confess to it, at any rate—someone had misinterpreted Captain Berry's coded transmission, "The Tiger is out of his cage." It was inferred that Ambassador Martin's arrival on the *Blue Ridge* meant that all Americans had been evacuated from Saigon. The airlift was now considered complete. The helicopters had been ordered grounded.

Frantic, Carey again telephoned Lieutenant General Wilson in Honolulu. Wilson was no less angry and frustrated than he had been at the earlier flight stoppage and once again in a position to do something about it. "General, I want you to inform the entire chain of command there of one important fact," Wilson told Carey. "I will personally court-martial anyone, regardless of service or rank, who halts any flights while Marines remain unaccounted for. Are you clear on that?"

Carey said he was.

It did not take long for hundreds of angry South Vietnamese to flood up the embassy stairwell, smashing the chain link barriers as they came. Steve Bauer could hear the gates crash, one by one, until the mob was directly outside the barricaded steel door leading to the roof.

Bauer glimpsed their faces, some pleading, some furious, before dozens of pounding fists cracked and finally smashed the thick, eight-by-eleven-inch window set high in the door. Shards of glass clung to its wire mesh. The hands and arms reaching through, some holding papers testifying to their employment at American agencies, were soon torn and bloody. Still, they did not stop. Slender brown fingers grasped for the outside door handle. Bauer sprayed a burst from one of the CS grenades, sending a shower of chlorobenzyllidenemalononitrile gas through the window. He heard coughing, screaming, gagging. But it felled only the first wave. More arms and hands followed. More flesh torn. He sprayed again. Some were so panicked that the mace was not even affecting them.

He stepped back at this and considered the men—and they were mostly men—he was gassing. He did not recognize their contorted faces as they pressed against the broken glass yelling unintelligible words, and he certainly did not know their names. But he knew there had to be people on the other side of that door with whom he had worked, perhaps even policemen and mission wardens in whom he had entrusted his life. He understood that it was too late to begin checking papers again, too late to change the course of this debacle. That door was now a floodgate, and if he opened it, no one, American or Vietnamese, would leave this roof alive. At the same time he wanted to reach out, back through that shattered window, to soothe them, to somehow let them know that this was not his fault, that important people, more powerful than a lowly Marine corporal, had set this tragedy in motion. It was the wrong thing to do. The wrong position for the United States of America to put him in.

He sprayed again. He had his orders, noxious as they were.

In the distance, he heard the beating rotors of a helicopter approaching. The poor souls in the stairwell heard it too. There was a brief pause in the pandemonium, and then the door's hinges creaked and began to buckle. The final shard of glass broke from the corner of the wire mesh as people on the other side screamed and begged. Bauer retrieved another CS canister from his camouflage web netting and pulled the pin.

"Everybody down. Flat on your stomachs."

Jim Kean crouched on the helipad, his colored paddles replaced by two large, glowing flashlights. A dozen Fleet Marines spread about the edges of the landing zone with the luminescent "H," with another dozen crouched behind them in a line snaking up the outside staircase.

Kean gestured toward their lieutenant. "Have all your men lose their helmets and flak gear. Less weight, more people. We'll cram as many as we can into each load."

The officer nodded, swiveled, and addressed his Marines. They continued to crouch as they stripped down.

Juan Valdez watched the scene with melancholy. He was transported back in time, back ten years, to the jungles surrounding Da Nang. Hollow cries for a medic. A medical chopper braving withering fire to land to evacuate the wounded. Charlie hiding in the tall trees shooting down at his AMTRACs. He scanned the windows of the British Embassy across the street for snipers. They were all dark.

They all heard the helicopters before they saw them—the *blat-blat-blat* of the rotors echoing off the exposed banks of the river at low tide. Kean and Steve Schuller raised their flashlights. Schuller dismissed a fleeting thought of the air traffic controller's course he had deliberately sabotaged. A lifetime ago.

Kean noticed that two or three of his exhausted MSGs had fallen asleep on the helipad and were only now stirring as the first Bird banked in for a landing. It was only twenty feet above the landing zone when one of them, one of the young kids, abruptly rose to his feet. Kean was so tired he'd forgotten the Marine's name. Before he could holler, the MSG was lifted off the pad by the upwash and dropped back to the roof twelve feet below. The major watched him execute a perfect parachute roll and stand up with a dazed and embarrassed look.

As the first Sea Knight's rear wheels bounced onto the helipad, the sky was the cool clear blue of watery ink, somewhere between night and dawn. A moment later, a small sliver of sun on the eastern horizon burst abruptly into a blooming red dahlia, blossoms ablaze in a cloudless sky. The helo's engine geared down, and Captain Claus Schagut, Gerry Berry's wingman, leaned out from the cockpit window and flashed a grand smile. Though his face betrayed no anxiety, Schagut was twirling his arm in a circular motion, exhorting the Marines to *move it, move it, move it!* Valdez noticed that the fuselage of Schagut's aircraft was riddled with bullet holes.

Berry's Lady Ace 09 hovered above, waiting to take his place. For a brief moment, as Berry gazed toward the southeast, he was certain that the sun had risen pocked with black dots, like a swarm of angry bees. It wasn't long before he realized that those "bees" darkening the skies above the South China Sea were hundreds of South Vietnamese helicopters issuing from the coast and the Mekong Delta and making for the fleet.

Meanwhile, Fleet Marines, Seabees, the Army officers, and an Air Force colonel who had accompanied them over from the DAO were among those who filed up the tailgate into Schagut's aircraft. The chopper was up and gone, out over the Saigon River, within ten minutes. Kean stood on the helipad waiving the last of the Fleet Marines up the staircase. This load was mixed with MSGs, including Doug Potratz, Kevin Maloney, and John Ghilain. As Berry's aircraft swooped down, the bright orange fireballs of NVA artillery far in the distance ringed Saigon's northern suburbs.

Kean took another head count. But he knew he was weary and asked Valdez to double-check his figures. They both came up with too many MSGs remaining.

"Never get us all in," Valdez said.

"Stripped of all gear?"

"I got them on each other's laps in there as is. Any more weight, he won't get air."

Kean looked around. The sky was a breathtaking blue. It was one of the most beautiful Saigon mornings he had ever seen. He was too tired to appreciate it. Exhausted men do not compose lyrical odes to radiant nature.

"Top," he said. "Give me nine guys I can bet my life on."

Gerry Berry gave Jim Kean the thumbs-up when Lady Ace 09 was loaded and ready to lift off. The pilot was checking his control panel when the major walked to the cockpit and tugged his sleeve. Berry pulled the headset away from his left ear and leaned out the window.

"Make sure you get back for us," Kean said. "Don't leave us here."

Five

The sun was beating down hard now, and everyone else was long gone. Juan Valdez, stooped low, walked the perimeter to be certain. The sniping had increased exponentially since dawn; the pinging of small arms concentrated on the helipad. NVA? ARVN Cowboys? North or South, it did not matter. Let them come. For the first time in a long time, Valdez wanted to fight.

He rechecked the magazine of his M-16 and racked the slide of his .45 sidearm. The last of his ammunition. He laughed to himself. He wished, again, that they had more firepower. He scanned the roof. Each MSG toted an M-16 rifle, and a few had .9-millimeter automatic pistols. There was a shotgun or two, and the two M-60s were set up below the landing zone. Against artillery? *A joke,* Valdez thought.

He eyed the other ten remaining Marines. The major. Mike Sullivan. And the handpicked MSGs. He'd tapped each one himself before the last chopper lifted off.

"Staying 'til the end." It wasn't a question.

"Yes, Top."

"Sure, Top."

"At your service, Top."

Steve Schuller, adjusting the crimson rag stuffed into the hole between the flaps of flesh exposing his ribs. Terry Bennington, his papery cheeks more hollow than ever, looking as if they could store nuts on the outside. Steve Bauer, pacing before the incinerator room like one of the queen's own Beefeaters at Buckingham Palace. Bobby Schlager out of Bien Hoa—

good man, showed what he was made of going back for that flag. Might need that kind of sand.

Across the roof Dave Norman and the Black Market King, Duane Gevers, were whispering in one corner. Probably making a bet on how long before Gevers was selling the deed to the Brooklyn Bridge to an NVA colonel. Phil Babel was sitting by himself, apart from the rest. Valdez would have liked to have known what Babel was thinking. He appeared to be taking this the hardest. Hard to say with him. Rumor had it he was leaving a Vietnamese girl behind, or she had gone and left him behind.

Not far from Babel squatted Bobby Frain, turning a spare magazine for his M-16 over and over in his hand. A little over four months ago, at the conclusion of the last Marine Corps Birthday Ball in Saigon, Frain had unpacked his trumpet and closed the evening with the most moving rendition of "Taps" Valdez had ever heard. On the final note he had bowed his head—a movement that had annoyed several of the salty officers present; a Marine trumpeter is always supposed to maintain his position. But to his fellow noncoms it had been an unforgettable moment. *Perhaps,* Valdez thought now, *a precursor.*

Valdez was proud of his kids—each and every one, including the Marines he'd already loaded onto choppers. He had asked them to do the impossible and they had succeeded in a war that had been lost in Washington. For days they'd been bone tired, working around the clock under the most agonizing physical and emotional stress. No one had flinched or griped. Each man had performed every task asked of him in an impossible situation. He wanted to tell somebody; he wanted to brag about his boys. Somebody should know. *Especially if we die up here.*

He thought back to his teenage years in the boxing ring. Boxing, for all its lies, was about the truth. As was war. And he didn't care what anyone at any Paris peace table said; this was still war. Like most squad leaders who had seen their men die, who had witnessed the flag-draped coffins loaded onto the aircraft, Valdez worshipped soldiers as the true salt of the earth—the men who sacrificed themselves in blood so that others could live at home in comfort. To contemplate that these same civilians, these politicians, cared not a whit for his young grunts had set off inside Valdez a kind of numbness. He would care for his flock now. That is all he could do.

He peered over the low wall toward the northwest skyline. Shells, short rounds from Bien Hoa, were still barraging Tan Son Nhut. *The same kind that killed Judge and McMahon. The same kind that could blow us all off this roof right now.*

"What if they lift those rockets toward us?"

Someone had read his mind. It was Schuller, crouching beside him, his face marinated in misery. A red pus was oozing through the bandage, and he was sweating like a wheel of cheese.

Valdez wordlessly calculated the range of the NVA guns. *Would take only a couple of clicks on the sights.* He smiled, and his mustache obscured his upper lip. He hadn't trimmed it in almost a week.

"Be pretty simple," he said. "Then we're dead."

"Hey, you know what?" Steve Bauer had tossed a canister of tear gas through the broken wire mesh window to buy himself a few moments; now he was hunched over and digging through his rucksack. He pulled out two quart bottles wrapped in old *Stars and Stripes*. Whiskey. Johnny Walker Red and Johnny Walker Black. From the fourth-floor liquor cabinet in the Marine House where he'd once tended bar. Where they'd all once laughed and drank and sometimes snuck women in.

"Rescued these soldiers," he said.

Eight men gathered around him, sitting cross-legged in a loose circle. Bauer was reminded of an old western movie, of Indians, about to smoke a peace pipe. He twisted the cap on the bottle of Red, took a swig, and passed it to his right.

Bobby Frain lifted the bottle to his lips. "To the ambassador," he said. No one laughed.

The quart made the full circle and came back empty. The Black next, in the same direction.

"What about Top and the Major?" Frain said.

Everyone turned. Valdez and Kean were huddled in conversation at the far end of the roof, beneath the big satellite dish.

Mike Sullivan said, "Not interested," with an authority no one contested.

The bottle of Black took longer to return to Bauer. They had saved him the last gulp. He drained it.

In Washington, D.C., Henry Kissinger had been assured that Graham Martin had finally departed the embassy, on the last American helicopter to leave Saigon, and was now safe with the Seventh Fleet. The secretary dictated a message to the ambassador to be delivered to the USS *Blue Ridge:* "I am sure you know how deeply I feel about your performance under the most trying circumstances. My heartfelt thanks."

Now Kissinger had one final task: to face a press corps that, he was certain, would go to any length to confirm "that everything that had ever happened [in Vietnam] had been an unforgivable mistake." As he crossed the passageway between the White House and the Executive Office Building, he studied the statement he was about to read, the statement he was certain would be ignored. He would try to tell the newspeople that it was too soon for a postmortem on Vietnam, that the wounds to the country were still too raw. They would not understand. They wanted blood. He would, he told himself, refuse to take their bait.

Moments later, after concluding his plea for a period of introspection, a reporter blurted the only question on anyone's mind: "Mr. Secretary, there are reports that there are still Marines at the embassy in Saigon. Can you confirm that, and why are they still there?"

Kissinger was visibly flummoxed. He had no idea. He could only stare at the upturned faces in the gallery. He turned abruptly and hurried from the podium. He found an aide and demanded a telephone. He needed to get in touch with CINCPAC in Hawaii, or the Seventh Fleet, anyone who could confirm this horrible error. And then he needed to speak to the president.

Jim Kean preferred to think that the NVA wanted nothing to do with starting another war with the United States. As a combat veteran, however, he also knew that the danger lay in the possibility of small troop units coming into contact with each other. He thought of the 9,000 frustrated and pissed-off Marines cramped together in the holds of the Seventh Fleet, armed to the teeth and itching for revenge over the killings of Judge and McMahon. He had seen it in their eyes when young Thompson-Powers's platoon had poured off the helicopters. They were almost twitching for action. A wayward shot now, he thought, was all it would take to light the fuse. He gathered his men in the center of the roof.

"People," he began, "Charlie, Cowboys, God knows who, are going to be throwing potshots up here to gauge our reaction. I want no return fire. No one—unless on my say-so. All weapons on safe. Round in the chamber. Dicks in the dirt."

Not a minute later, a bullet ricocheted off the incinerator room not far from where Steve Schuller was nearly asleep on his feet. He dove into Bobby Schlager's lap.

"I been shot at all fucking night. I'm tired of people fucking shooting at me."

"So who you want to shoot back at?" Schlager was goading him.

"I don't give a fuck. Just, just . . . somebody."

Schlager kicked the toe of his combat boot at the backup ammunition stuffed into Schuller's belt. "Wouldn't last too long. Specially against tanks."

"We could make a run downstairs to the gun room." Duane Gevers had joined the conversation. He was fingering the safety of his sidearm, nervously clicking it off and on. "Got rifles, shotguns, pistols. Maybe a couple of .60s."

Schlager jerked a thumb over his shoulder toward the incinerator room door. Steve Bauer had returned to his post and was spraying a gas grenade at the disembodied hands still clawing through the broken wire-mesh window. "Through that?" Schlager asked.

"Climb over and down the rocket shield?" Gevers said.

Schlager laughed. He was still staring at the door. "You think they left any weapons for us?"

"Hell with weapons," Schuller said. "Could make a run for it." He thought back to the long nights during boot camp. Everyone else in his platoon beat to shit after humping a pack all day, racking out, or crowding around the pool table and crappy television set in the recreation room. While he was out running mini-marathons.

"Yeah," he said softly. "Make a run for it."

"What about the French Embassy?" Gevers said. "The hole in the wall? Don't they have to grant us asylum or something?"

Schlager just laughed. "We ain't getting off this roof," he said.

They had all heard the horrible stories about North Vietnamese prison camps. The Hanoi Hilton. The Tiger Cages. Mike Sullivan intuited the thoughts running through each man's mind. It wasn't supposed to end like this. Vietnam was supposed to be another Korea, a country divided in the middle. The southern half kept safe by an uneasy truce backed by American might. Better yet, he thought, we'd go back in and kick some Communist ass. Drive them right back into China. "Everybody bring it in," he said.

One by one the Marines gathered about him. Schlager was the first to break the tense silence. "You think the fleet's even still out there?"

"Of course, it is," Sullivan said.

Schlager gave him a look. "Then what's taking them so long?"

"I ain't ending up in no camp," Bennington said. He motioned toward one of the machine guns. "I got my spot picked out."

"Then we'll die up here." It was Babel. The first words he'd uttered all morning.

"So be it," said Bobby Frain.

"We better take a vote," Sullivan said. He had no doubt how it would come out. But he wanted to make it official.

One by one, each man voted to fight.

Kean and Valdez stood thirty feet away, watching. The two men eyed each other, the silence broken only by the muffled crumps of artillery, now resonating from all directions. Kean knew the Marines would not ask for an officer's vote. The Corps was not a democracy. Valdez, however, was another matter. He may have been their commander and de facto leader, but he was still an enlisted man. The Major jerked his chin.

"Go see what's up, Top."

Valdez reached the circle just as Bobby Frain was finishing a speech. ". . . and so anyway, that's what I say." His hand brushed the dog tags hanging from the thin metal chain around his neck. "It may not be a long fight, but when they pull these off me, I want them to have to dig through a pile of gooks to get them."

Valdez was struck by the matter-of-fact tone of Frain's voice. By all of their voices.

The sun was higher now, and the humidity weighed on the top sergeant like an anvil. All eyes were on him. Everyone else had voted to make a last stand, and his was the final ballot. Somebody had said that it had to be unanimous.

Valdez, too, was certain this was the end. But he knew it would not arrive in an Alamo-like siege. There would be no enemy infantrymen storming up the stairs, no Davy Crockett moment. Why would the NVA waste soldiers like that? He peered out again at the artillery explosions rocking Tan Son Nhut. No, he thought, when the final blow comes, it will fall from above. One well-placed round is all it will take. But there would be more, just to make certain. There was no need for the North Vietnamese to start conserving ammunition now. He thought of his two sons. What would they be told? What would everyone back home know about what happened today? He raised his right hand.

"Aye, we fight," he said.

Terry Bennington had settled into his "spot," slumped behind one of the M-60s, with clear fields of fire toward both the stairwell door and the windows of the abandoned British Embassy. He looked around at his fellow Marines and felt as if he could physically feel the tug of the bond among each of them.

He had never been much for introspection, but now he thought about how the Marine Corps had changed his life. It had accepted him like no one else before—not family, not friends—and, he guessed, like no one else would again. He knew he could not have put his feelings into words if someone put his own machine gun to his head, likely because the trust he felt for every one of these men trapped on this roof went deeper than words allowed. To the point of love. No, he thought, what he felt went even beyond the word *love*. It was as if there was an invisible cord stretched among them, splicing them together like the ends of eleven raw nerves. They were all brothers this morning, motivated by a sense of valor and courage and duty. Brothers sharing the same beliefs, the same challenges, the same fears. Together. Maybe for the last time. He racked the slide on the big gun.

Up on the helipad, Dave Norman was having similar thoughts. A warm feeling had suddenly washed over him; he was at peace with the fact that he was going to die on this roof with a good bunch of Marines. He had never felt so serene before, although his one regret was that he would never see his mom and dad back in Ohio again. He was certain they would understand.

He could tell the NVA was close. Not just the artillery and ground troops pouring into the city, but he could hear the rumbling of their tank treads. *Whoever wants us first, come and get us.* It was only a matter of time. He sat up straight and gazed about the rooftop. He felt as if he should say something. Instead he rechecked the clip of his rifle for the twentieth time.

Mike Sullivan found a piece of shade next to Phil Babel on the west side of the helipad. He was seated with his back against the wall of the incinerator room, and he knew the men were stealing glances at him. They were scared and alone; he could read it on their faces. They were also wondering why he'd humped that damn "Prick 25" around with him all morning if he wasn't going to use it. He didn't have the heart to tell them that not only were the radio's batteries almost dead, but even at full power it wouldn't broadcast much farther than three or four miles, depending on obstructions. Moreover, the Fleet had never given him a call sign. Without a call sign, he knew, no American would reply even if they could hear him.

He lifted the black handset, wrapped in cellophane, that was attached to the blocky radio by a spiral cord. It looked like the handset of a pay telephone from a 1930s gangster movie. He could imagine James Cagney or Edward G. Robinson growling into such a handset. Instead, in clipped syllables that spilled out of his mouth as if slipped through a mail slot, Sullivan said, "United States Navy, Navy, this is Embassy. Over."

No answer. He tried again. "Navy, hello United States Navy. This is the Marine Security Guard detachment at the United States Embassy in Saigon. Over. Hello Navy, can you hear me? Over."

While he spoke into the dead radio, he studied the concerned faces of his young MSGs. *What could it hurt?*

"Navy, U.S. Navy, this is Embassy. Eleven Marines requesting extraction. Repeat, eleven packs. Over."

A pause. "Yes, sir. I understand. Perfectly, sir. No problem, sir. We will indeed hold the fort, sir. Over."

Sullivan cupped the headset against his chest. "They're on their way," he said. He ignored the skeptical glances from Kean and Valdez.

"They're on their way," he repeated. "Just gotta fuel up and change crews."

Phil Babel turned and pretended to look down into the compound. "Bullshit," he said under his breath.

"Shut up," Sullivan whispered. "You talk too much."

Valdez made his way over to a corner of the roof where Jim Kean sat by himself. The major was peering over the parapet, watching a motorcade speeding down Thong Nhut Boulevard toward the bunker-like facade of the Presidential Palace. *Big Minh's last ride,* Kean thought. *Wants to meet his conquerors with all due pomp and ceremony.*

As the convoy neared the palace gates, the riot police in Minh's Jeep escorts began firing into the knots of looters along Mac Dinh Chi Street. Kean jumped to his feet and emptied his .45 into the big radio satellite dish.

"Major!"

Kean turned, arms akimbo, his Colt now at his side. "Top?"

"Sir, uh, maybe somebody hears those gunshots and figures we're looking for a fight."

"Aren't we?" Kean said. He was scared to death, but determined to keep it to himself. "Point taken, Top. I just didn't want to leave any coms material intact for the NVA."

"Pretty sure the thermite grenades in the Bubble Room took care of that, sir." Valdez stroked his massive chin. By now Kean knew the unconscious gesture meant something was troubling the big man.

"Top?"

"Major, you think they forgot us?"

Kean looked about the roof. The whiskey was gone, the two bottles standing empty on the asphalt. Mike Sullivan was still hunched over the Prick 25, pretending to receive messages. By now he was fooling no one. The remainder of his MSGs had dispersed to their own private islands, slumped with their backs literally against the low wall. Dragging deep on cigarettes. Alone with their thoughts. Even if General Carey thought all his Marines were out of the city and scattered among the fleet, Kean thought, certainly by now he would be looking for my debrief. And what about Gerry Berry? He had been flying for over eighteen hours, and that was enough to give a man bugs on the brain. But enough to forget the last eleven Americans?

"There is that possibility," Kean said.

There was a long silence. The Major broke it. "No rope?"

Valdez shook his head.

"Sure as hell can't jump."

"Climb down that rocket screen?" Valdez said.

Both men peered over the side. The jutting edges of the rough concrete latticework might provide a man with handholds and toeholds. But then what? The angry Vietnamese below them in the compound resembled swarming insects.

"Human chain, maybe," Valdez said.

Kean ran his hands through his filthy hair. "Out the back door and dash to the river . . ."

"And steal a boat," Valdez said, finishing the thought.

"Could be done," Kean said. "The vote to stand and fight? Unanimous?"

Valdez shrugged. *What do you think?*

Kean nodded, and again looked over the rampart. He checked his watch. It had been just over an hour.

Terry Bennington, squatting behind his M-60, and Dave Norman, lying on his back on the helipad, spotted it almost simultaneously—a slender white contrail painting the blue sky far to the southeast.

"Major Kean."

In the time it took Kean to raise his binoculars, the contours of the CH-46 became visible to the naked eye. Four Marine AH-Cobra gunships flew cover on the compass points—above, below, and to either side of the Sea Knight, criss-crossing in attack formation every half mile.

The sniping turned into a barrage as the chopper banked for its final approach and HMM-164, call sign Swift 22, set its great black tires down on the rooftop helipad. Its crew chief dropped the tailgate. The glass in the side windows had been shot out.

Kean ran to the cockpit and shouted above the beating blades. "Waitin' for you. Didn't think you were coming."

The Marine pilot, Captain Tom Holben, grinned and gave the thumbs up. The Cobra gunships, nose down for optimal firing, swooped like hawks above the embassy. High above them, a Navy A-7 Corsair attack jet left its own vapor trail in the form of interlacing circles.

Kean turned and raised both arms. "Strip down," he hollered. "Lighten up. Lose grenades, helmets. Just leave them." He looked toward Bauer. "Two minutes, Corporal. Then get your ass up here."

Kean led the Marines up the ramp—ducking and zigzagging; no one wanted to be killed now—and took a canvas sling seat behind the pilot. Valdez waited outside the tail ramp. On Kean's signal, he shouted for Bauer. Bauer took one more slow, sentry walk in full view of the faces on the other side of the broken window and edged out of sightline. He bolted up the stairs two at a time, losing his flak jacket as he ran. He flung his helmet away before stepping in through the tailgate.

Sergeant Juan Valdez, the last American serviceman to depart Vietnam, snapped a group photo with a small Brownie camera before scuttling aboard.

"Pop the gas," someone yelled, and Bobby Schlager pulled the pins on two canisters of CS. He rolled them out the gunner's door. They hissed, tumbled off the helipad, and came to a stop in front of the incinerator room door.

It took a moment for everyone to realize the mistake. The rotors were sucking the gas vapors into the cockpit and cabin of the helicopter. The pilots were blinded. The helicopter hopped and lurched, its skids bouncing once, twice, three times off the landing zone. The ramp was still down, and on the third bounce Juan Valdez rolled out of the chopper.

Three sets of hands shot out of the clam shell. Valdez waved them off and got to his knees, embarrassed. He clambered back aboard.

"Planning on staying, Top?" Mike Sullivan yelled.

Valdez grinned and strapped himself into a sling seat. Through the fog of CS, he could just make out the door to the incinerator room. It bulged, buckled, and then broke. He thought of Da Nang, the civilians fighting to pile aboard the Birds, clutching at the skids. If it happened now, the weight would surely force the aircraft over the side of the building.

Holben and his copilot Captain Doug Cook's eyes were red with fatigue and the effects of the tear gas, but in a moment most of it had blown off. They could see if they squinted. Holben lifted off just as the mob surged up the outside staircase and onto the sun-baked roof. He banked the aircraft southeast, toward the river. The rotors drowned out the sounds of small arms fire. Jim Kean checked his watch: 0758. Twenty-three hours after he had found out his wife was pregnant. Bobby Frain grabbed a field radio in the back of the cabin. It was broken, disabled by a bullet. He put the handset to his mouth anyway.

"Hey, Major," he hollered above the rotors, "they want to know what kind of pizza you want when we get to Manila."

Swift 22 passed low over the Presidential Palace where Big Minh awaited his fate. Then the downtown hotels hove into view beneath the skids, their terraces and roof bars eerily deserted.

"Look," Bobby Schlager hollered. He pointed to a half-dozen Russian-made T-32 tanks, flanked by armored NVA vehicles, lumbering across the Newport Bridge.

Each Marine in the helicopter craned for a view, each thinking of what might have been.

General Dung had no idea what to expect when one of his tank commanders radioed him that they were crossing the Newport Bridge. He could hear gunfire echoing in the background, and he hoped it was merely scattered resistance. Better yet, he thought, perhaps it was celebratory gunshots. He did not want to inherit a destroyed Saigon. He wanted to enter a city with its buildings intact, with electricity, with running water. With as few civilian casualties as possible.

His spies and forward observers had kept for him a running tally of the evacuation flights, and he was still adding up the numbers. But as of this moment, it appeared that over the preceding eighteen hours, the American helicopters had made well over 600 runs in and out of the city.

As his staff celebrated—turning the NVA's jungle headquarters into a romper room of whooping cries, impromptu dancing, and parading about the camp ground on each other's shoulders—Dung thought of his wife in Hanoi. Her mother lived in Saigon. They had not seen each other in over twenty-one years. His subordinates were not aware that tomorrow was his fifty-eighth birthday. He had already received his present, and his salutations, in the form of an unusually terse cable from Hanoi: "Political Bureau is most happy."

He also mused over the opportunities he had all afternoon, night, and, now, morning, to blow the Americans out of the sky. He lighted a cigarette. He wondered if they knew that.

Swift 22 banked right, passed over the city docks, and followed the twists and bends of the Saigon River. Tracer fire from antiaircraft guns—a warning? a good-bye and good riddance?—flew perilously close to the aircraft, but within moments the helicopter was over the Rung Sat, the "Swamp of Death" that separated the city from the South China Sea.

Someone lit a cigarette and passed the pack around. When the helicopter passed over the coast—"Feet Wet"—the door gunner and crew chief cleared their weapons and left them slack as, one by one, the escorting Cobra gunships swooped down next to Swift 22 and each pilot in succession saluted the Marines. With that, Mike Sullivan made his way to the front of the cabin and slapped Jim Kean's knee.

"We made it, Major. We made it."

The words were barely out of his mouth when he noticed the fuel gauges. The needles on both read empty. "But you better take your shoes off, sir." He pointed. "Bingo fuel. We might have to swim."

Kean passed the word for each MSG to lighten an already depleted load. A few stray flak jackets that his Marines had forgotten to leave behind were passed to the crew chief standing at the gunner's window. He tossed them into the sea.

Steve Schuller stood and craned his neck out the window. A flotilla of rusting boats stretching from the Vung Tau peninsula to the horizon fought through the rolling combers. He could make out sampans, fishing smacks, tramp steamers, even the occasional pleasure craft, each packed to the gunwales with escaping Vietnamese. Bobby Frain noticed that a shrimper was on fire, and Bobby Schlager yelped and pointed to another trawler that looked as if it was sinking. Soon, the sorry sight gave way to the American armada, the three dozen ships of the Seventh Fleet, and the MSGs watched from above as Navy crewmen heaved million-dollar helicopters into the shallow waters of the South China Sea.

Forty-three minutes after they had been evacuated from the U.S. Embassy roof, Major Jim Kean, Master Sergeant Juan Valdez, and their squad of nine exhausted Marines stepped off Swift 22 onto the hot steel deck of the USS *Okinawa* with mixed emotions.

The long Vietnam War was over. There was a sadness to the moment, a sense of loss. Yet at the same time, each Saigon MSG felt buoyed by the knowledge that he had helped to secure one small triumph in the war's final crucible. Their country may have lost something that it might never recover. But they had persevered with dignity and courage. It was all that the Marine Corps could have asked of them. It was all that they could have asked of themselves.

Epilogue

USS *Okinawa*, 0845, 30 April 1975

When it was all over, I was never sure whether or not I was going to get
an award or a good kick in the ass.
—Major Jim Kean, USMC

Jim Kean surprised himself. He hadn't thought he'd have the energy to laugh. Yet here he was grinning like a jack-o-lantern as he stood on the deck of the amphibious assault ship USS *Okinawa*. They had not been able to reach the USS *Blue Ridge*, where Swift 22 had been expected to land—the flagship of Task Force 76 was too far out to sea and the helicopter hadn't enough fuel. And now Kean watched with a grin as his ten bedraggled Marine security guards stepped off the helicopter, one by one, only to be disarmed by a squad of Fleet Marines.

Kean had already handed over his own Marine-issue M-16 rifle, a .9-millimeter automatic pistol he'd picked up near the embassy pool, and his personal Gold Cup Colt .45. Yet some of his MSGs, reluctant to surrender their guns, were not quite so obliging. Kean recognized that the Fleet Marines had their orders: every weapon carried by anyone boarding a U.S. ship was to be tossed over the side. Still, he found the scene bizarre. Not including hand grenades, Kean counted thirty-six confiscated rifles and pistols of varying makes and sizes taken from his men and heaved into the South China Sea, including a couple of Czech-made machine pistols his men had picked up from God knows where and even a little chromium-plated .32. He thought he may have to intervene once, when he noticed Steve Schuller jawing with a Fleet Marine. But before he could take action, Schuller turned an about-face, strode to the edge of the flight deck, and flung his own weapons overboard. If they were going to drown, he would do it himself.

Yes, Kean thought again, *Pancho Villa's raiders.*

All about the MSGs, hundreds of South Vietnamese refugees, military and civilians, were lined up for processing. Dozens of Royal South Vietnamese Air Force helicopters continued to hover overhead, destined for the same watery grave as the MSGs' guns whether or not they found deck space to set down. Some of Kean's Marines remained topside to watch the show, but the major was too spent. He was processed in, found a cot below decks, and fell into a deep slumber for six hours.

A little before 3 P.M., a sailor shook him awake. General Carey had summoned him to the USS *Blue Ridge.* As his chopper lifted off the USS *Okinawa* for the fifteen-minute hop, Kean wondered how much hot water he was in for deploying the tear gas on the roof. *Well, it was a good career while it lasted. Maybe it will be the last casualty of the Vietnam War.*

His only property was a half-smoked cigar, and when General Carey debriefed him, Kean was still wearing his Arnold Palmer golf shirt and his blue slacks. To the major's relief, Carey congratulated him on a job well done, and then Kean went on to meet "The Bulls"—the battalion commander and the operations officer of the Marine landing force, as well as the regimental landing team leader Colonel Al Gray. It was during this session that he learned that the remains of Corporal Charles McMahon and Lance Corporal Darwin Judge were still somewhere in Saigon and that Gray was leading the investigation into the failure to recover their bodies.

This brutal piece of information spurred anew his anger at having to split his detachment three days earlier and send the squad to the DAO. But he said nothing. What was left to say? Kean further discovered that the U.S. Army colonels Madison and Summers, also aboard the USS *Blue Ridge,* had charged the embassy Marines with panicking "and leaving behind people who otherwise might have been saved," including the inebriated Koreans. Kean was annoyed at what he considered a slander but measured his words carefully.

Epilogue

"We probably could have emptied the compound," he told Colonel Gray. "But we would have had to ignore President Ford's orders to do it."

Meanwhile, although his MSGs had no such administrative red tape or interservice sniping to deal with, they were finding they did have one problem: the Navy sailors, cognizant of the historic occasion, were regularly trying to swipe what little gear they had carried out, including their clothes, as souvenirs. After they were processed and escorted below decks, they stripped off their stinking utilities and lurched in search of their first showers in a week. Schuller was peeling off his socks—pieces of flesh tore off with them—when he noticed a swabbie make a grab for Terry Bennington's blouse. He stopped the sailor, and from there on in, the MSGs tried to take turns in the shower room, guarding each other's uniforms.

The entire Saigon Marine security detachment reached the American naval air station at Subic Bay in the Philippines on May 6. At the American Embassy in Manila, they were billeted and supplied with shaving kits, toothbrushes, and, a godsend, hot meals. To their chagrin, however, with their passports, service records, and pay books long lost, the next few days were spent seated at trestle tables filling out piles of forms—their official "welcome home" to the joys of bureaucracy.

Finally, following a small mutiny, Kean arranged for the embassy paymaster to advance $200 to each of his men, and they were allowed off-base to purchase clean clothes. Naturally, after stocking up on shoes, dungarees, and T-shirts, most gravitated to the capital city's notorious "Pig Alley"—Manila's version of Tu Do Street. Everywhere they went in town, however, they were followed by reporters clamoring to hear the "real story" of the final moments on the roof. Finally, after one too many encounters with inquiring newsmen, most of the detachment commandeered a bar, paid its owner to toss everyone out who was not an MSG, and spent eight hours eating, drinking, and reliving what many had assumed would be the last moments of their lives. Numerous Philippine bar girls were among the curious onlookers pausing outside the gin mill to gawk in, and rumor had it that the money the Marines had been advanced was not spent entirely on food and alcoholic beverages.

During the party, Master Sergeant Juan Valdez spent much of the evening brooding by himself off in a corner. After two days aboard the USS

Epilogue

Okinawa, Valdez had also been flown to the USS *Blue Ridge* to be debriefed by General Carey and Colonel Gray, and it was there that he, like Kean, discovered that the bodies of Corporal McMahon and Lance Corporal Judge had never left Saigon.

Valdez had initially been incensed with Gunnery Sergeant Vasco Martin, whom he had placed in charge of the MSG squad siphoned off to the DAO. His anger at Martin soon ebbed, however, when he put himself in the squad leader's shoes and thought through the utter chaos that had encompassed the DAO during and after the NVA shellings. There was nothing Martin could have done to bring the remains of those boys home, and by the time the MSGs had reached Manila, Valdez's fury was directed inward. He was, after all, "Top" Sergeant as well as old school; he believed to the depths of his soul in the credo that Marines never leave one of their own behind. The incident would haunt him for years.

The next day, back at the Manila embassy, Kean was preparing for his return to Hong Kong when he encountered Graham Martin in the office of the American ambassador to the Philippines. It was the last time they would meet. The two exchanged awkward small talk—Martin remained terribly gaunt and wan—and Kean was relieved to head to the airport when their brief conversation concluded. Soon after, back in Hong Kong, he began the task of typing from memory a nine-page, single-spaced after-action report as well as writing the recommendation narratives that would form the basis for the forty-two Navy Achievement and Navy Commendation medals subsequently awarded to Marine Security Guards from the Saigon, Can Tho, Phnom Penh, Nha Trang, Da Nang, and Bien Hoa detachments.

As he pieced together his Marines' exploits, he thought of Napoleon, who had once noted the brave deeds men will perform for a little piece of ribbon. His own question about his fate was also answered when, instead of a good kick in the ass, he was awarded the Bronze Star for meritorious achievement for his actions in Saigon during the last week of April 1975.

The merchant ship SS *Pioneer Contender,* trailed by Terry McNamara's two converted landing craft, reached the Vung Tau peninsula and the outlying warships of the Seventh Fleet around 9:30 A.M. on April 30. The first thing that the former American consul to Can Tho and his former Can Tho MSG noncommissioned officer in charge, Staff Sergeant Steve Hasty, noticed was that all about them, the green water of the South China Sea was littered with the wreckage and flotsam of fleeing refugee boats. The two men were sharing a cold breakfast on the merchant ship's deck when a messenger informed McNamara that his two battered LCMs would not be needed to evacuate Vietnamese from the peninsula beaches.

Shortly after noon, McNamara and Hasty were transferred by Japanese tug to a larger ship being leased by the Americans, an oceangoing Korean LST built to land tanks. They spent a cold night sleeping under the stars, and twenty-four hours later, a squadron of Marine helicopters retrieved McNamara and his American compatriots and Hasty and his small Marine contingent and ferried them to the USS *Blue Ridge*. Their do-it-yourself odyssey was over.

As McNamara's Huey soared high above the Seventh Fleet, the veteran Foreign Service officer took in the length and breadth of the American armada. He had one thought: *How could a nation with so much strength end a war by abandoning its allies and saving its own citizens in such ignominious circumstances?* As the USS *Blue Ridge* sailed on to the Philippines, McNamara sent a message to the State Department in Washington as to his and his staff's whereabouts and settled in to make his own notes on the river journey.

Meanwhile, Steve Hasty sought out Jim Kean, his commanding officer, in the ship's Marine billet. When a grinning Kean spotted his young staff sergeant, he shouted, "You did the good job we expected of you." Hasty was then hustled up into the ship's superstructure to be personally debriefed by General Carey, a heady experience for such a green trooper. Over glasses of iced tea, the general thanked the staff sergeant for the good job he had done. A million thoughts raced through Hasty's mind. The CIA's double-cross. The ARVN Navy's boarding. The attack on the river. The blinding rainstorm that likely saved their lives. Their despair at not finding a U.S. Navy ship waiting for them in the river delta.

Yet when the general asked about the journey, the staff sergeant knew to keep his opinions to himself and stick to the bare facts. He walked from the general's stateroom thinking, *You don't know the half of it, Sir.*

At twilight on April 30, a traditional burial at sea was conducted on the deck of the USS *Hancock.* The coffins were empty. The bodies of Captain William Nystul and Lieutenant Michael Shea were never recovered from their helicopter, Swift 14, which crashed and sank in approximately seventy feet of water.

After Swift 14's crew chief, Stephen Wills, and its first mechanic, Richard Scott, were rescued from the South China Sea, the only other items recovered from the aircraft were four flight crew helmets and the helicopter's front landing strut, with its tires still attached. The cause of the accident was never determined, but as the Marine Corps historians Major George Dunham and Colonel David Quinlan were to write, "crew inexperience and unfamiliarity with the mission may have been factors."

The former North Vietnamese soldier-turned-journalist Colonel Bui Tin, deputy editor of the official NVA newspaper *Quan Doi Nhan Dan,* was with the leading tank column that smashed through the grillwork of the gates to Saigon's Presidential Palace on the morning of April 30. As Tin climbed the steps to the ornate building amid awed young North Vietnamese foot soldiers, bewildered tank operators, and junior officers from General Dung's 2nd Army Corps, he was mistaken for a Communist leader. He was directed by a presidential aide to the private office of General Duong Van "Big" Minh. There he found President Minh, dressed in a short-sleeve shirt and surrounded by his ministers. Minh had already addressed the South Vietnamese people and army by radio—ordering them to cease fighting and assuring them that "a national reconciliation and concord" was at hand.

Now he greeted Tin with another brief pronouncement: "I have been waiting since early this morning to transfer power to you."

Tin was taken aback. He asked an NVA tank commander for the whereabouts of General Dung. No one knew. So Tin seized the moment.

Epilogue

"There is no question of your transferring power," he told Minh. "Your power has crumbled. You have nothing in your hands to surrender, and so you cannot surrender what you cannot possess."

As if to fit a capstone to the proceedings, just then a burst of automatic weapons fire rattled the windows. Minh's ministers flinched; the North Vietnamese barely budged. "Our men are merely celebrating," Tin told the room. "Between Vietnamese there are no victors and no vanquished. Only the Americans have been beaten."

The flag of the National Front for the Liberation of Southern Vietnam, the Vietcong, was raised over the Presidential Palace at 12:15 P.M., and as the day progressed, Bui Tin toured the defeated city. He photographed the large pieces of the tamarind tree spread across the grounds of the American Embassy compound, and accompanied a group of North Vietnamese soldiers to the embassy roof, which was empty except for a littering of discarded weapons, helmets, and flak vests. From there, atop the tallest building in Saigon, he could see fires still burning all about the city, including at Tan Son Nhut Airport and the adjacent DAO compound.

Later that evening, Tin disappeared into a small office in the Presidential Palace to compose his newspaper dispatch. He wrote a four-page story but did not know how to send it to his editors in Hanoi. He hitched a ride to the DAO, hoping to find a working telex but discovered that all communications equipment had been destroyed by the U.S. Marine demolition team.

On a hunch, he walked over to a small, outlying building in the complex, one of the first structures to be erected by the Americans in Saigon when the base was known as Camp Davis. It was occupied by an NVA communications team setting up shop. He left his news report with them, and it was eventually filed to Hanoi.

The opening lines of his story were thus: "I am writing this article while sitting at a desk on the second floor of the Presidential Palace in Saigon. The long war is over."

Frequent Wind, the last U.S. military operation in Vietnam, was the largest and most successful helicopter evacuation ever conducted. It has not been duplicated since. During the weeks before Frequent Wind was launched on April 29, fixed-wing aircraft had evacuated 50,493 people, including 2,678 orphans, from Saigon's Tan Son Nhut Airport. The exact number of refugees who put out to sea in Royal Vietnamese Air Force helicopters, private aircraft, barges, trawlers, and other boats that April, and how many reached safety, is impossible to calculate.

Given the crowded skies above Saigon, General Dung's intelligence officers proved remarkably accurate in their assessment of what many were already referring to as the "American Dunkirk." U.S. Marine helicopter pilots flew 682 sorties into Saigon during Operation Frequent Wind. A total of 395 Americans and 4,475 Vietnamese and third-country nationals were evacuated from the DAO, with another 978 Americans and 1,220 Vietnamese and others rescued from the U.S. Embassy. Altogether, over 7,000 people were lifted out of the city before it was occupied by North Vietnamese troops and the Vietcong. Of the 420 people left behind at the embassy, over 100 were South Korean citizens.

Of the 1,054 flight hours flown by Marine helicopter pilots on April 29 and 30, Captain Gerry Berry in his CH-46 Lady Ace 09 logged the most, flying 18.3 hours over a 20-hour span. Before the return of their mother ship, the USS *Dubuque,* from the Gulf of Thailand, Berry's squadron remained without a "home port," and he and his crews spent the next twenty-four hours hitching a ride on the USS *Duluth* until, on May 1, the *Dubuque* steamed back into the South China Sea. Berry's four choppers subsequently returned to the *Dubuque,* and then sailed to Okinawa. For their heroic effort during the evacuation, Berry's Sea Knights were named the Marine Corps' Squadron of the Year for 1975.

One more helicopter note: The one that Steve Schuller observed landing atop the building on Gia Long Street the afternoon of the 29th was turned into an iconic photograph that to this day is mistakenly believed to portray the last Americans leaving Saigon. The UPI office was on the top floor of the Peninsula Hotel, four blocks from the Pittman Apartments. The UPI station chief was Alan Dawson, and there were several staff and freelance reporters as well as Hubert van Es, a Dutch photographer who had decided to remain and cover the takeover by the North Vietnamese and Vietcong.

Van Es had just returned from shooting pictures and was in the darkroom processing film. He was alerted to a chopper on the roof of a building. He grabbed a camera and a 300 mm lens, the longest in the office, and dashed to the balcony. He took ten frames of O. B. Harnage, a CIA operative, helping civilians onto the helicopter. After processing the film, van Es selected a print to be transmitted by radio signals to Tokyo from the Saigon telegraph office. The 5 x 7 black-and-white photo took twelve minutes to send. Van Es went to his grave in 2009 insisting that he wrote the correct information in the caption, but that editors erroneously assumed it was the U.S. Embassy roof and the last American helicopter to evacuate Saigon.

In his memoir, *A Time to Heal,* Gerald Ford reflected on America's unheralded triumph in the closing hours of the Vietnam War. "When it was all over, I felt deep satisfaction and relief that the evacuation had been a success," he wrote. "The problem of what to do with the refugees, however, remained. More than 120,000 of them had managed to escape, but they had nowhere to go. Thailand didn't want them. Neither did Malaysia, Indonesia nor the Philippines. The United States, I felt, had a special obligation to them, and on April 30 I asked Congress to approve a bill that would provide $507 million for their transportation and care. The House rejected my request on May 1. Unbelievable! After World War II we had opened our gates and offered a new life to 1.4 million displaced persons plus 50,000 after the Hungarian revolution in 1956 and half a million Cubans after Castro came to power. In 1975, refugee camps were established around the country. With the help of local citizens and volunteer organizations, the 120,000 Vietnamese began a new life in America, as had other refugees before them."

Others were not so lucky. Although nothing is officially known regarding the fate of the 300-odd Vietnamese refugees abandoned in the embassy compound—the South Koreans left behind were eventually repatriated to their country—according to the Hanoi government, more than 200,000 South Vietnamese government officials, military officers, and soldiers were sent to "reeducation camps," where torture, disease, and malnutrition were widespread.

South Vietnam's ex-president, Duong Van Minh, fared better. Several days after the fall of his capital city, he was permitted to return to his villa. He lived there for the next eight years in seclusion, raising birds and tending exotic orchids. In 1983 he was allowed to emigrate to France, where he lived near Paris until again emigrating, to Pasadena, California, where in August 2001 he fell ill and died at the age of eighty-five.

Minh lived long enough to see the United States reestablish formal diplomatic relations with Vietnam under President Bill Clinton in July 1995. The old U.S. Embassy property was returned to the United States, and the historic staircase that led to the rooftop helipad was salvaged and is now on display at the Gerald R. Ford Museum in Grand Rapids, Michigan.

On the morning of April 29, 1975, at 9 A.M. Eastern Standard Time—seventeen hours after the North Vietnamese artillery barrage of Tan Son Nhut Airport commenced—twenty-eight-year-old Marine Captain Michael Maloney received a telephone call in the trailer used as a Marine Corps recruiting office behind the Postal Annex in downtown Boston, Massachusetts. Aside from his duties as a recruiting officer, Maloney was also the area's casualty officer.

"I have a casualty notification, KIA," the caller from the Casualty Section of the First Marine Corps District at Garden City, New York, began. "Are you ready to copy?"

Maloney readied a pencil and pad.

"Name—McMahon, Charles," the voice continued. "Rank—Corporal. Multiple fragmentation wounds."

Within ninety minutes, Captain Maloney and Gunnery Sergeant Hilliard Crosswhite had arrived by car at the pink and white two-family home of Edna and Charles McMahon Sr., in Woburn. Charles McMahon Sr., a night-shift factory worker, was asleep and did not hear their knocks. After consulting with local police, the two Marines returned to the McMahon home just as Edna McMahon and her younger son, Scott, a recently recruited Marine still on inactive duty, were entering the house. Scott McMahon stopped to speak with them—"Can I help you, sir? Is it about my brother?"—but Maloney and Crosswhite asked to be allowed into the house. Edna McMahon woke her husband, and the family gathered in the kitchen.

Epilogue

Maloney steeled himself. "Mr. and Mrs. McMahon," he said. "I'm sorry to have to tell you that your son Charles has been killed in Vietnam."

Maloney did not say—because he did not know—that the body of Charlie and Edna McMahon's oldest son remained in Saigon.

Halfway across the country, at 11:30 A.M. Central Standard Time on the same day, a black Chevrolet carrying two Marines intercepted Henry Judge as he was close to finishing his morning postal rounds in Marshalltown, Iowa. The car pulled to the curb, the Marines exited, and one of them informed him that his son, Darwin, had been killed in Vietnam. They walked with him to his white clapboard house and waited outside while Henry told his wife that their boy was dead. That afternoon, the Judges addressed the first gaggle of reporters who had begun to camp out on their front yard.

"All I can say is that Darwin felt he had to be there to keep the Communists from coming here," Ida Judge told the gathered newsmen and women as her husband, Henry, stood silent off to her side. "We're proud of that boy. We're good Christian folk, you see, and the good Lord will take care of us. I love my boy, but when it's your time to go . . ."

The "welcome aboard" letter Juan Valdez had written to the McMahon family reached them days after they had learned of the death of their son. Corporal Charles McMahon USMC, Lance Corporal Darwin Judge USMC, Captain William Nystul USMC, and Lieutenant Michael Shea USMC were the last four of the 58,151 Americans to die in the Vietnam War that also cost the United States over 300,000 casualties and $670 billion in inflation-adjusted dollars. The war saw the death of untold millions of Vietnamese.

At eight years, five months, and three days—from the 1964 Gulf of Tonkin Resolution in August 1964 to the signing of the Paris Peace Accords in January 1973—the Vietnam War also stood as America's longest official military conflict until June 2010, when it was surpassed in length by Operation Enduring Freedom in Afghanistan.

On May 1, 1975, Ambassador Graham Martin, who had agreed to hold a top-side press conference on the USS *Blue Ridge,* received one last back-channel cable from Secretary of State Henry Kissinger. It read, "I think it advisable that you avoid all public comment until you have made your report to the President."

Kissinger's long-ago words crossed Martin's mind. *You've got to get back out there because the American people have got to have somebody to blame.* Martin cancelled the press conference. Yet when caught by reporters below decks, the last U.S. ambassador to South Vietnam declared, "I think the Americans have a right to be proud of this evacuation. I have absolutely nothing for which I apologize at all."

Postscript

On April 30, 2010, many of the Marine Security Guards who were present during the final hours of the existence of the country of South Vietnam gathered in Quantico, Virginia, to commemorate the thirty-fifth anniversary of the historic event. The epic evacuation three and a half decades earlier had been figuratively set in motion by the deaths of Darwin Judge and Charles McMahon, and the reunion commemorating it would end with somber remembrances of the two young Marines by the men who served with them and to whom the fates had granted the gift of middle age. In between and among other festivities, the gathered Marines attended the 2010 MSG School graduation ceremony as honored guests, and visited the Vietnam Veterans Memorial in Washington, D.C., where they located the names of Judge and McMahon on the brooding stone edifice.

Although widely scattered after their harrowing adventures, most of the Saigon Marines remained personal friends or kept in touch through the Fall of Saigon Association, which was cofounded and incorporated by the attorney Doug Potratz in 2000. More than a number of them had gone on from their service in Vietnam to fashion a career in the Corps. Not all of the men could make this reunion—three of the "Final Eleven," including Jim Kean, had since passed away—but as the event's organizer, the former Saigon MSG Ken Crouse, noted, "They are still with us, in our hearts and minds."

Though hardly mentioned, two spectral presences hung over that thirty-fifth reunion weekend. The first was the last ambassador to Saigon, Graham Martin. Upon his return from Vietnam, Martin, who never again served overseas in any State Department capacity, was appointed a special assistant to Secretary of State Henry Kissinger. He retired shortly thereafter, in 1977, suffering from chronic emphysema and tethered to an oxygen tank. He and his wife, Dorothy, returned to their home in Winston-Salem, North Carolina, where they boarded one of Martin's young cousins who was attending college in the area. Martin died in 1990 at the age of seventy-seven. In 2002 the cousin, who requested that his name be withheld, penned a letter to the Fall of Saigon Association Web site in which he wrote, "I would spend night after night listening to his recollections, his version of what went awry and his regrets. According to Dorothy, Graham never fully recovered from the April 1975 events. She said it took him 15 years to die."

The other reunion presence never discussed, but viscerally felt, was that of General Van Tien Dung, the Communist commander who in 1975 represented everything U.S. Marines had fought against in Vietnam. Dung's book, *Our Great Spring Victory*, written in a surprisingly entertaining style, has become the standard work from North Vietnam's perspective of the war and its final days, and the old MSGs were not surprised to learn that following his capture of Saigon, Dung directed Vietnam's invasion of Cambodia as well as the resultant 1979 border conflict with China. The following year he became Vietnam's defense minister, a position he held for seven years before being ousted. Thereafter, Dung lived quietly until his death in March 2002.

Ironically, at a Saturday night dinner in the replica of the famous Tun Tavern on the grounds of the National Museum of the Marine Corps, both thoughts and glasses were raised in memory of another deceased lion whose political sympathies were once viewed by many Marines as not so dissimilar to the Communist leaders in North Vietnam. For it was the late Senator Edward M. Kennedy of Massachusetts who, beginning in May 1975, spearheaded the intense, behind-the-scenes negotiations with Hanoi that resulted in the release of the remains of Corporal McMahon and Lance Corporal Judge, which were turned over to two of the senator's aides in Ho Chi Minh City in March 1976 and flown back to the United States for military burial.

Similarly, one more civilian held a special place in the hearts and minds of the veteran MSGs: the former American consul in Can Tho, Francis Terry McNamara. Although the Saigon contingent was unfamiliar at the time with McNamara's notorious "river run," his exploits have since gone down in unofficial State Department and Marine Corps annals. True to his love for Vietnam and its people, following the Saigon diaspora McNamara signed on as the director of the Task Force for the Resettlement of Indochinese Refugees at the State Department. From that post he went on to serve as consul general to Quebec, Canada; deputy chief of mission at the U.S. Embassy in Beirut, Lebanon; and deputy assistant secretary of state for public affairs. McNamara also served as a foreign affairs fellow with the Hoover Institution at Stanford University and as a senior research fellow at the National Defense University. After thirty-seven years of public service he retired to McLean, Virginia, in 1993, to write his memoir, recounting his adventure down the River of Poems.

When someone at the reunion asked Steve Hasty when he would sit down to write his own seafaring yarn about the "Can Tho Yacht Club," he smiled ruefully and said, "Maybe when I have time in my next life." He may not have been joking. Before retiring in February 2009 after a distinguished forty-one-year military career, Hasty had become the senior active-duty colonel in the entire Marine Corps, as well as the longest continuously serving Marine on active duty. A year after departing Can Tho, Hasty was selected to appointment as a warrant officer, and thereupon began a journey that included deployments in military intelligence, Scout-Sniper School, and counterterrorism. In 1988 he graduated magna cum laude from George Washington University with degrees in Middle East studies and international relations, and two years later volunteered for combat duty during Operation Desert Shield and continued in that capacity throughout Operation Desert Storm.

He honed his intelligence-gathering and counterterrorism expertise during subsequent postings to Turkey, the Kurdistan region of northern Iraq, Somalia, Cairo, Haiti, Bosnia, Cuba, Peru, Norway, and Kosovo, and, three weeks before the September 11 attacks, he assumed command of all Marine Security Guards at U.S. diplomatic facilities throughout the world. Following this command, he again volunteered for combat duty, in Iraq, and followed that assignment with two deployments to Afghanistan.

Postscript

Hasty's trunk full of decorations includes the Defense Superior Service Medal, the Legion of Merit, the Bronze Star Medal with Valor Device and three Gold Stars, the Defense Meritorious Service Medal with three Oak Leaf Clusters, the Meritorious Service Medal, the Joint Service Commendation Medal, the Navy Commendation Medal with Valor Device and Gold Star, the Joint Service Achievement medal, the Combat Action Ribbon with three Gold Stars, the Department of State Meritorious Honor Award Medal, and seventeen U.S. and foreign unit citations.

During that same celebratory dinner at the Tun Tavern, as more than a few conversations inevitably turned to tales of the evacuation from the U.S. Embassy compound, the name Gerry Berry passed quite a few lips. At that very moment Berry, who had been invited to Quantico by the association, was a continent away, being feted as the guest of honor at the Flying Leatherneck Aviation Museum in Miramar, California, where his old CH-46 Sea Knight, Lady Ace 09, was being put on permanent display.

Following the fall of Saigon, Berry rose steadily through the ranks of the service, serving in posts around the world and attending both the Marine Corps Command and Staff College and the Naval War College, from which he earned a master's degree in strategic studies. In his last posting in 1991, by then promoted to colonel, Berry commanded over sixty aircraft and 3,000 Marines and sailors supporting fleet operations during Operation Desert Shield. Along the way he also found time to earn a master of arts from Salve Regina College, the better, perhaps, to appreciate the intricate designs on his three Distinguished Flying Crosses, two Meritorious Service Medals, two Single Mission Air Medals, a Navy Commendation Medal and Combat Action Ribbon, and forty-six Air Medals. By the time of his retirement from the Corps in 1993 after twenty-five years of service, Berry had amassed over 4,800 total flight hours. Today Berry, who went on to found an aviation security company, splits time between Florida and his home state of Montana.

The fates of the Marines who were the very last men out of Saigon ranged from joyous to bittersweet. At the reunion, silent prayers were said for the two deceased "Bobbys"—Schlager and Frain. The former, whose service in Saigon was his third tour of duty in Vietnam, served twenty-three years in the Marine Corps before retiring and becoming quality control supervisor for a company in the state of Washington. He remained an avid outdoorsman, hiking and camping throughout the Pacific Northwest until his life was cut short by cancer, in February 2003, at the age of sixty-two.

In Frain's case, he left the Marines soon after Saigon, and his former comrades had lost touch with him until in 1992, shortly before his death, "The Body Beautiful" reached out in a letter to his old top sergeant, Juan Valdez. Frain wrote that following his discharge from the Corps in 1975, he moved back to the Pacific Northwest, attended college, received a bachelor of science in business finance and business management, and began a civilian career as a budget analyst for the Washington State Department of Energy. Over the subsequent decades he fathered four "beautiful daughters," yet also underwent thirty surgeries for cancer and Crohn's disease.

"We were all thrown together at a time and place that will remain part of history," Frain ended his letter to Valdez. "There is a bond that cannot be put into words that will always link us." The pain of these maladies apparently too much to take, Frain committed suicide in 1993.

Bobby Frain and Bobby Schlager are both buried in the Willamette National Cemetery in Richland, Washington.

Similarly, whenever "Silent" Phil Babel's name came up at the reunion, it was always in hushed tones. Soon after the evacuation, his Marine colleagues lost touch with Babel, and in response to their inquiries, he made it clear that he wanted nothing to do with them. After learning of Frain's death, Valdez made a concerted effort to reach out to Babel by traveling to his home outside San Antonio. Babel refused to see him, and Valdez was shooed off his front porch by Babel's wife.

The name Duane Gevers, on the other hand, evoked nothing but smiles and laughs. After Gevers left the Marines in 1977, he seemed to disappear from the face of the earth until, in the 1980s, his fellow former MSGs began receiving calls from him imploring them to join him in Saudi Arabia, where the Black Market King had secured a contract from a prominent Saudi prince to provide security. Today Gevers is still handling and transporting goods as a long-haul trucker.

Not a few of the Saigon MSGs followed their Marine service with careers in law enforcement. "Big" John Ghilain, who departed Saigon on the second-to-last chopper, received his discharge in 1977 and joined the Medford, Massachusetts, Police Department, where he still serves as a patrol officer as well as a member of the department's Honor Guard. Ghilain is also the vice president of the Fall of Saigon Association and remains active in scholarship charities dedicated to the memories of McMahon and Judge.

Dave Norman left the Corps in 1976 to pursue a college degree, and while a student he was recruited by the Greene County (Ohio) Sheriff's Office to work undercover drug operations. Three years later, he was hired as a full-time officer by the Piqua, Ohio, police department and four years later transferred to the Miami County Sheriff's Office, also in Ohio. He earned a master's degree in criminal justice and remains a detective in Miami County.

Steve Bauer took a more roundabout route to his law enforcement badge. He served twenty years with the Corps, following his Saigon MSG deployment with postings to San Diego, Alaska, Okinawa, and Coronado, California, in positions as varied as infantry platoon sergeant, drill instructor, Marine liaison to the U.S. Army, and NCOIC of an Amphibious Recon unit. He was selected to warrant officer and in Operation Desert Storm served as the 1st Marine Division's nuclear, biological, and chemical officer. Following Desert Storm, he returned to Camp Pendleton as the executive officer of an instructor company and retired in 1992. Along the way, Bauer married a U.S. Navy sailor, and when she was transferred to Newport, Rhode Island, he moved east and began law school. But when his wife was again transferred, to Pensacola, Florida, he dropped out of law school and began a second career with the Pensacola Police Department, where he still serves as a patrol sergeant.

Terry Bennington, who was present at the reunion, went from Saigon to a Marine Security Guard posting in Vienna, Austria. He was one of the MSGs on duty the following year when President Ford famously tripped coming down the airplane ramp during his Austrian visit. When Ford learned that Bennington had been one of the last Marines to depart Saigon, the president invited the noncom to meet with him privately for a thirty-minute conversation during which Bennington "thanked him for getting us out of there." Later that night, Betty Ford called him to get his parents' address so she could send them a photo of him and Ford.

Bennington retired from the Corps as a sergeant major in 1995, having served twenty-four years. He became a Junior ROTC instructor in Henrico County in Virginia and four years later began working for the federal government in Quantico as a simulations analyst. Bennington is currently the deputy director of the Training Simulations Division, Training and Education Command, which develops methods to save lives of American personnel serving in Afghanistan and Iraq, where his son has served two tours as a Marine.

Steve Schuller put in his twenty years (plus twenty-four days) of service and retired from the Marine Corps in 1991 with the rank of gunnery sergeant—but not before realizing his dream and deploying to Okinawa as a "super grunt" with the 3rd Marine Division's Recon outfit. He said he "spent the best years of my life" living in the bush "ambushing" Marine infantry companies rotating through the Okinawa jungle, but the closest he came to combat was live-fire training with Republic of Korea Marines. He sandwiched his Recon posting with one last post-Saigon MSG deployment to New Delhi, India, and afterward performed several duties stateside ranging from drill instructor on Parris Island to recruiting officer in both his home state of Connecticut and at Marine headquarters in Washington, D.C.

As a civilian, Schuller began a home improvement construction company and in 2001, nearly thirty years to the day after he left his mother's farm to begin his Marine Corps odyssey, he returned to the property in northwest Connecticut when he and his wife moved into the house they built across the field from the family homestead, where they still live.

Mike Sullivan continued in the Marine Corps and retired in January 1988 after serving for twenty-one years. He returned to college and earned a master's degree in public administration at the same time he worked at National University as a financial advisor to students. After receiving his degree, Sullivan worked for the Orange County, California, court system in both the small claims and criminal divisions. He left this job in 1993 to become the full-time caregiver to his son, Sean, who had muscular dystrophy. He did this until December 2009, when Sean died. According to

Sullivan, "Since then my wife and I are still trying to come to grips with life without Sean."

Following the evacuation of Saigon, Jim Kean remained in the Corps for eight more years, retiring as a lieutenant colonel in 1983 after more than twenty-three years of service. He used his fluency in Chinese and his experience in Southeast Asia to found Yankee Traders, an import-export company for Asian goods, and parlayed the success of that venture into the purchase of another company, Pacific Grinding Wheel, in Marysville, Washington. In 1998, he retired from the civilian workforce and, with all of their five children grown and on their own, he and Rosanne moved to Cummaquid, Massachusetts, where he planned to write his autobiography. His daily regimen included morning laps at a local pool, and on May 5, 2008, as he emerged from the pool, he suffered a fatal heart attack. He is buried in the Massachusetts National Cemetery in Bourne.

Sorely missed at the 2010 reunion was Sergeant Juan Valdez. At seventy-two the "Frito Bandito"'s thick, bushy mustache is now completely gray, but otherwise he remains in battle-ready condition. Valdez, who presides as president of the Fall of Saigon Association from his home in Southern California, had planned on attending the weekend event after a short stopover in his hometown of San Antonio, Texas. But he fell ill with the flu on the train bringing him east and reluctantly returned to California. He fully recovered.

Top spent thirty years in his beloved Marine Corps, including MSG postings in Vienna and Brussels. He also served as a motorcycle traffic MP in Hawaii, and during a billeting post to Camp Pendleton he was promoted to the Corps' highest enlisted rank, master gunnery sergeant. He completed his active-duty military career at Camp Pendleton in June 1985 and made the area just north of San Diego his home. For twelve years following his retirement, Valdez was the assistant housing manager with the camp's Family Based Housing Authority until his final retirement from civil service in 1997.

An inveterate student of anything and everything that intrigued him, over his long career Valdez earned associate degrees in art history and criminal justice supervision and management, real estate, and hospitality management. He continues to attend Palomar and MiraCosta Community Colleges, with plans to transfer to the University of California at San Marcos "in the near future."

After the dinner at the Tun Tavern on the night of May 1, 2010, some of the men weren't ready to turn in. A dozen or so wandered over to the Command Post, a popular bar on the Quantico base, where tables were pushed together so everyone could sit and talk. New photos were taken and older ones passed around, memories were shared and debated, drinks were ordered (and reordered). There was plenty of laughter as men well past their fighting trim exaggerated to each other about an event that had shaped their lives thirty-five years earlier.

Toward the end of the spontaneous gathering, the mood suddenly turned somber when John Ghilain and Dwight McDonald, seated at the head of the extended table, expressed regret that the Saigon MSG detachment had left two behind when they departed the city. "To this day I wish we had brought those Marines home with us," McDonald murmured, and heads about the table nodded silently.

Then there was nothing more to say. It was time to return home, and for these veteran Marines to continue with their lives.

Source Notes and Selected Bibliography

As we have noted in our previous collaborations, *Halsey's Typhoon* and *The Last Stand of Fox Company,* all historical records are complicated, none more so than accounts of any war's individual small-unit actions, be they firefights or evacuations. *Last Men Out* is a narrative account of the final hours of U.S. involvement in the Vietnam War as experienced by a handful of American Marines and civilians. Nothing has been invented or recreated here for the sake of that narrative. This story needs no embellishment.

In addition to relying on official U.S. and Marine Corps historical records, previously classified government documents, troves of material housed at the Vietnam Center and Archive at Texas Tech University, the Oral History Archives at Rutgers University, the Graham Martin Papers and other valuable collections at the Gerald R. Ford Library and the Gerald R. Ford Museum, contemporary media accounts, and the works referenced in this selective bibliography, we have reconstructed the events surrounding the evacuation of Saigon, particularly the dialogue between and among the participants, from contemporary journals, diaries, and personal letters written by the participants soon after the occurrence. We have found that official (and nearly immediately written and submitted) after-action reports by Marine commanders—in this case, particularly those penned by James Kean regarding his command at the embassy, Boyette "Steve" Hasty in Can Tho, Gunnery Sergeant Vasco Martin at the defense attaché's office near Tan Son Nhut Airport, and the "unofficial" report filed soon after by Master Sergeant Juan Valdez for *Leatherneck* magazine—have been most helpful in defogging so many memories clouded by the mists of time.

Defeat in war is a bitter pill—especially for men, civilian and military, who fear (often rightfully) that they will become scapegoats. In justifying their actions, these people often display a candor regarding their personal experiences that cannot be found in any official record. One such document that immediately springs to mind—"Walking Around with My Head in a Basket," captured in Larry Engelmann's fine oral history, *Tears Before the Rain*—was written by the former (and final) U.S. ambassador to South Vietnam, Graham Martin. Similarly, as the last U.S. defense attaché to South Vietnam, the U.S. Army's Major General Homer Smith's effort to "represent a mixture of facts and my own thoughts" in his 1975 paper, "The Final Forty-Five Days in Vietnam," was a cache of personal insights not generally found in postwar reports. In addition, numerous recollections by men such as those found in General Richard Carey's collected papers at the Marine History Branch in Quantico, Virginia, were most insightful as well as informative.

Conversely, as the adage has it, the histories of wars are written by the victors, and of the North Vietnamese sources cited below, none allowed us as closely into the mind-set of "the enemy" as the insights of the NVA chief of staff General Van Tien Dung's *Our Great Spring Victory.* Rather than being a stilted account of battle after battle and explanations of strategy, Dung's book is a colorfully written memoir of the last few months of the Vietnam War that bluntly celebrates the motivations and eventual triumph of North Vietnam.

Finally, all of the accounts, documents, and resources listed above and below were crucial to unlocking the recollections of the surviving Saigon Marine Security Guards and others with whom, over the course of the last two years, we conducted multiple interviews in person, by telephone, and by e-mail—often to their utter consternation. All that said, we acknowledge that thirty-five-year-old memories can play tricks, so whenever possible, we have tried to confirm these conversations with each participant.

Books

Arnett, Peter. *Live from the Battlefield.* New York: Simon & Schuster, 1994.
Brady, James. *Why Marines Fight.* New York: Thomas Dunne Books, 2007.
Burchett, Wilfred. *At the Barricades.* New York: Times Books, 1981.

————. *Grasshoppers and Elephants.* New York: Urizen Books, 1977.

Butler, David. *The Fall of Saigon.* New York: Simon & Schuster, 1985.

Buttinger, Joseph. *Vietnam: The Unforgettable Tragedy.* New York: Horizon Press, 1977.

Carhart, Tom. *Battles and Campaigns in Vietnam.* Buckinghamshire, U.K.: Military Press, 1994.

Colby, William. *Honorable Men: My Life in the CIA.* New York: Simon & Schuster, 1978.

Cosmas, Graham A., and Murray, Terrence R. *U.S. Marines in Vietnam: Vietnamization and Redeployment 1970–1971.* Washington, D.C.: History and Museums Division, Headquarters, U.S. Marine Corps, 1986.

Dawson, Alan. *55 Days: The Fall of South Vietnam.* Englewood Cliffs, N.J.: Prentice Hall, 1977.

DeForest, Orrin, and Chanoff, David. *Slow Burn.* New York: Simon & Schuster, 1990.

Dung, Van Tien. *Our Great Spring Victory: An Account of the Liberation of South Vietnam.* London: Monthly Review Press, 1977.

Dunham, George R., and Quinlan, David A. *U.S. Marines in Vietnam: The Bitter End 1973–1975.* Washington D.C.: History and Museums Division, Headquarters, U.S. Marine Corps, 1990.

Engelmann, Larry. *Tears Before the Rain: An Oral History of the Fall of South Vietnam.* New York: Da Capo Press, 1997.

Ford, Gerald. *A Time to Heal.* New York: Harper & Row, 1979.

Goldstein, Gordon M. *Lessons in Disaster: McGeorge Bundy and the Path to War in Vietnam.* New York: Times Books/Henry Holt, 2008.

Hackworth, David H. (and Sherman, Julie). *About Face: The Odyssey of an American Warrior.* New York: Simon & Schuster, 1989.

Hartmann, Robert. *Palace Politics.* New York: McGraw-Hill, 1980.

Henderson, Charles. *Goodnight Saigon: The True Story of the U.S. Marines' Last Days in Vietnam.* New York: Berkeley Publishing Group, 2005.

Herrington, Stuart. *Peace Without Honor?* New York: Presidio Press, 1983.

Hosmer, Stephen, Kellens, Konrad, and Jenkins, Brian M. *The Fall of South Vietnam: Statements by Vietnamese Military and Civilian Leaders.* New York: Crane, Russak, 1980.

Hung, Nguyen. *The Palace File.* New York: Harper & Row, 1986.

Isaacs, Arnold R. *Without Honor: Defeat in Vietnam and Cambodia*. Baltimore, Md.: Johns Hopkins University Press, 1983.

Karnow, Stanley. *Vietnam: A History*. New York: Viking Press, 1983.

Kissinger, Henry. *Crisis: The Anatomy of Two Major Foreign Policy Crises*. New York: Simon & Schuster, 2003.

———. *Ending the Vietnam War: A History of America's Involvement in and Extrication from the Vietnam War*. New York: Simon & Schuster, 2003.

———. *The White House Years*. Boston: Little, Brown, 1979.

Ky, Nguyen Cao. *Twenty Years and Twenty Days*. New York: Stein and Day, 1976.

Lee, J. Edward, and Haynsworth, Toby. *White Christmas in April: The Collapse of South Vietnam*. New York: Peter Lang Publishing, 1999.

McNamara, Francis Terry (with Hill, Adrian). *Escape with Honor: My Last Hours in Vietnam*. Washington D.C.: Brassey's, 1997.

Ngan, Nguyen Ngoc. *The Will of Heaven*. New York: Dutton, 1982.

Pilger, John. *The Last Day: America's Final Hours in Vietnam*. New York: Vintage Books, 1976.

Robbins, Christopher. *Air America*. New York: Putnam, 1979.

Santoli, Al. *Everything We Had*. New York: Ballantine, 1985.

———. *To Bear Any Burden*. New York: Dutton, 1985.

Sheehan, Neil. *A Bright Shining Lie: John Paul Vann and America in Vietnam*. New York: Random House, 1988.

Snepp, Frank. *Decent Interval*. New York: Random House, 1977.

Steinman, Ron. *The Soldiers' Story: Vietnam in Their Own Words*. New York: Barnes & Noble Books, 1999.

Summers, Harry G., Jr. *The Vietnam War Almanac*. New York: Ballantine Books, 1985.

Terzani, Tiziano. *Giai Phong!* New York: St. Martin's Press, 1999.

Thi, Lam Quong. *The 25-Year Century*. Denton: University of North Texas Press, 2002.

Todd, Olivier. *Cruel April*. New York: Norton, 1990.

Vien, Cao Van. *The Final Collapse*. Washington, D.C.: Center for Military History, 1983.

Warner, Dennis. *Certain Victory: How Hanoi Won the War*. Kansas City, Mo.: Sheed Andrews & McMeel, 1978.

Weiner, Tim. *Legacy of Ashes*. New York: Doubleday, 2007.

Zinn, Howard. *A People's History of the United States: 1492–Present.* New York: Harper Perennial, 1980.

Magazine and Newspaper Articles

"178 Die on Babylift." *Pacific Stars and Stripes*, April 6, 1975.

"As Marine Choppers Flew and Saigon Fell They Played 'White Christmas.'" Sergeant Steven A. Davis, *Leatherneck,* October 2002.

"Escape from Saigon." Suzanne Goldenberg, *Guardian*, April 28, 2005.

"Evacuation of Saigon Tumultuous at the End." George Esper, *New York Times*, April 30, 1975.

"Frequent Wind." Tom Bartlett, *Leatherneck,* September 1975.

"Frequent Wind Organization and Assembly." General Richard E. Carey and D. A. Quinlan, *Marine Corps Gazette*, February–April 1976.

"From Defeat, Lessons in Victory." Gordon M. Goldstein, *New York Times,* October 18, 2009.

"Getting It Wrong in a Photo." Fox Butterfield with Karl Haskell, *New York Times*, April 23, 2000.

"Graham Martin, 77, Dies; Envoy at Saigon's Fall." Alfonso Narvaez, *New York Times,* March 15, 1990.

"Henry Makes the Best of It." Hugh Sidey, *Time Magazine*, May 12, 1975.

"How South Vietnam Died—By the Stab in the Front." Fox Butterfield, *New York Times,* May 25, 1975.

"How to Lose a War: The Press and Viet Nam." Robert Elegant, *Encounter*, August 1981.

"It's Over." *Pacific Stars and Stripes*, May 1, 1975.

"Journey to North Vietnam." Frances FitzGerald, *New Yorker,* April 28, 1975.

"Last Chopper Out of Saigon." *Time Magazine*, May 12, 1975.

"The Last Day: Local Men Look Back a Decade to Fall of Saigon." David Parrish, *Blade Tribune,* April 28, 1985.

"Last Hope for Vietnam; U.S. to Take 2,000 Orphans." *Pacific Stars and Stripes*, April 5, 1975.

"Marine Pilot Recalls Evacuation of U.S. Embassy in Saigon in '75." Joan Oleck, *News and Observer*, April 30, 1985.

"Marines Among Last to Leave Saigon." Terry L. Colvin, *San Diego Union*, May 5, 1985.

"Minh Surrenders, Vietcong in Saigon." Associated Press, April 30, 1975.

"Operation Frequent Wind: The Final Mission." Al Hemingway, *VFW Magazine*, April 1995.

"Panic Rises in Saigon, But the Exits Are Few." Fox Butterfield, *New York Times*, April 24, 1975.

"Reporter's Notebook: Six Days in the Evacuation of Saigon." Fox Butterfield, *New York Times*, May 5, 1975.

"Saigon Apparently Braces for a Direct Thrust by Foe." Malcom Browne, *New York Times*, April 18, 1975.

"Saigon Defenses Attacked; Airport Under Rocket Fire." Fox Butterfield, *New York Times*, April 29, 1975.

"Saigon Remembered." Sally MacDonald, *Seattle Times*, March 12, 1995.

"Saigon Survivor: Marine Remembers Last Copter Trip Out of Vietnam." Eileen Mead, *Fredericksburg Free Lance-Star*, March 29, 1994.

"Saigon Under the VC Flag; Reds in Orderly Takeover." *Pacific Stars and Stripes*, May 2, 1975.

"The End of a Thirty Years' War." *Time Magazine*, May 12, 1975.

"The Freedom Bird Flies Again." *Pacific Stars and Stripes*, April 4, 1975.

"The Last Casualty." Donovan Moore, *Boston Magazine*, December 1975.

"The Last Grim Goodbye." *Time Magazine*, May 12, 1975.

"The Last Ones Out." Terry Sforza, *Orange County Register*, April 30, 2005.

"The Last Ones to Leave." Kirsten Scharnberg, *Chicago Tribune*, April 30, 2005.

"The Other Side." Le Ly Haslip with Jay Wurts, *The Los Angeles Times Magazine*, February 5, 1989.

"The Vietnam War We Ignore." Lewis Sorley, *New York Times*, October 17, 2009.

"Thirty Years at 300 Millimeters." Hubert van Es, *New York Times*, April 29, 2005.

"This Is It! Everybody Out!" Roy Rowan, *Time Magazine*, May 12, 1975.

"U.S. Withdrawing Americans from Saigon by Helicopter Under Marine Protection." John W. Finney, *New York Times*, April 29, 1975.

"VC Launch Attack on Tan Son Nhut." *Pacific Stars and Stripes*, April 30, 1975.

"Victor's Final Strategy." Rod Paschal, *Vietnam Magazine*, April 2000.

"Vietnam: Long Time Passing: 30 Years After the Fall of Saigon," Kirsten Scharnberg, *Chicago Tribune*, April 30, 2005.

Source Notes and Selected Bibliography

"Vietnam 20 Years Later: Last Marines to Leave Vietnam Remember Chaos of Last Day." Dennis Camire, *Gannett News Service*, April 22, 1995.

Video and Electronic Sources

"The Fall of Saigon." *Vietnam, a Television History.* PBS, 1983.
"The Fall of Saigon 1975: An Eyewitness Report." John Pilger, zmag.org, 2005.

Other Sources

Burke, Marius. *Vietnam Report.* Air America Log, January–March 1990.

Kean, James. "Jim Kean Remembers." Unpublished recollection of events, December 1994.

Lavalle, Lt. Col. A. J. C. *Last Flight from Saigon.* USAF Southeast Asia Monograph Series, Volume IV, Monograph 6.

Lehmann, Wolfgang J. Interviewed May 9, 1989, before the Association for Diplomatic Studies and Training, Foreign Affairs Oral History Project, Foreign Affairs Series.

Martin, Graham. Testimony Before the Special Investigations Subcommittee of the House International Relations Committee, January 27, 1976.

Acknowledgments

There was much to find in documents, files both electronic and dusty, and in other research sources, but we would not have been able to tell this story, especially the deeply human part of it, without the help and cooperation of many people. We will endeavor to thank all of them, and it is our oversight if we do not.

First and foremost are the last men out, and our thanks go to those Marines who stayed at their posts and followed their orders until the final evacuation of Saigon. We are particularly indebted to Ken Crouse and Doug Potratz, who flew on those last Birds and are especially active members of the Fall of Saigon Association. We also thank Phil Keith of the U.S. Navy for his eyewitness accounts of Saigon.

Essential to our understanding of the personal dramas of those final twenty-four hours were the recollections generously shared with us by men who were on the ground and in the air to experience them: Steve Bauer, Terry Bennington, Gerry Berry, Marius Burke, Ron Duffey, John Ghilain, Greg Hargis, Steve Hasty, Stuart Herrington, Steve Johnson, Dave Leet, Kevin Maloney, Dwight McDonald, Francis McNamara, John Moore, Bill Newell, Don Nicholas, Dave Norman, John Rhodes, Steve Schuller, John Stewart, Mike Sullivan, Juan Valdez, Steve Wills, and Chris Woods. We thank you.

Also providing much help and information were John Balboa, Warren E. Blow, Bill Collier, Bob Gabelein, Joel Gardner, Valerie Hanley, J. "Huge" Heffernan, "Slick" Katz, Dick Rosser, Tony Tucci, and the members of the Fox 2/7 Association.

The seed for what became this book was planted at the Gerald R. Ford Museum in Grand Rapids, Michigan, and much material was collected at the Gerald

Acknowledgments

R. Ford Library in Ann Arbor, Michigan. We are very grateful to Elaine Didier and her helpful staff, particularly William McNitt and Nancy Mirshah, at both institutions for the inspiration as well as the information. We were also aided by information gleaned from the Rutgers University Oral History Archives and the Vietnam Center and Archive at Texas Tech University. Once again, not only were the materials at the Colonel Alfred Gray Research Center and the Marine History Branch in Quantico, Virginia, made available to us for in-depth research, but Dr. Charles Neimeyer and Robert Aquilina were always ready to provide help and answers to numerous questions.

Martin Beiser was our loyal editor who guided this book through the process from the very beginning. In addition, we are also grateful to the many others at Free Press who have also contributed so much, especially Martha Levin, Emily Loose, Eric Fuentecilla, Leah Miller, and Alexandra Pisano. A debt we can never repay for his support and encouragement is owed to Nat Sobel and, by extension, to Adia Wright and others at Sobel-Weber Associates.

Support and encouragement also came our way from Joan and Fred Baum, John and Corinne Bonfiglio, Heather Buchanan, Ed Butscher and Paula Trachtnan, Anne Drager, Michael and Shelly Gambino, Joan Geroch, Scott Gould, Michael Griffith and Nancy Grigor, Ken Moran, Danny Peary and Suzanne Rafer, Bob Rosen, Tony and Patty Sales, Lynne Scanlon, Bob Schaeffer and Fred Smith, Val and Min-Myn Schaffner, Alison Thompson, and David Winter.

Our deepest thanks go to those who remain up on the writing roof with us: Denise McDonald, Liam-Antoine DeBusschere-Drury, and Leslie Reingold.

Index

Index

Index

Index

Index

surrounding embassy, 28, 130–31, 133–35, 136–41, 155–56, 158, 169, 179, 204, 223–26, 229–30, 246

Rockefeller, Nelson, 105, 113

Roosevelt, Franklin D., 71, 218

Route One, 42

Royal Cambodian Army, 229

Royal South Vietnamese Air Force, 50, 62, 73, 122, 252, 258

Royal South Vietnamese Marine Corps, 18, 41, 107–8

Saigon. *See also* Evacuation; United States Embassy (Saigon)
date for "liberation" refixed, 105
Ford advised of impending fall, 56
martial law declared in, 88
North Vietnamese surrounding of, 3
sacking of, 132–33

"Santa Fe Trail," 93, 141

Schagut, Capt. Claus, 214–15, 217, 235

Schlager, Sgt. Bobby, 114–15, 138–39, 165, 208–9, 225
evacuation of, 247, 250
in "Final Eleven," 237–38, 241–42
flag retrieved by, 90–92, 146, 237–38
postwar life and death of, 266–67

Schlesinger, James, 24, 69

Schuller, Jennie, 44–45

Schuller, John, 45

Schuller, Cpl. Steve, 29, 43–49, 75–76, 114, 153–55, 163, 168–71, 173–76, 179, 203–4, 226, 229–30, 234, 252, 253, 258
air traffic controller training, 45, 187–88

background of, 44–45
bayonet wound of, 169–71, 173, 176
evacuation of, 250
in "Final Eleven," 237, 239, 241
postwar life of, 269

Scott, Cpl. Richard, 180, 182, 183, 184, 196, 197–99, 256

Scowcroft, Lt. Gen. Brent, 56, 66

Segura, Sgt. Clemon, 159, 163, 216, 218–19

September 11 terrorist attacks, 265

Seventh Fleet, 10, 28, 35, 83, 91, 94, 105, 122, 134, 152–53, 186, 193, 208, 212, 240, 250, 255

7th Regiment, 19

Shea, 1st Lt. Michael, 182, 196, 200, 256, 261

Singh, Mr. (evacuee), 132

Smith, Maj. Gen. Homer, 64–66, 72, 107, 109, 111, 113, 142, 195

Snatch, Operation, 215

Snepp, Frank, 29–31, 35, 36, 49, 88, 95, 112–13, 156, 177–78, 203–4

South Koreans, 205–6, 252, 258, 259

Soviet Union, 70

Sparrow Hawk assault team, 167

Spring Offensive, 63

St. Paul, USS, 123

Stargell, Willie, 20

Stars and Stripes (newspaper), 49, 54, 219

State Department, U.S., 16, 17, 23, 85, 86, 118, 255

Steele, V. Adm. George, 96, 97, 130, 155, 186, 193, 208

Stewart, Cpl. John, 142–43

About the Authors

BOB DRURY is a contributing editor for *Men's Health* magazine and has reported from numerous war zones. His last solo book, *The Rescue Season,* was made into a documentary by the History Channel.

TOM CLAVIN is the author of twelve books, including *Roger Maris: Baseball's Reluctant Hero* (with Danny Peary) and *One for the Ages: Jack Nicklaus and the 1986 Masters.*

The authors' most recent collaboration, *The Last Stand of Fox Company,* was awarded the 2010 General Wallace M. Greene Jr. Award by the Marine Corps Heritage Foundation for "outstanding nonfiction book pertinent to Marine Corps history." They are also the authors of *Halsey's Typhoon: The True Story of a Fighting Admiral, an Epic Storm, and an Untold Rescue.*